2

Hiro Mashima

Translated and adapted by William Flanagan
Lettered by North Market Street Graphics

Ballantine Books · New York

Fairy Tail volume 2 is a work of fiction. Names, characters, places, and incidents are the products of the author's imagination or are used fictitiously. Any resemblance to actual events, locales, or persons, living or dead, is entirely coincidental.

A Del Rey Manga/Kodansha Trade Paperback Original

Published in the United States by Del Rey Books, an imprint of The Random House Publishing Group, a division of Random House, Inc., New York.

Publication rights arranged through Kodansha Ltd.

First published in Japan in 2007 by Kodansha Ltd., Tokyo

ISBN 978-0-345-50330-5

Printed in the United States of America

www.delreymanga.com

9 8 7 6 5 4 3

Translator/Adapter—William Flanagan
Lettering—North Market Street Graphics

Contents

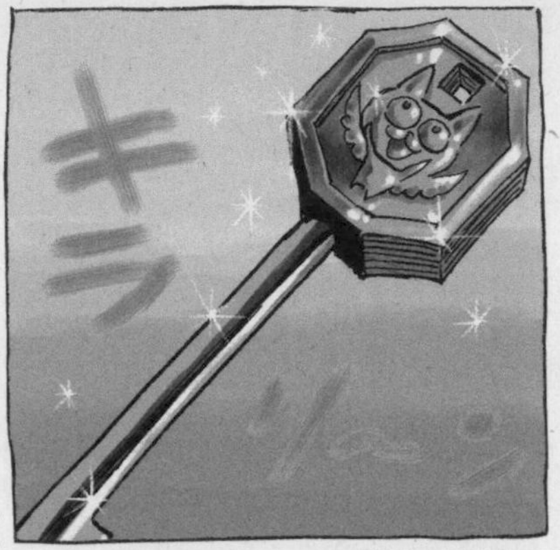
キラ

It's so much fun to come up with all the different kinds of magic...or at least it *should* be!! But aside from Natsu and Lucy, there are so many characters, and I have to think up different types of magic and abilities for each of them! That's what it means to build a world, and it's pretty rough work!
Still, there are some very intricate backgrounds for the supporting characters, and someday I'd like to go into these in detail.

—Hiro Mashima

Honorifics Explained

Throughout the Del Rey Manga books, you will find Japanese honorifics left intact in the translations. For those not familiar with how the Japanese use honorifics and, more important, how they differ from honorifics in American English, we present this brief overview.

Politeness has always been a critical facet of Japanese culture. Ever since the feudal era, when Japan was a highly stratified society, use of honorifics—which can be defined as polite speech that indicates relationship or status—has played an essential role in the Japanese language. When addressing someone in Japanese, an honorific usually takes the form of a suffix attached to one's name (example: "Asuna-san"), is used as a title at the end of one's name, or appears in place of the name itself (example: "Negi-sensei," or simply "Sensei!").

Honorifics can be expressions of respect or endearment. In the context of manga and anime, honorifics give insight into the nature of the relationship between characters. Many English translations leave out these important honorifics and therefore distort the feel of the original Japanese. Because Japanese honorifics contain nuances that English honorifics lack, it is our policy at Del Rey not to translate them. Here, instead, is a guide to some of the honorifics you may encounter in Del Rey Manga.

-san: This is the most common honorific and is equivalent to Mr., Miss, Ms., or Mrs. It is the all-purpose honorific and can be used in any situation where politeness is required.

-sama: This is one level higher than "-san" and is used to confer great respect.

-dono: This comes from the word "tono," which means "lord." It is an even higher level than "-sama" and confers utmost respect.

-kun: This suffix is used at the end of boys' names to express familiarity or endearment. It is also sometimes used by men among friends, or when addressing someone younger or of a lower station.

-chan: This is used to express endearment, mostly toward girls. It is also used for little boys, pets, and even among lovers. It gives a sense of childish cuteness.

Bozu: This is an informal way to refer to a boy, similar to the English terms "kid" and "squirt."

Sempai/
Senpai: This title suggests that the addressee is one's senior in a group or organization. It is most often used in a school setting, where underclassmen refer to their upperclassmen as "sempai." It can also be used in the workplace, such as when a newer employee addresses an employee who has seniority in the company.

Kohai: This is the opposite of "sempai" and is used toward underclassmen in school or newcomers in the workplace. It connotes that the addressee is of a lower station.

Sensei: Literally meaning "one who has come before," this title is used for teachers, doctors, or masters of any profession or art.

-[blank]: This is usually forgotten in these lists, but it is perhaps the most significant difference between Japanese and English. The lack of honorific means that the speaker has permission to address the person in a very intimate way. Usually, only family, spouses, or very close friends have this kind of permission. Known as *yobisute*, it can be gratifying when someone who has earned the intimacy starts to call one by one's name without an honorific. But when that intimacy hasn't been earned, it can be very insulting.

FAIRY TAIL

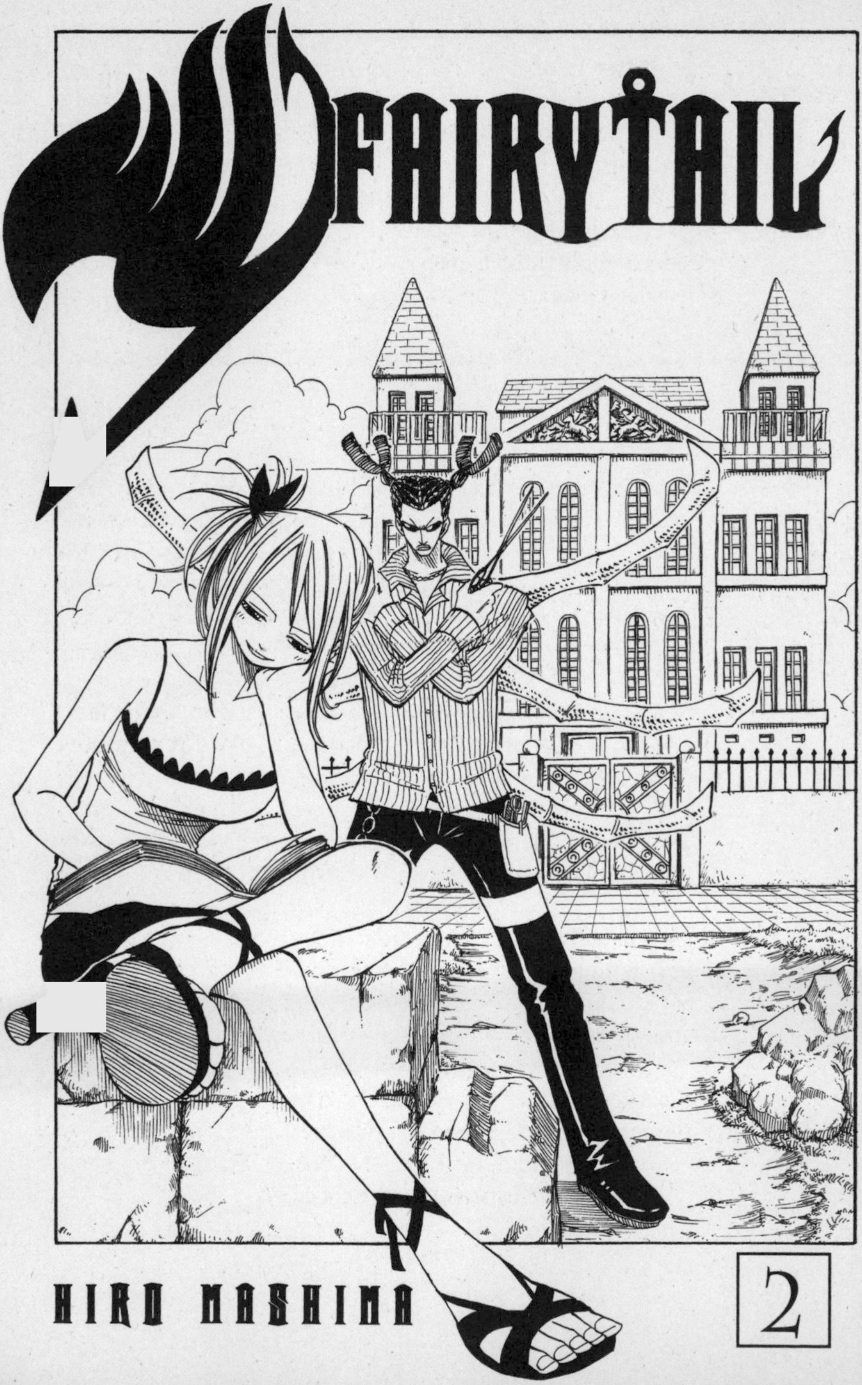

HIRO MASHIMA

2

If you please, Master, these are the contents for *Fairy Tail* volume 2!

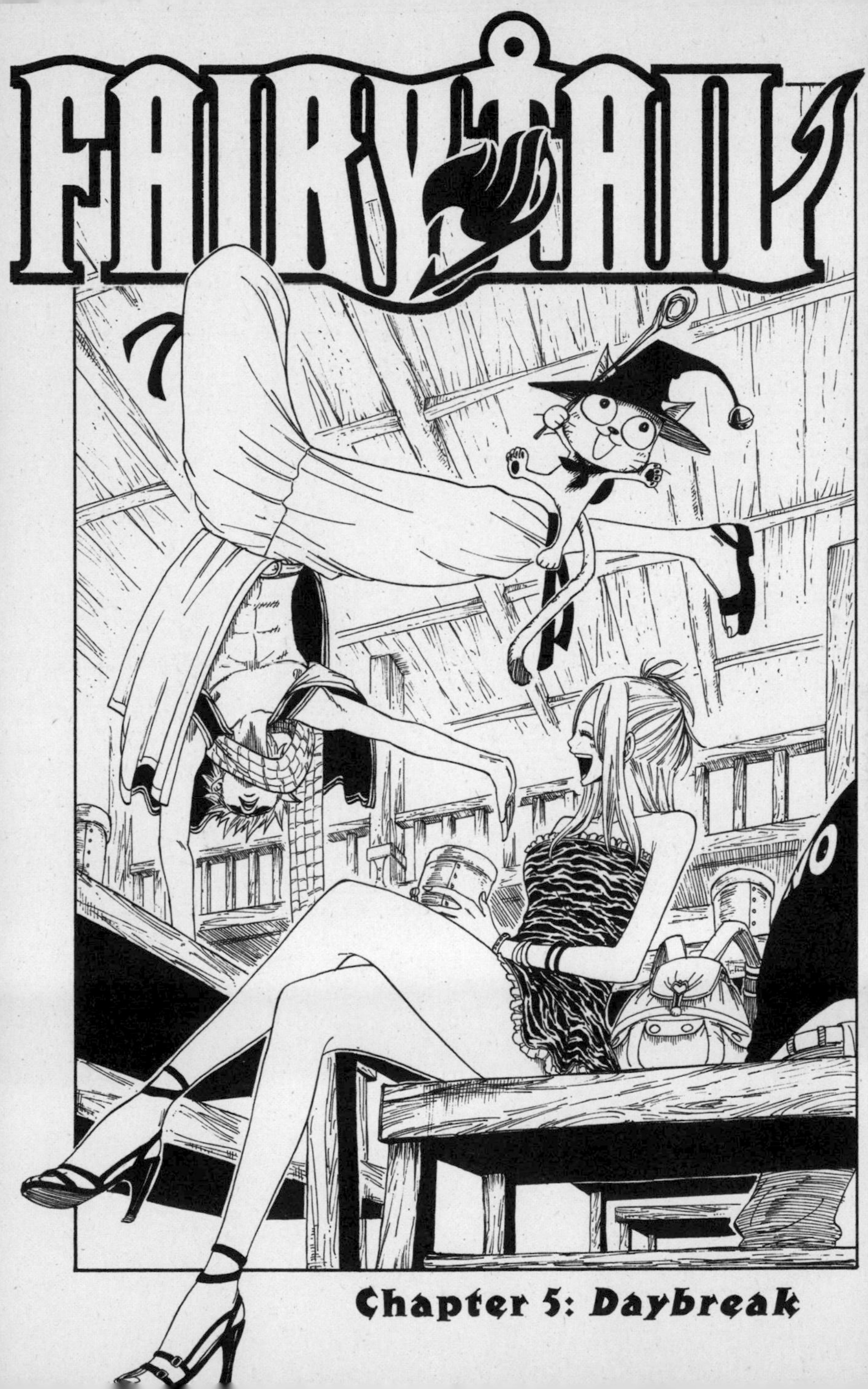
FAIRY TAIL
7

Chapter 5: *Daybreak*

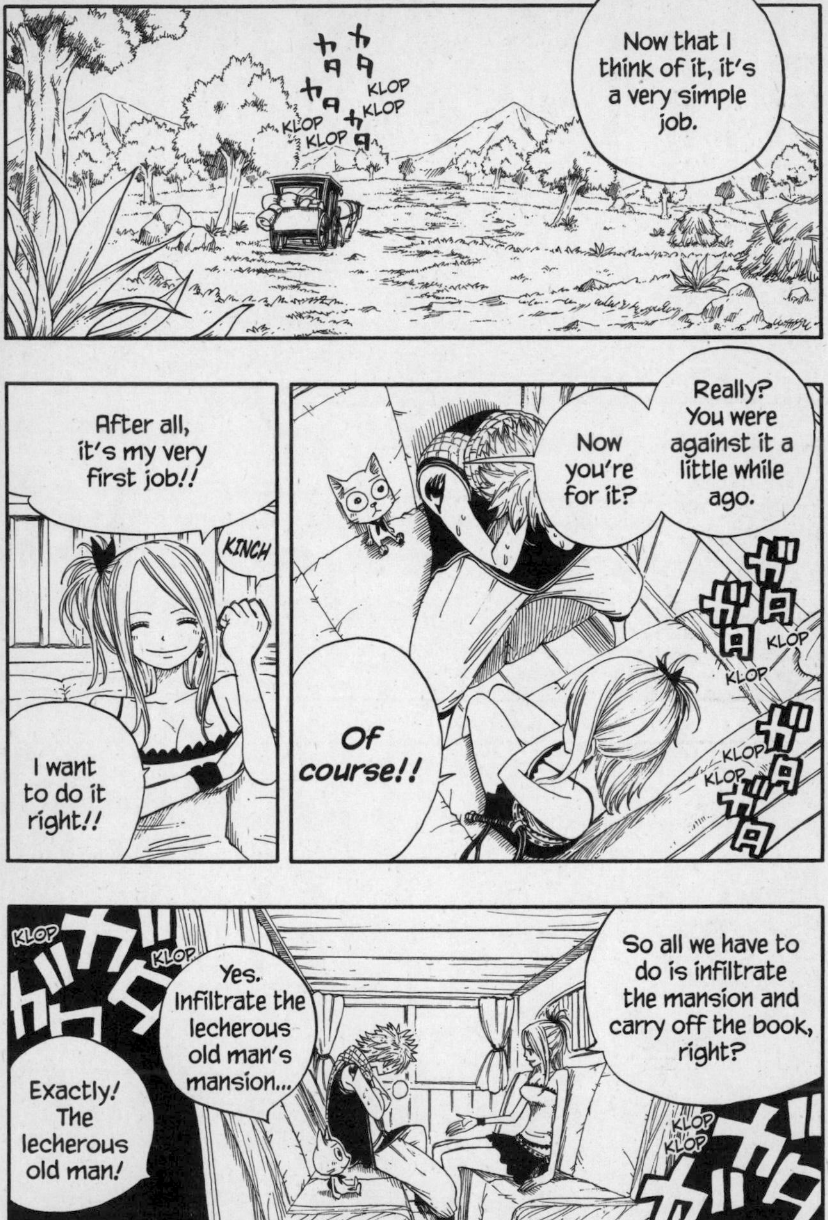

Now that I think of it, it's a very simple job.
KLOP KLOP
KLOP KLOP
Really? You were against it a little while ago.
Now you're for it?
Of course!!
KLOP KLOP
KLOP KLOP
After all, it's my very first job!!
KINCH
I want to do it right!!
So all we have to do is infiltrate the mansion and carry off the book, right?
KLOP KLOP
Yes. Infiltrate the lecherous old man's mansion...
KLOP KLOP
Exactly! The lecherous old man!

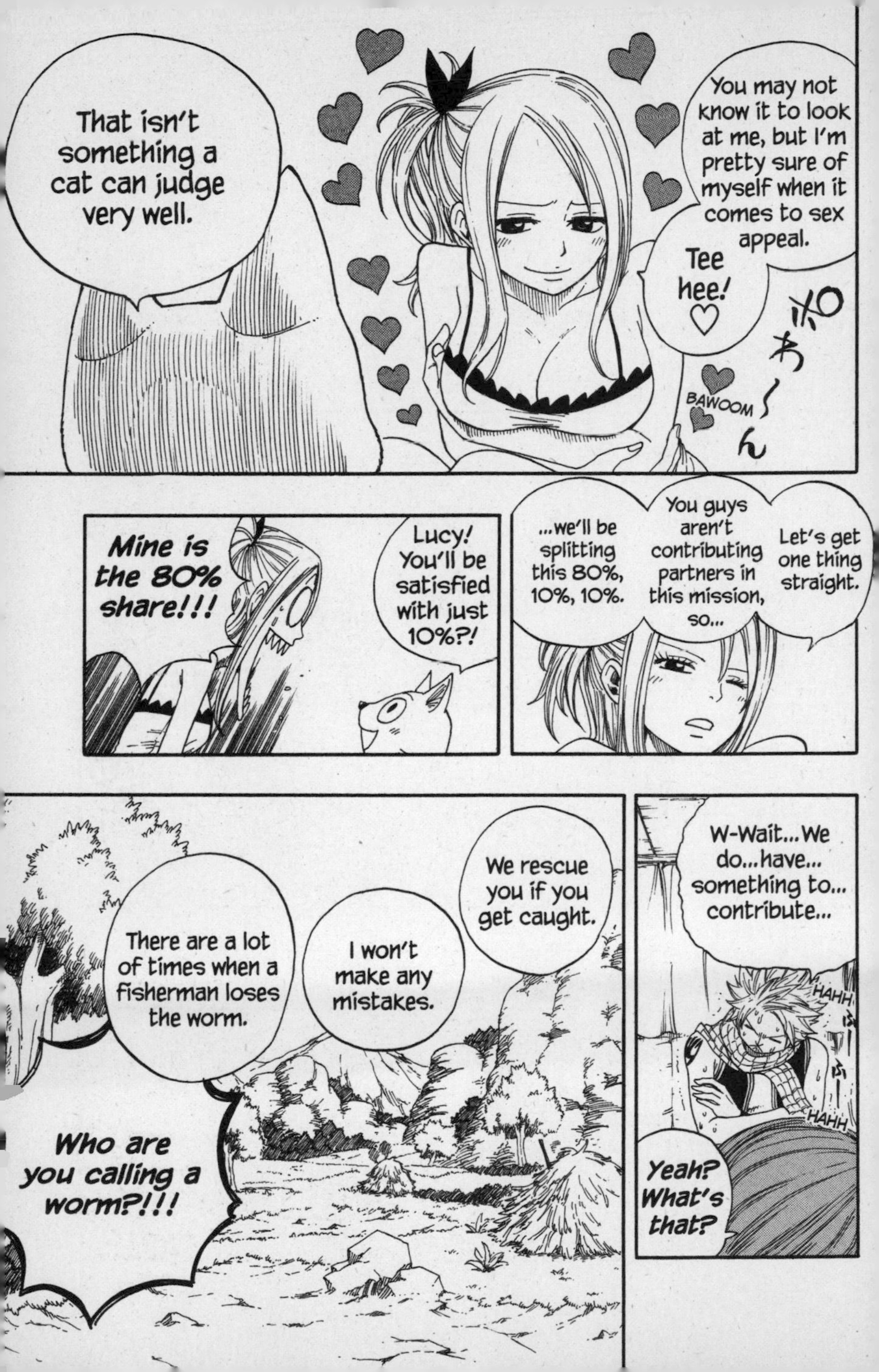
You may not know it to look at me, but I'm pretty sure of myself when it comes to sex appeal.
Tee hee! ♡
BAWOOM
That isn't something a cat can judge very well.
Let's get one thing straight.
You guys aren't contributing partners in this mission, so...
...we'll be splitting this 80%, 10%, 10%.
Lucy! You'll be satisfied with just 10%?!
Mine is the 80% share!!!
W-Wait...We do...have... something to... contribute...
HAHH
HAHH
Yeah? What's that?
We rescue you if you get caught.
I won't make any mistakes.
There are a lot of times when a fisherman loses the worm.
Who are you calling a worm?!!!

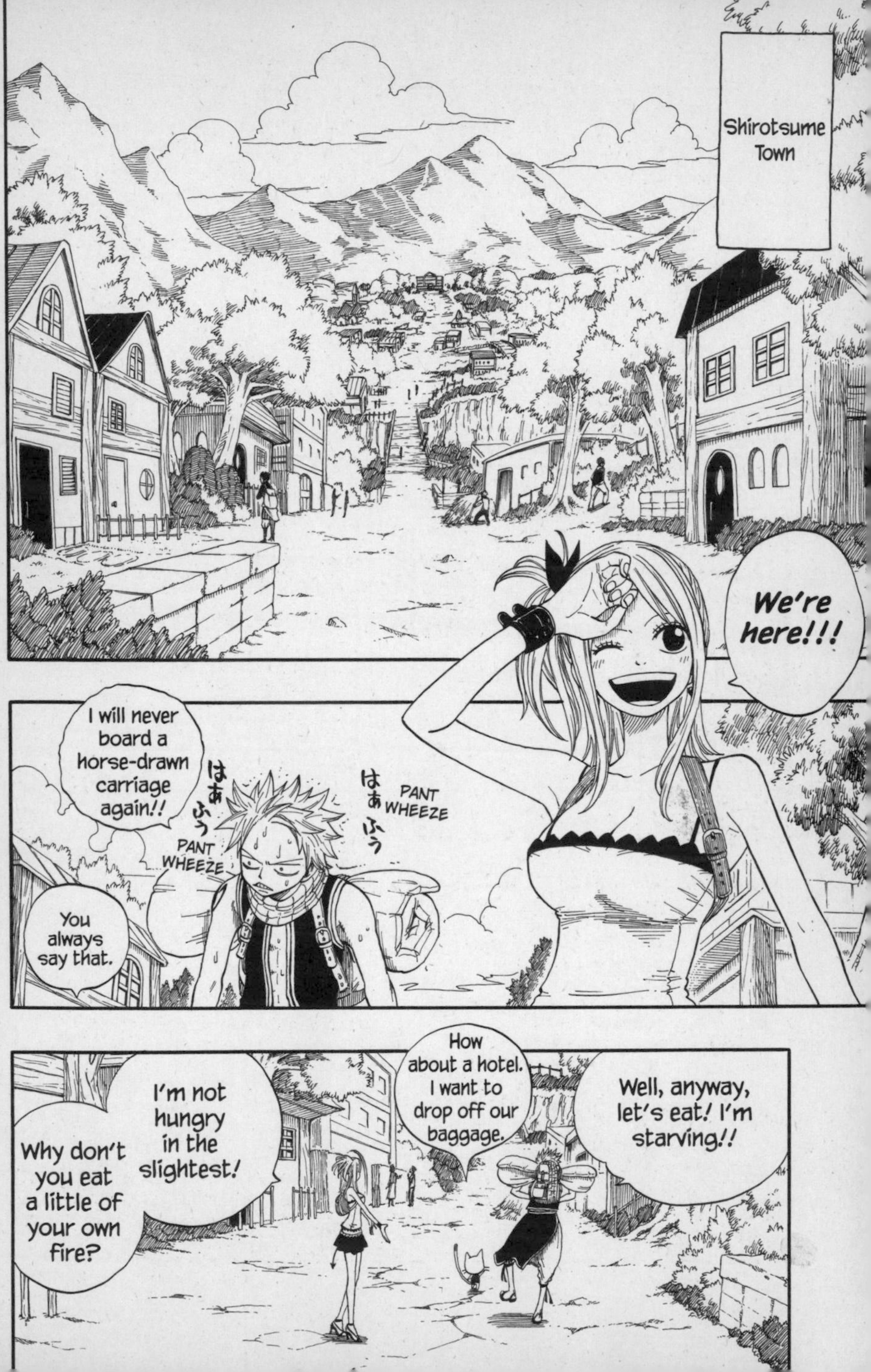
Shirotsume Town
We're here!!!
はぁ ふぅ PANT WHEEZE
はぁ ふぅ PANT WHEEZE
I will never board a horse-drawn carriage again!!
You always say that.
Well, anyway, let's eat! I'm starving!!
How about a hotel. I want to drop off our baggage.
I'm not hungry in the slightest!
Why don't you eat a little of your own fire?

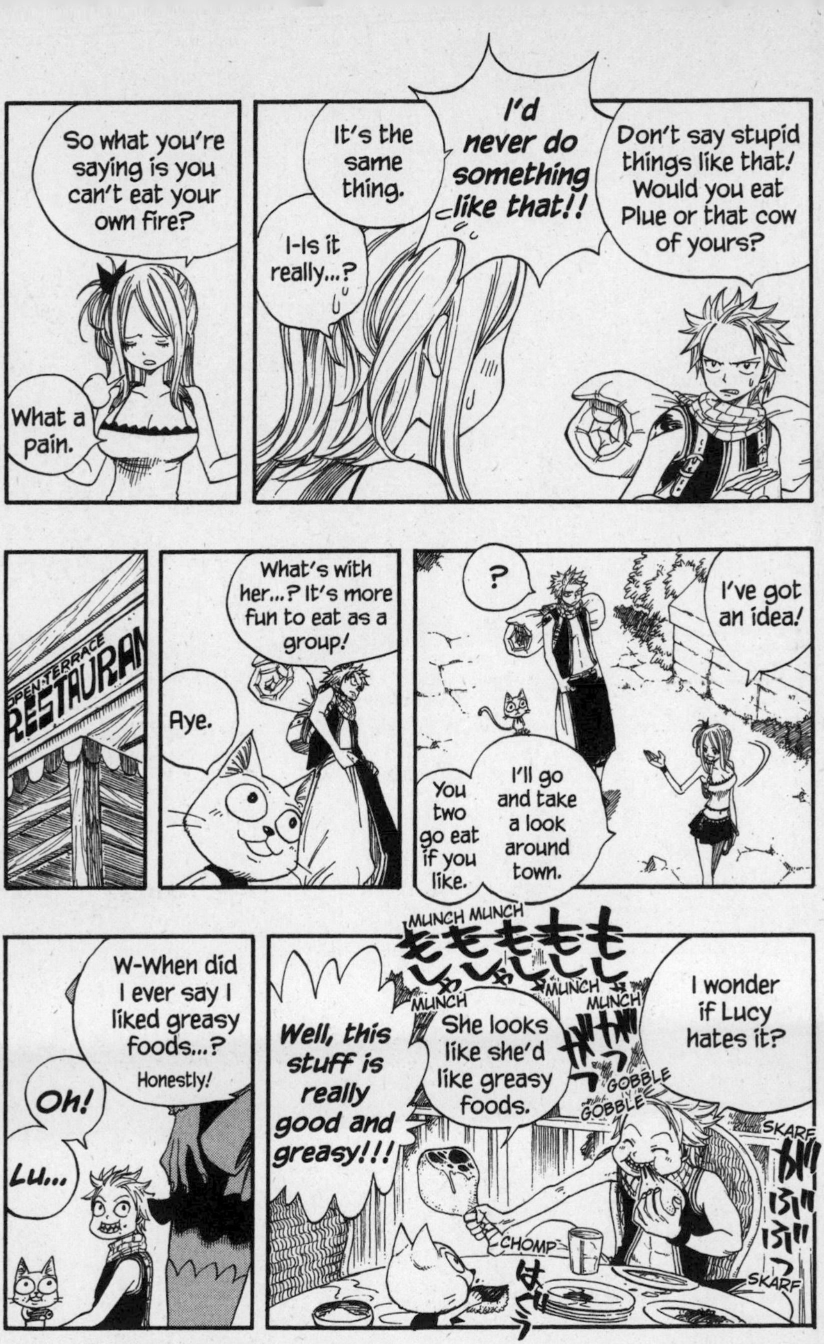
Don't say stupid things like that! Would you eat Plue or that cow of yours?
I'd never do something like that!!
It's the same thing.
I-Is it really...?
So what you're saying is you can't eat your own fire?
What a pain.
I've got an idea!
?
I'll go and take a look around town.
You two go eat if you like.
What's with her...? It's more fun to eat as a group!
Aye.
OPEN TERRACE
RESTAURAN
I wonder if Lucy hates it?
MUNCH MUNCH
MUNCH
MUNCH
MUNCH
She looks like she'd like greasy foods.
Well, this stuff is really good and greasy!!!
GOBBLE
GOBBLE
SKARF
SKARF
CHOMP
W-When did I ever say I liked greasy foods...?
Honestly!
Oh!
Lu...

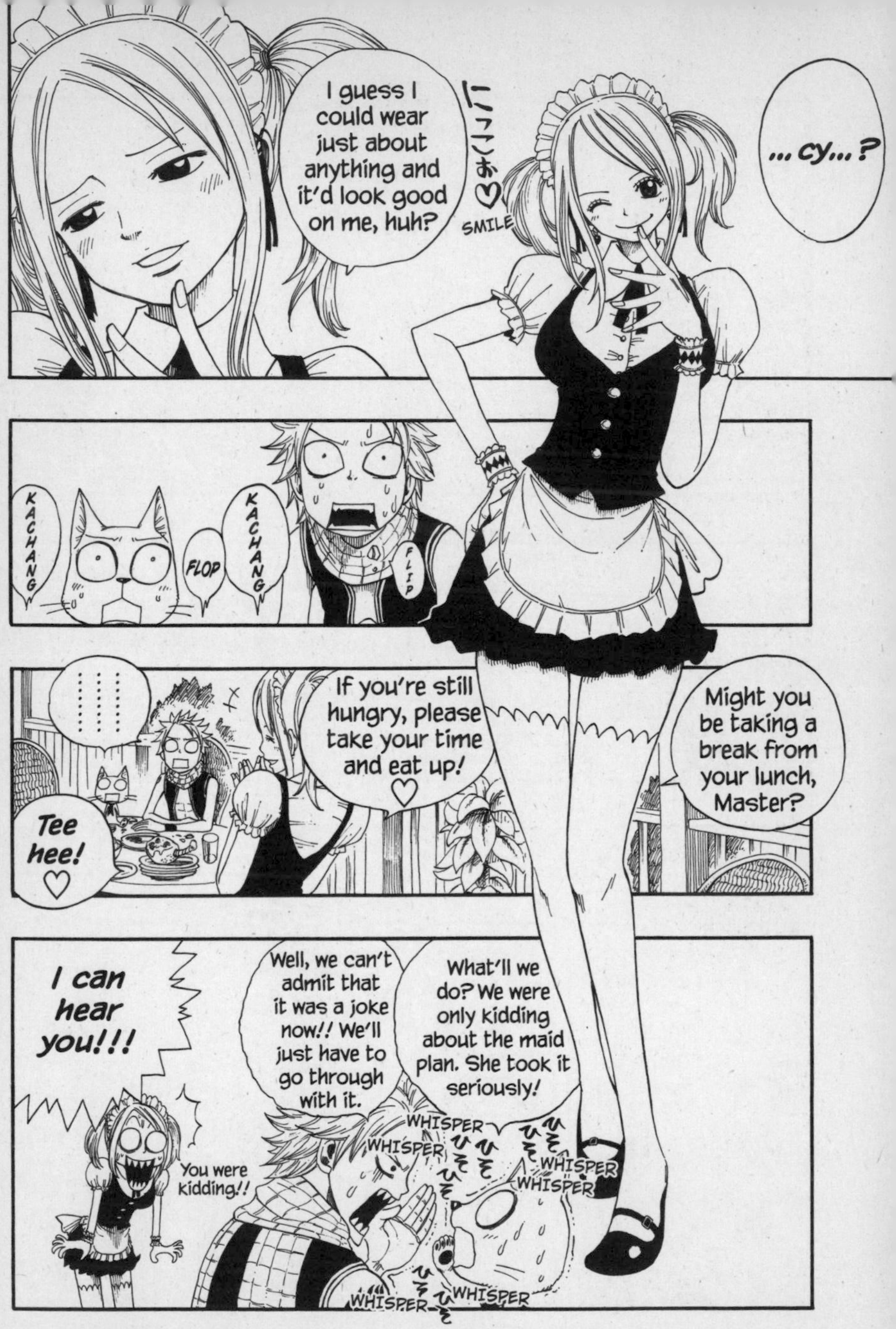
... cy... ?
にっこぉ♡
SMILE
I guess I could wear just about anything and it'd look good on me, huh?
FLIP
KACHANG
FLOP
KACHANG
Might you be taking a break from your lunch, Master?
If you're still hungry, please take your time and eat up! ♡
......
Tee hee! ♡
What'll we do? We were only kidding about the maid plan. She took it seriously!
Well, we can't admit that it was a joke now!! We'll just have to go through with it.
WHISPER
WHISPER
WHISPER
WHISPER
WHISPER
WHISPER
You were kidding!!
I can hear you!!!

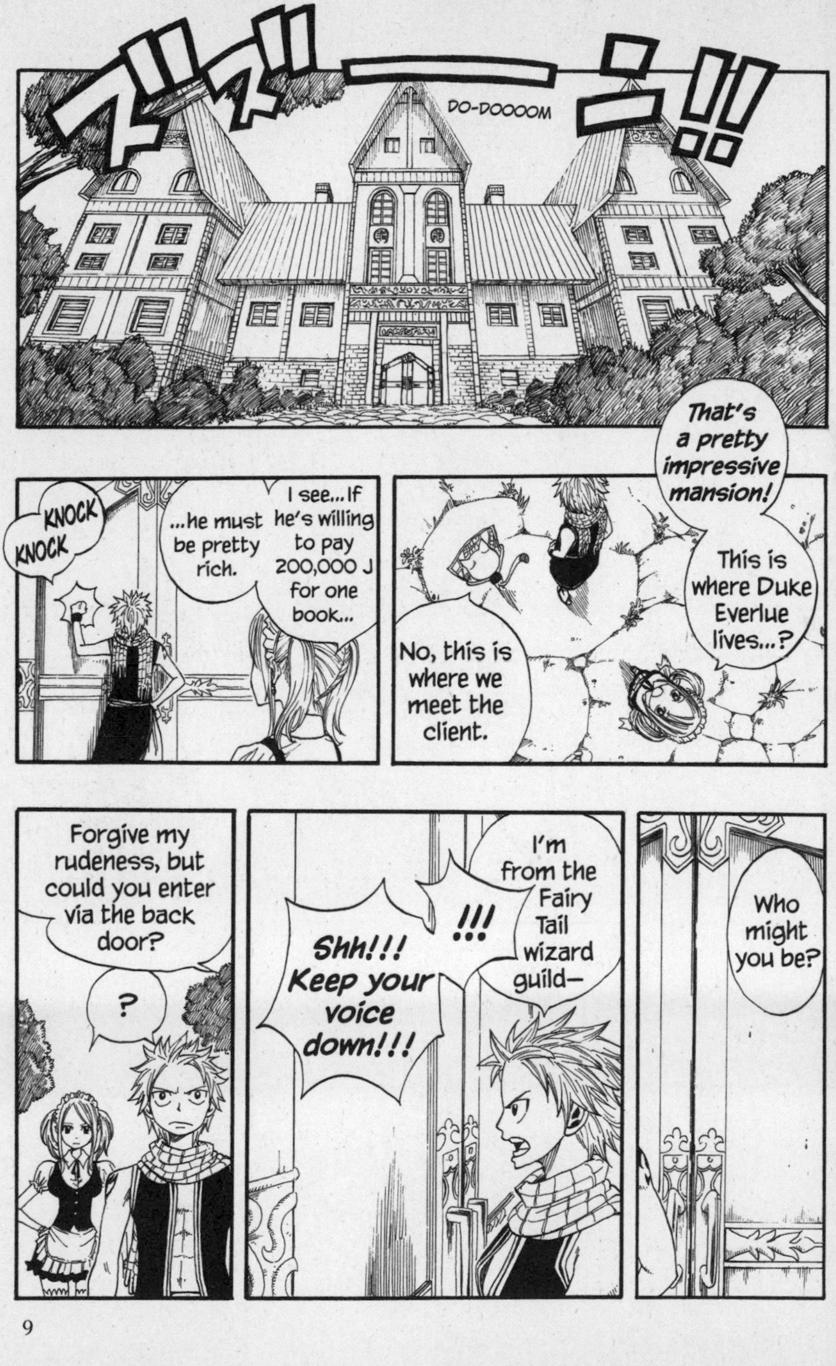
DO-DOOOOM
That's a pretty impressive mansion!
This is where Duke Everlue lives...?
No, this is where we meet the client.
I see... If he's willing to pay 200,000 J for one book...
...he must be pretty rich.
KNOCK KNOCK
Who might you be?
I'm from the Fairy Tail wizard guild—
!!!
Shh!!! Keep your voice down!!!
Forgive my rudeness, but could you enter via the back door?
?

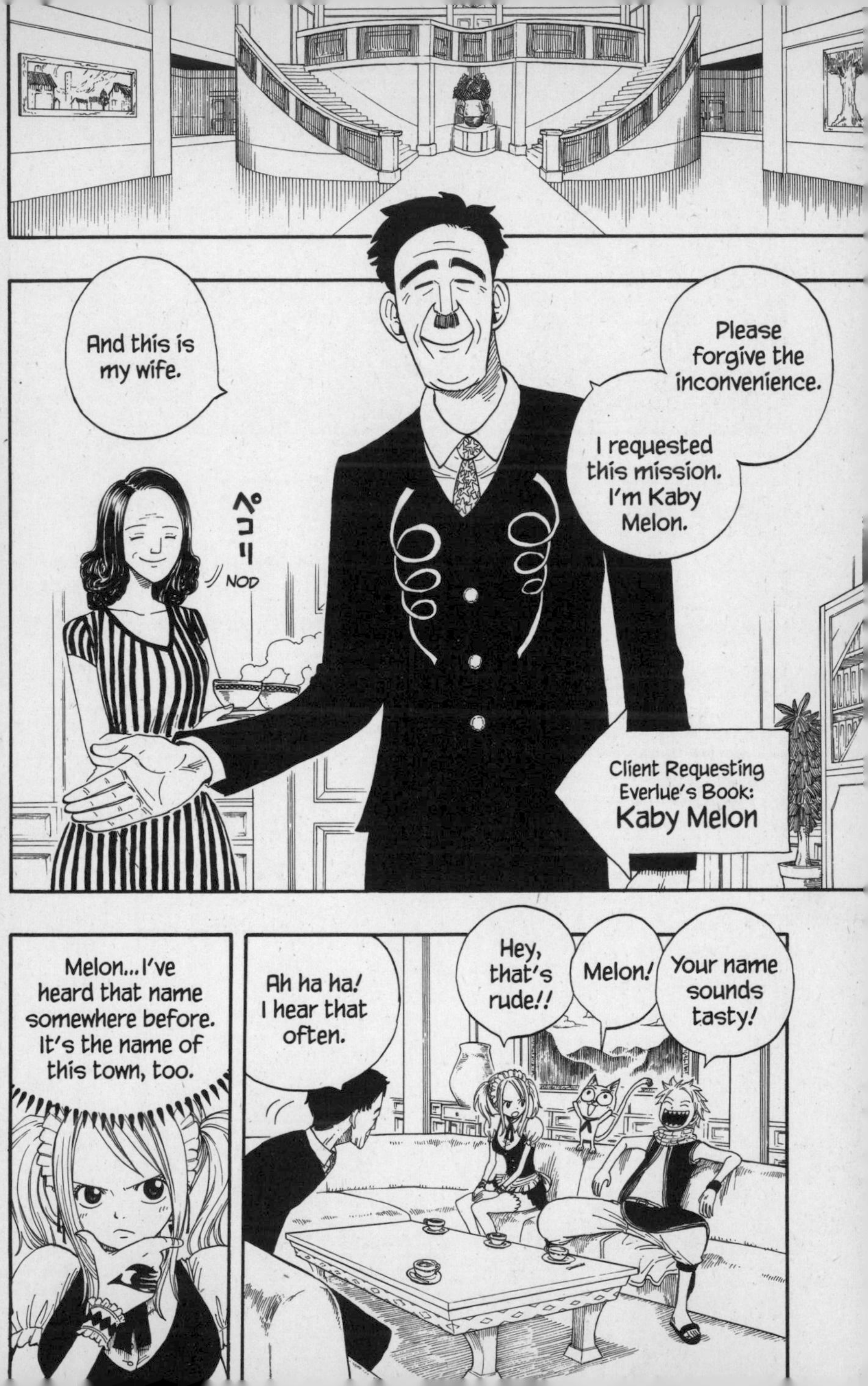

Please forgive the inconvenience.
I requested this mission. I'm Kaby Melon.
And this is my wife.
ペコリ
NOD
Client Requesting Everlue's Book: Kaby Melon
Your name sounds tasty!
Melon!
Hey, that's rude!!
Ah ha ha! I hear that often.
Melon...I've heard that name somewhere before. It's the name of this town, too.

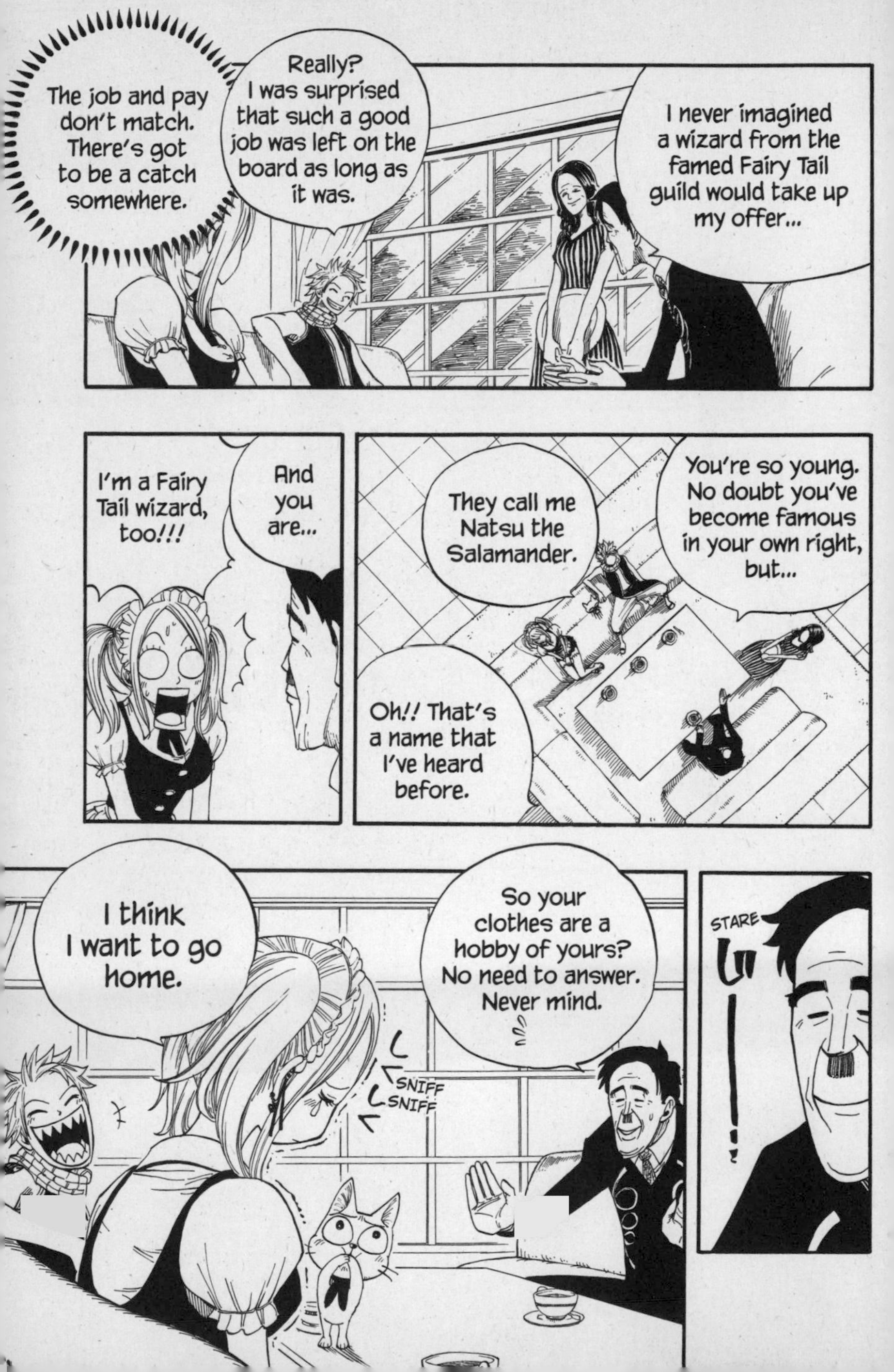
I never imagined a wizard from the famed Fairy Tail guild would take up my offer...
Really? I was surprised that such a good job was left on the board as long as it was.
The job and pay don't match. There's got to be a catch somewhere.
You're so young. No doubt you've become famous in your own right, but...
They call me Natsu the Salamander.
Oh!! That's a name that I've heard before.
And you are...
I'm a Fairy Tail wizard, too!!!
STARE
So your clothes are a hobby of yours? No need to answer. Never mind.
SNIFF
SNIFF
I think I want to go home.

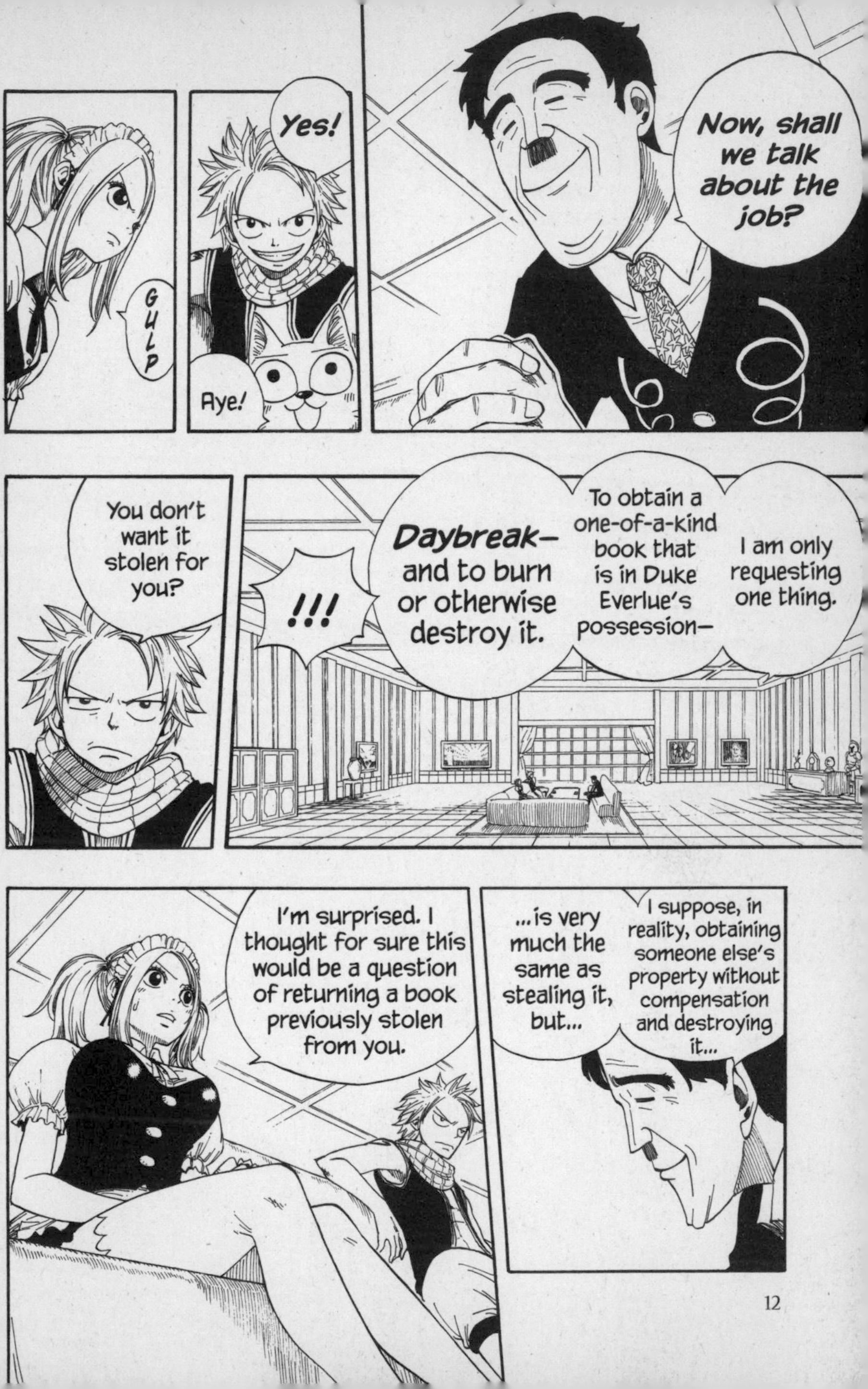
Now, shall we talk about the job?
Yes!
Aye!
GULP
I am only requesting one thing.
To obtain a one-of-a-kind book that is in Duke Everlue's possession—
Daybreak— and to burn or otherwise destroy it.
!!!
You don't want it stolen for you?
I suppose, in reality, obtaining someone else's property without compensation and destroying it...
...is very much the same as stealing it, but...
I'm surprised. I thought for sure this would be a question of returning a book previously stolen from you.

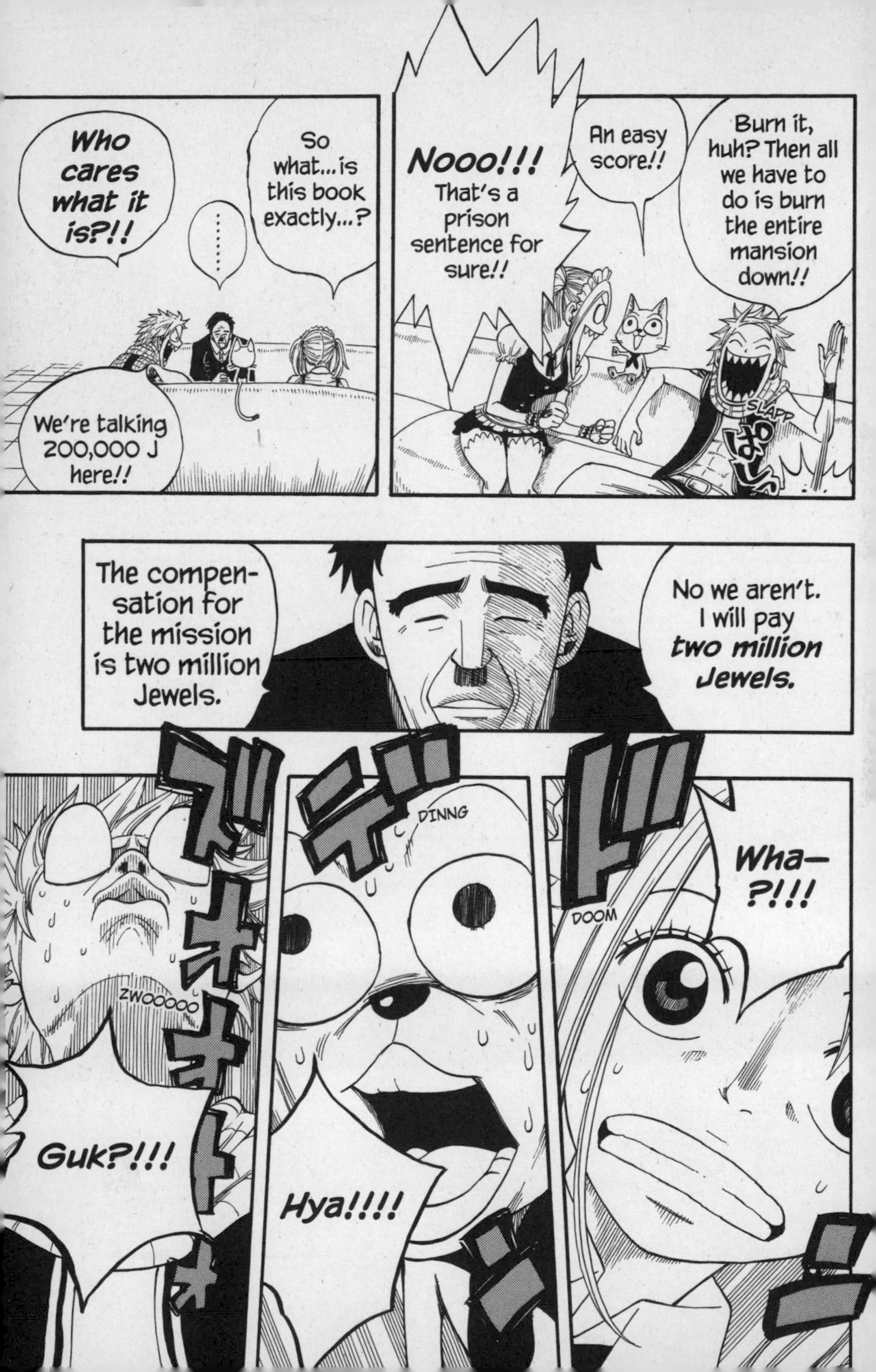
Burn it, huh? Then all we have to do is burn the entire mansion down!!
An easy score!!
Nooo!!! That's a prison sentence for sure!!
SLAPP
So what...is this book exactly...?
......
Who cares what it is?!!
We're talking 200,000 J here!!
No we aren't. I will pay two million Jewels.
The compensation for the mission is two million Jewels.
Wha—?!!!
DOOM
DINNG
Hya!!!!
ZWOOOOO
Guk?!!!

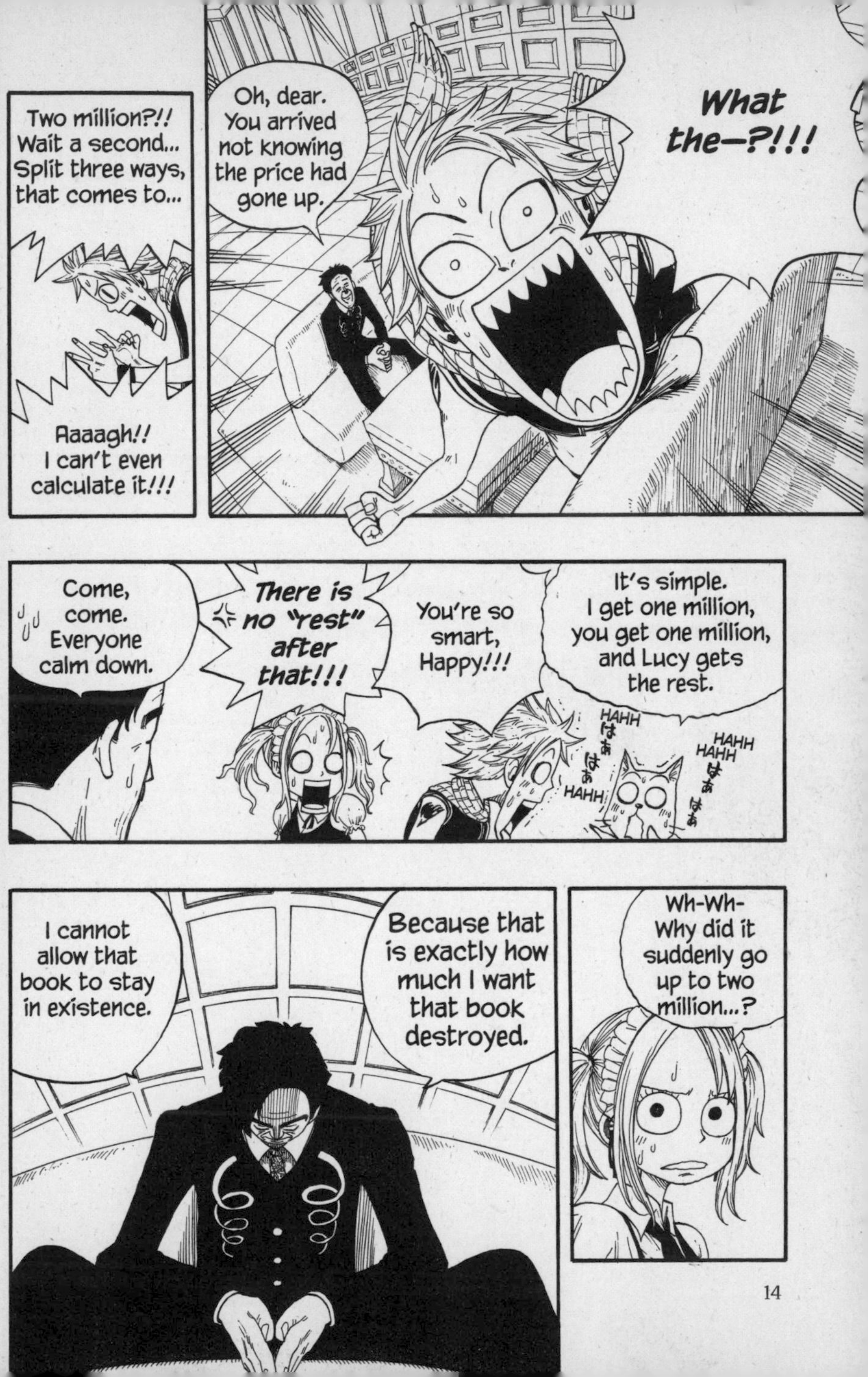
What the—?!!!
Oh, dear. You arrived not knowing the price had gone up.
Two million?!! Wait a second... Split three ways, that comes to...
Aaaagh!! I can't even calculate it!!!
It's simple. I get one million, you get one million, and Lucy gets the rest.
HAHH はあ HAHH はあ
HAHH はあ はあ
You're so smart, Happy!!!
There is no "rest" after that!!!
Come, come. Everyone calm down.
Wh-Wh- Why did it suddenly go up to two million...?
Because that is exactly how much I want that book destroyed.
I cannot allow that book to stay in existence.

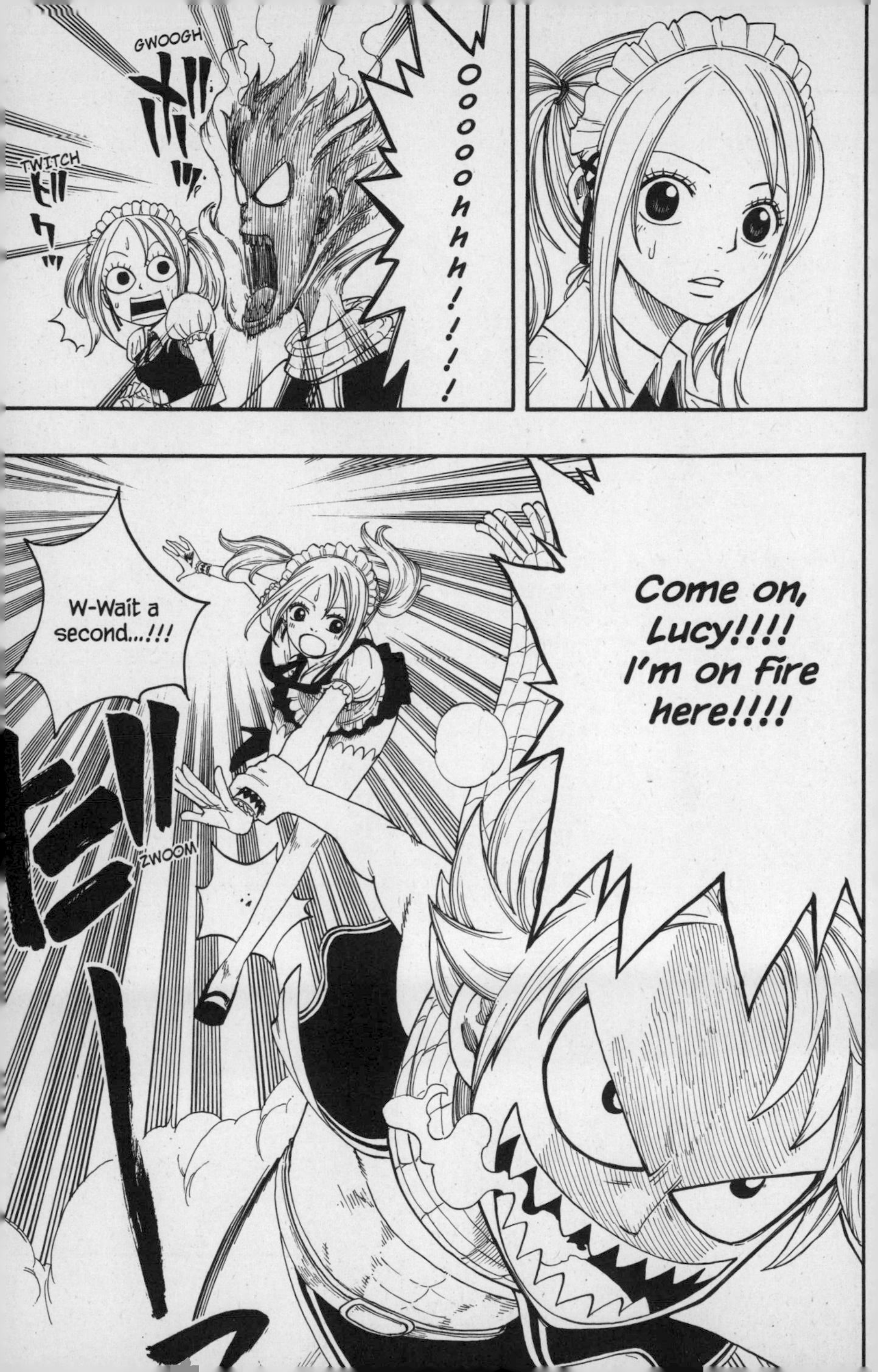
Ooooohhh!!!!
GWOOGH
TWITCH
Come on, Lucy!!!! I'm on fire here!!!!
W-Wait a second...!!!
ZWOOM

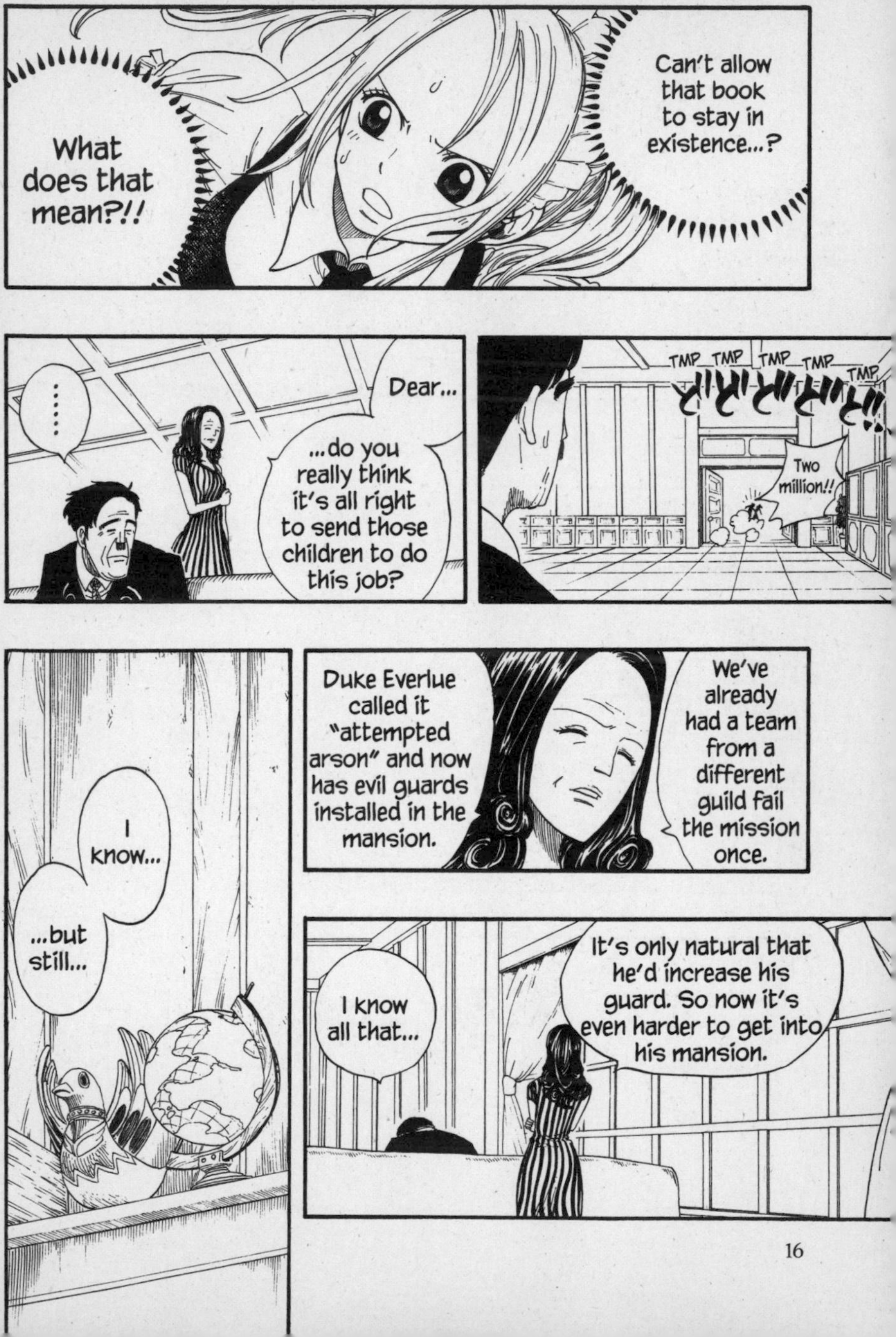

Can't allow that book to stay in existence...?
What does that mean?!!
TMP TMP TMP TMP TMP
どどどどど!!
Two million!!
Dear...
...do you really think it's all right to send those children to do this job?
......
We've already had a team from a different guild fail the mission once.
Duke Everlue called it "attempted arson" and now has evil guards installed in the mansion.
It's only natural that he'd increase his guard. So now it's even harder to get into his mansion.
I know all that...
I know...
...but still...

That book is the one thing...

...that I must erase from this world!!

The residence of Duke Everlue.

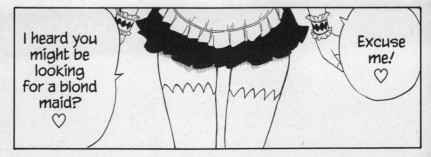

I heard you might be looking for a blond maid? ♡

Excuse me! ♡

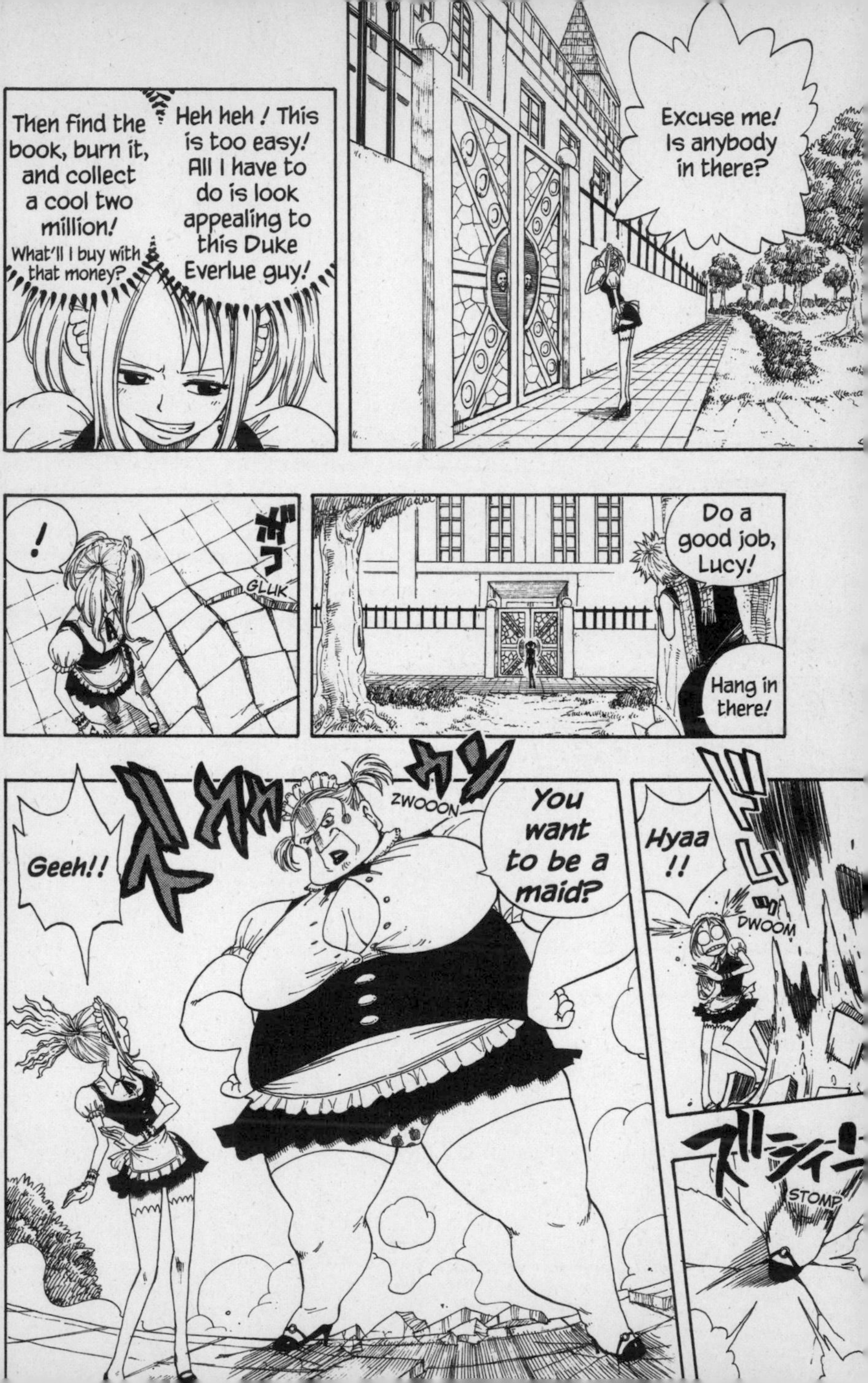
Excuse me! Is anybody in there?
Heh heh! This is too easy! All I have to do is look appealing to this Duke Everlue guy!
Then find the book, burn it, and collect a cool two million!
What'll I buy with that money?
Do a good job, Lucy!
Hang in there!
!
GLUK
Hyaa!!
DWOOM
STOMP
ZWOOON
You want to be a maid?
Geeh!!

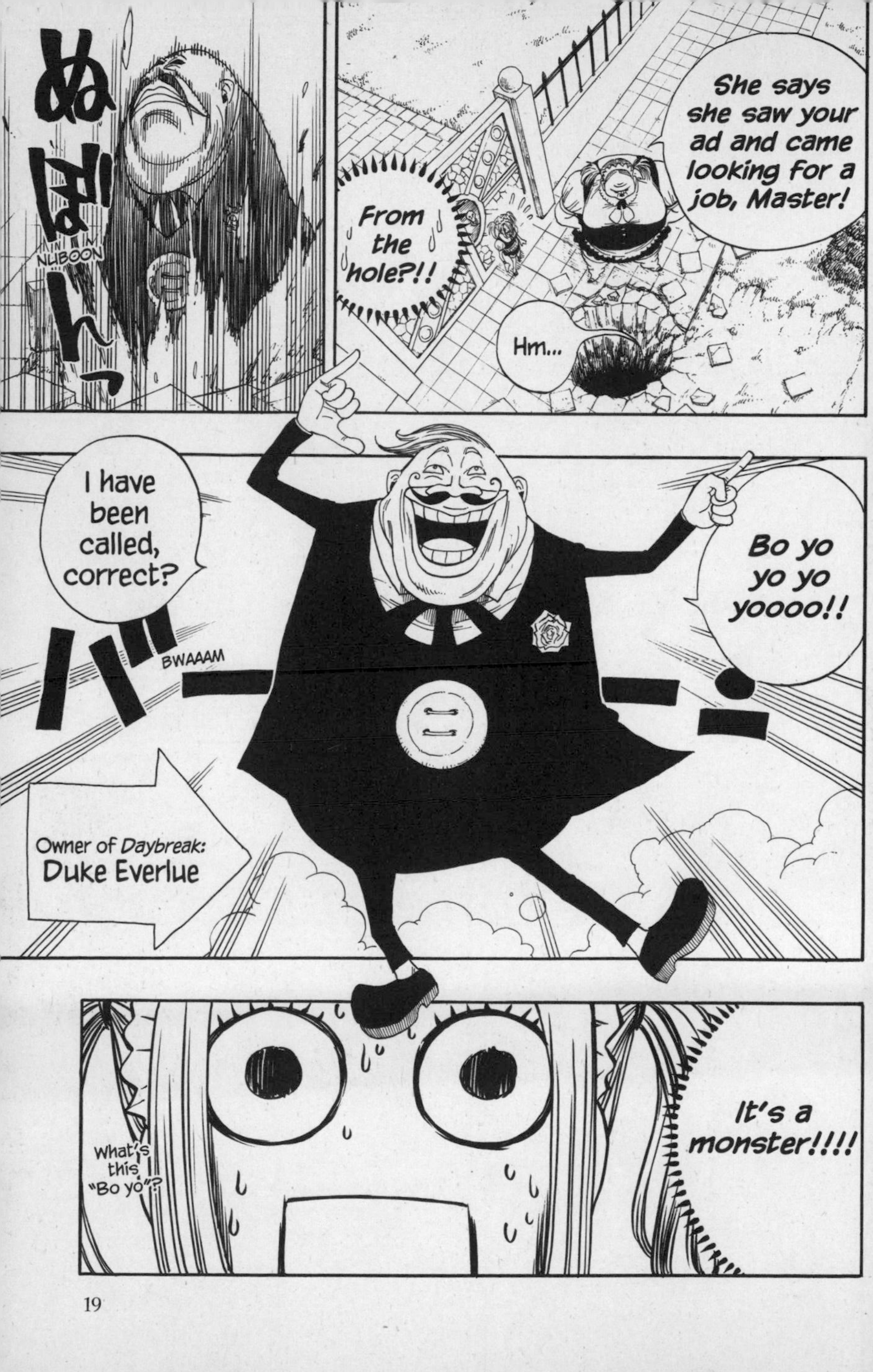
She says she saw your ad and came looking for a job, Master!
From the hole?!!
Hm...
ぬぼーんっ
NUBOON
Bo yo yo yo yoooo!!
I have been called, correct?
バーン
BWAAAM
Owner of Daybreak: Duke Everlue
It's a monster!!!!
what's this "Bo yo"?

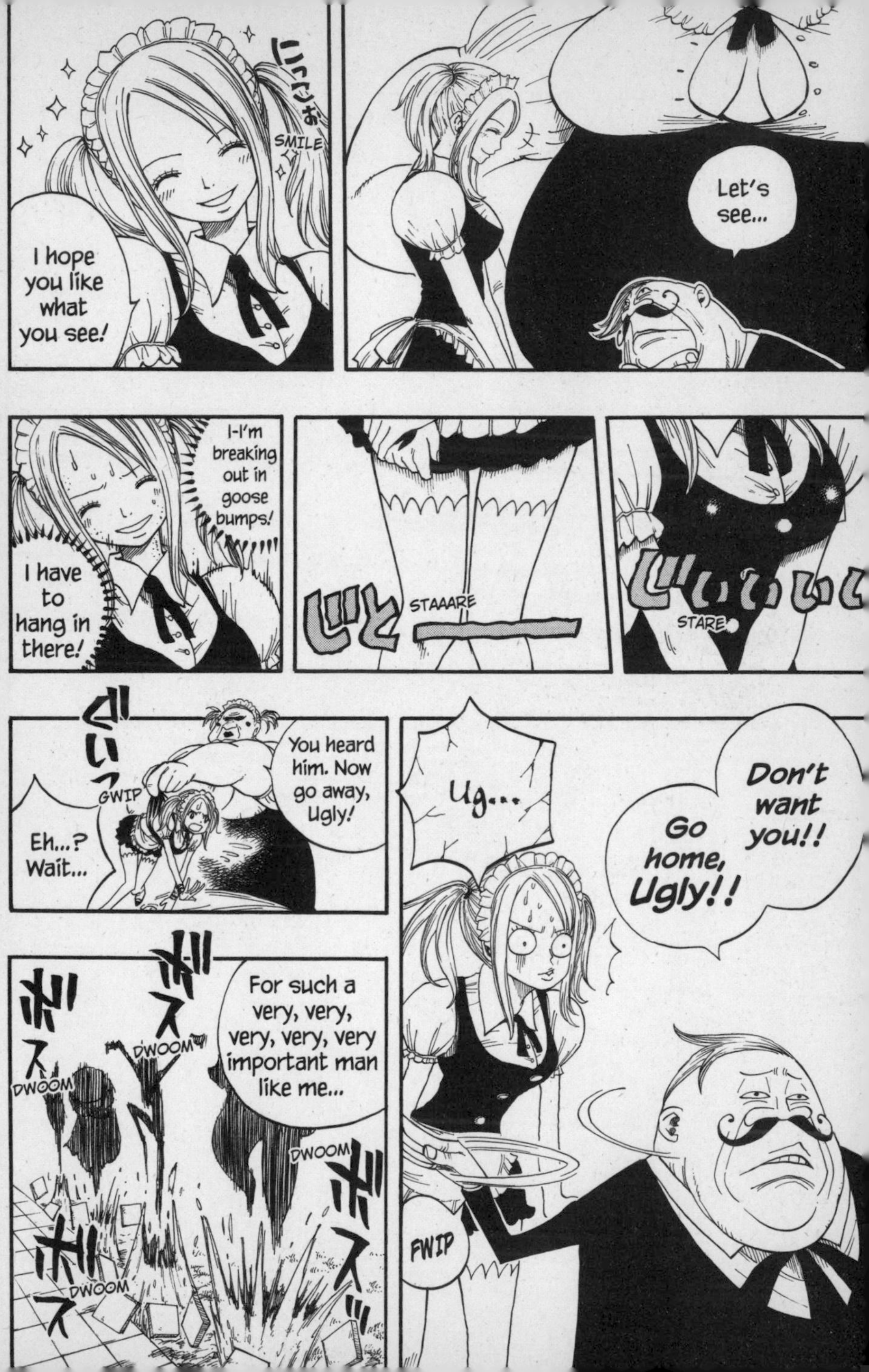
Let's see...
SMILE
I hope you like what you see!
STARE
STAAARE
I-I'm breaking out in goose bumps!
I have to hang in there!
GWIP
You heard him. Now go away, Ugly!
Eh...? Wait...
For such a very, very, very, very, very important man like me...
DWOOM
DWOOM
DWOOM
DWOOM
Don't want you!!
Go home, Ugly!!
Ug...
FWIP

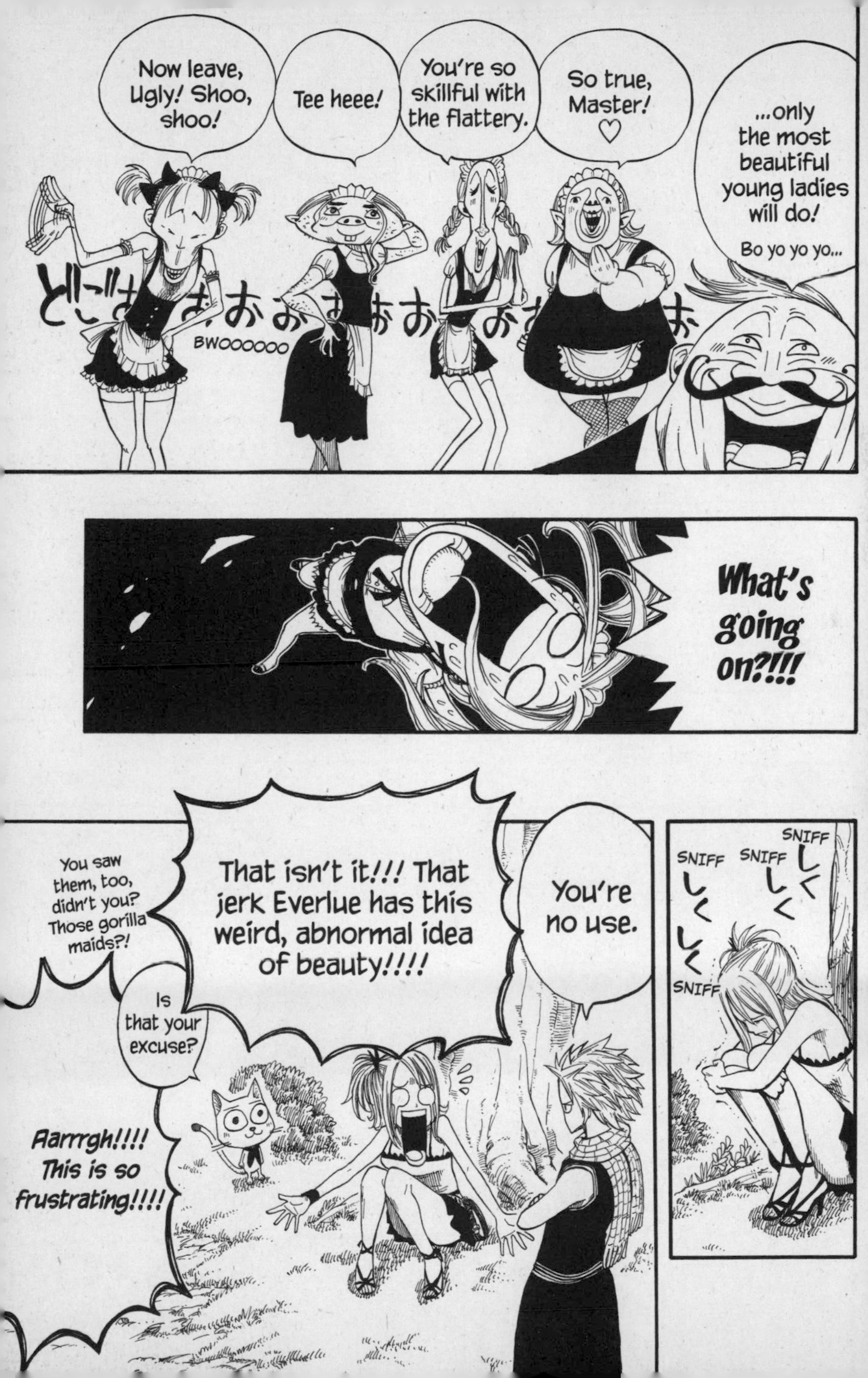
...only the most beautiful young ladies will do!
Bo yo yo yo...
So true, Master! ♡
You're so skillful with the flattery.
Tee heee!
Now leave, Ugly! Shoo, shoo!
BWOOOOOO
What's going on?!!!
SNIFF
SNIFF
SNIFF
SNIFF
You're no use.
That isn't it!!! That jerk Everlue has this weird, abnormal idea of beauty!!!!
You saw them, too, didn't you? Those gorilla maids?!
Is that your excuse?
Aarrrgh!!!! This is so frustrating!!!!

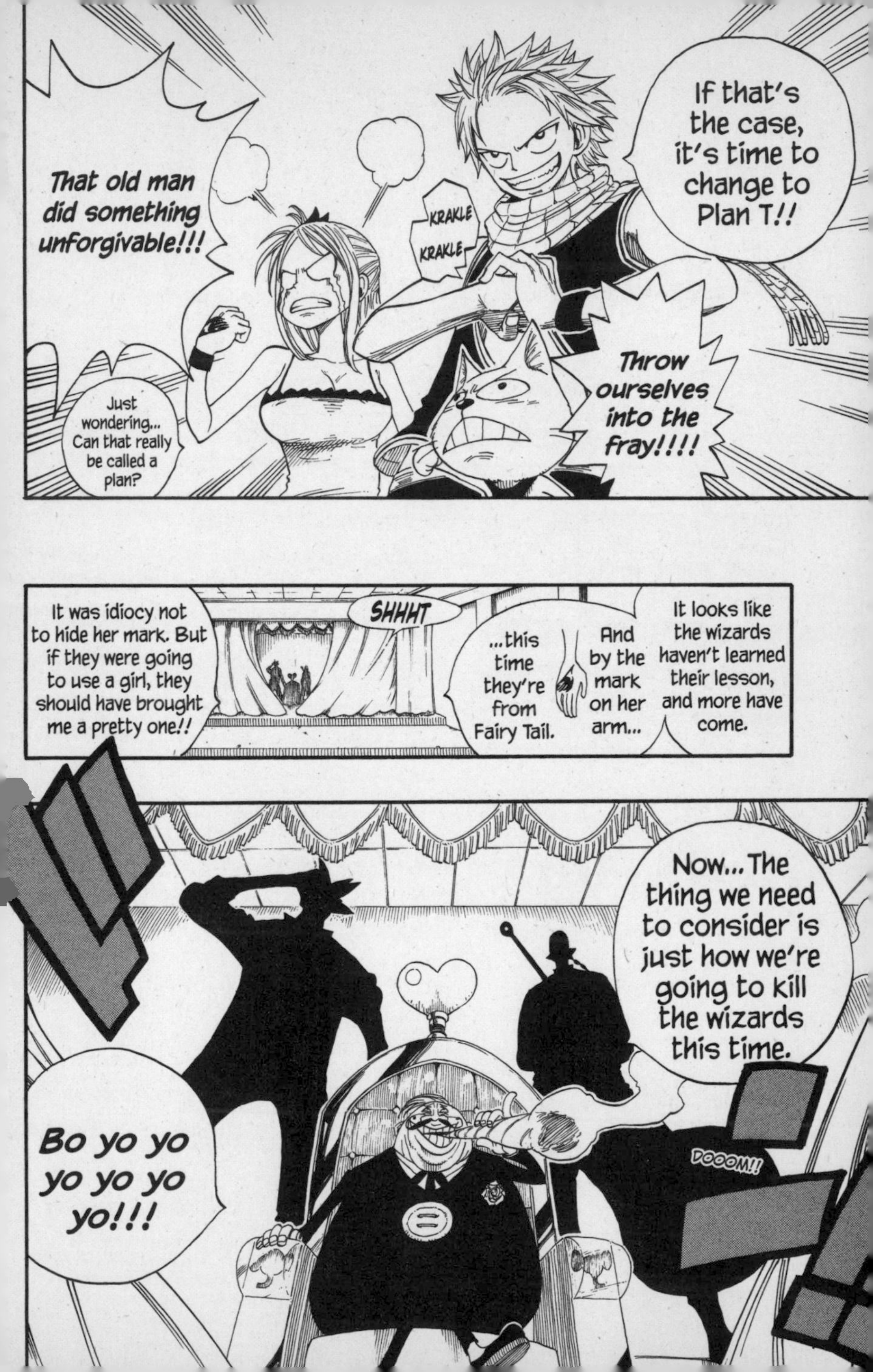
If that's the case, it's time to change to Plan T!!
KRAKLE KRAKLE
That old man did something unforgivable!!!
Throw ourselves into the fray!!!!
Just wondering... Can that really be called a plan?
It looks like the wizards haven't learned their lesson, and more have come.
And by the mark on her arm...
...this time they're from Fairy Tail.
SHHHT
It was idiocy not to hide her mark. But if they were going to use a girl, they should have brought me a pretty one!!
Now... The thing we need to consider is just how we're going to kill the wizards this time.
DOOOM!!
Bo yo yo yo yo yo yo!!!

FAIRY TAIL

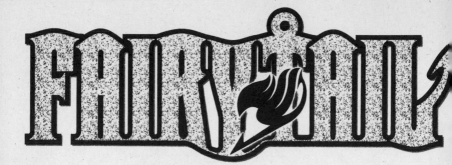

Chapter 6: Invade!! The Everlue Mansion

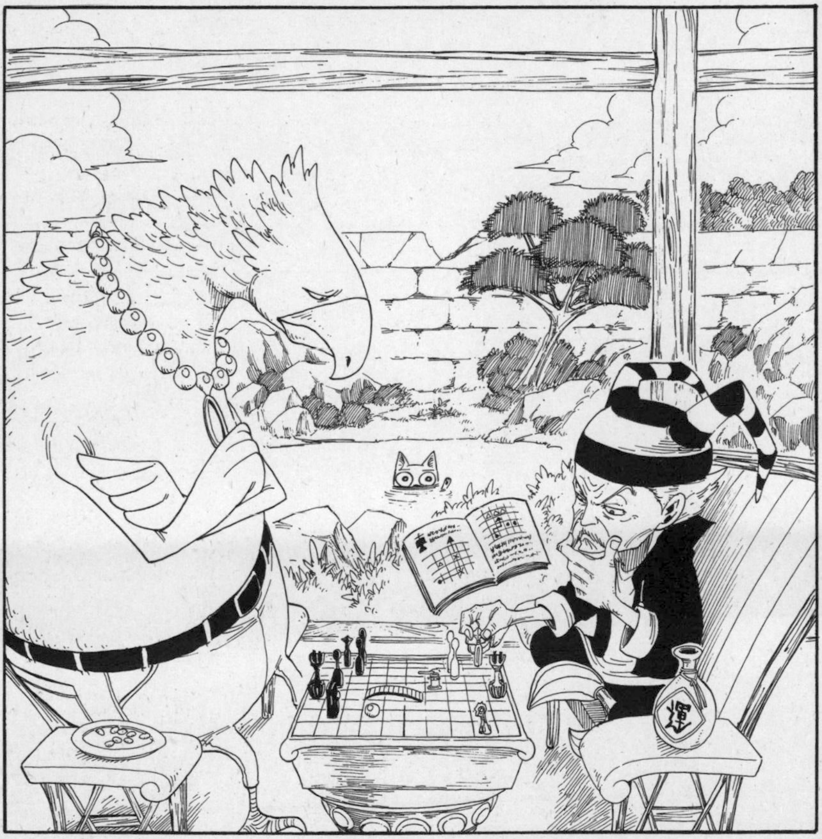

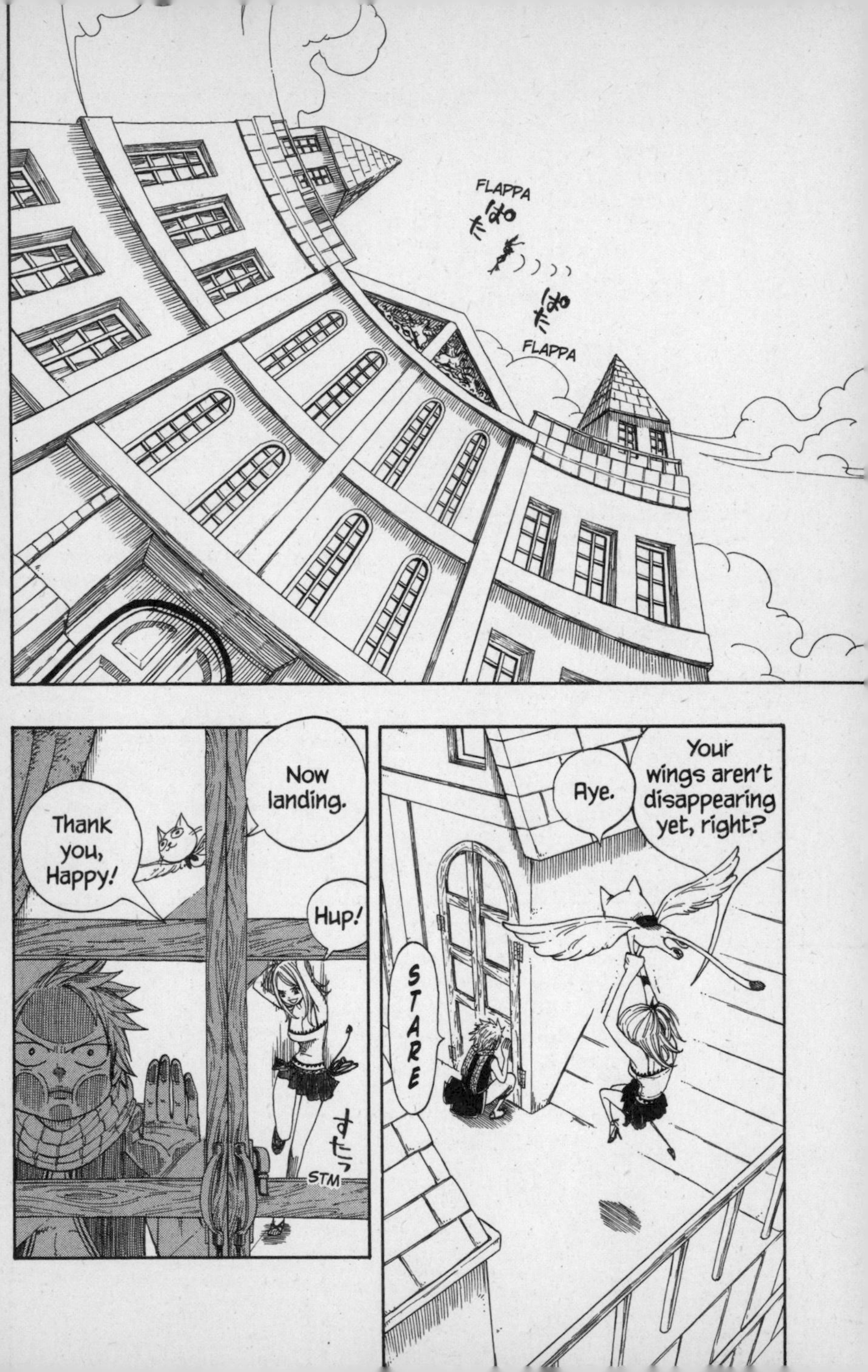
FLAPPA
FLAPPA
Your wings aren't disappearing yet, right?
Aye.
STARE
Now landing.
Thank you, Happy!
Hup!
STM

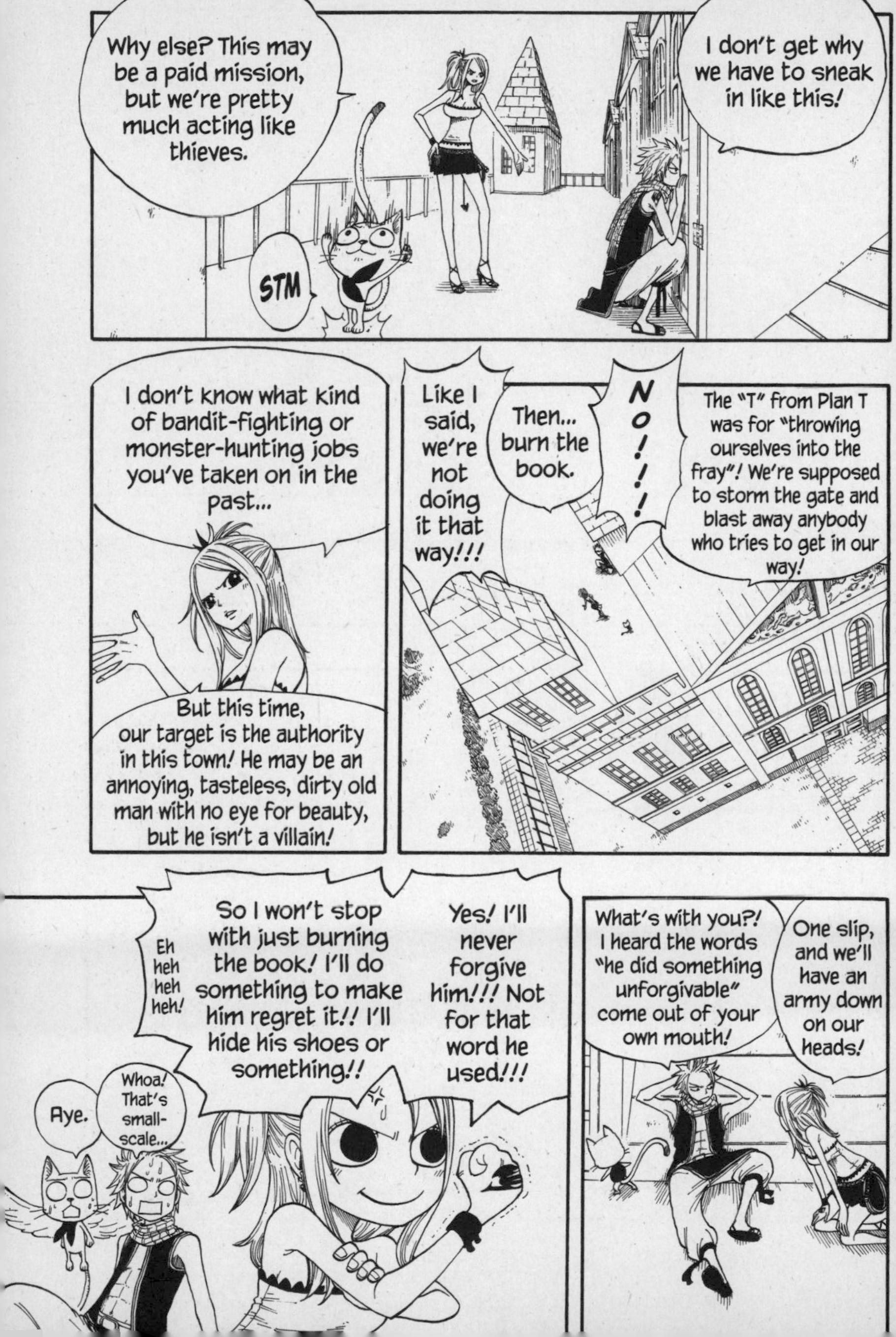
I don't get why we have to sneak in like this!
Why else? This may be a paid mission, but we're pretty much acting like thieves.
STM
The "T" from Plan T was for "throwing ourselves into the fray"! We're supposed to storm the gate and blast away anybody who tries to get in our way!
No!!!!
Then... burn the book.
Like I said, we're not doing it that way!!!
I don't know what kind of bandit-fighting or monster-hunting jobs you've taken on in the past...
But this time, our target is the authority in this town! He may be an annoying, tasteless, dirty old man with no eye for beauty, but he isn't a villain!
One slip, and we'll have an army down on our heads!
What's with you?! I heard the words "he did something unforgivable" come out of your own mouth!
Yes! I'll never forgive him!!! Not for that word he used!!!
So I won't stop with just burning the book! I'll do something to make him regret it!! I'll hide his shoes or something!!
Eh heh heh heh!
Whoa! That's small-scale...
Aye.

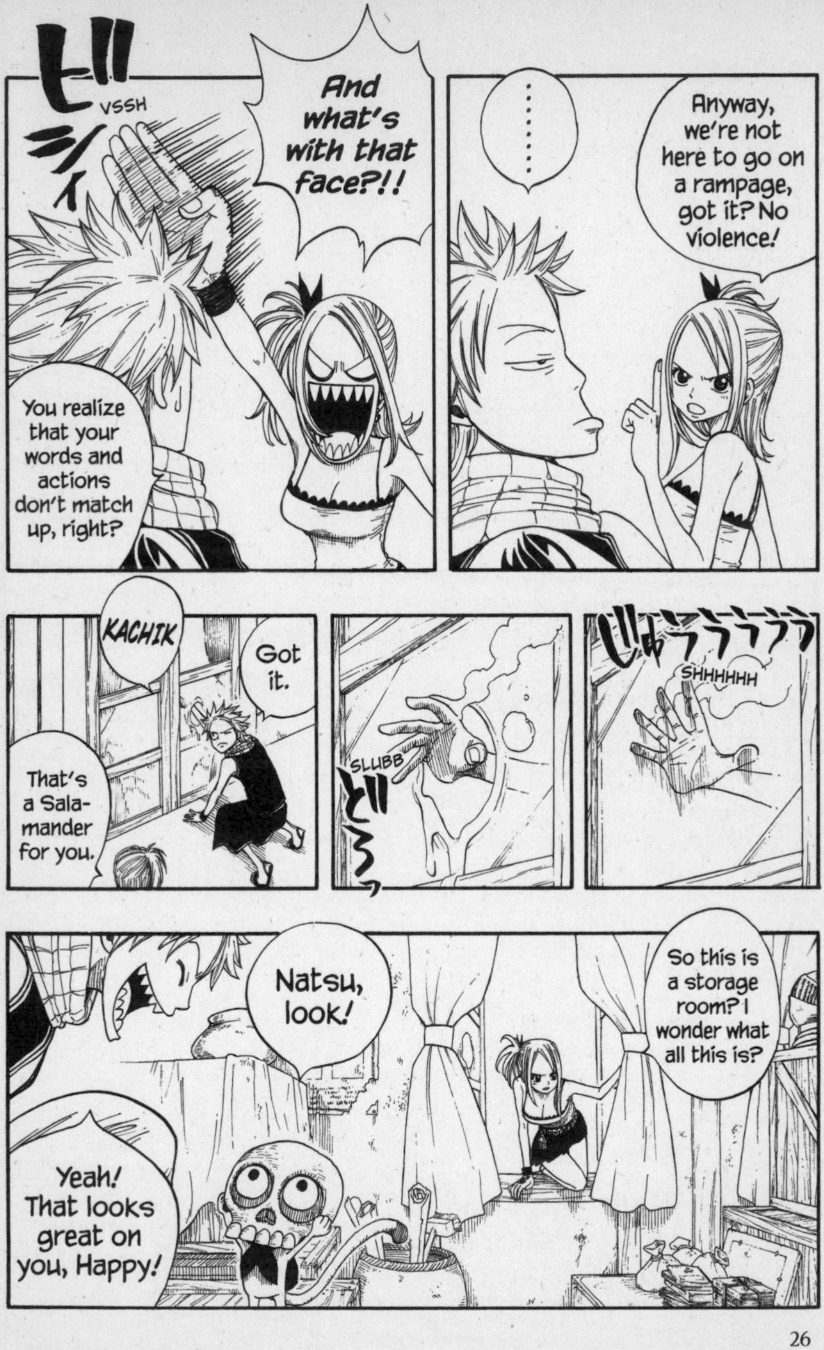

Anyway, we're not here to go on a rampage, got it? No violence!
....
And what's with that face?!!
VSSH
You realize that your words and actions don't match up, right?
SHHHHHH
SLUBB
KACHIK
Got it.
That's a Salamander for you.
So this is a storage room? I wonder what all this is?
Natsu, look!
Yeah! That looks great on you, Happy!

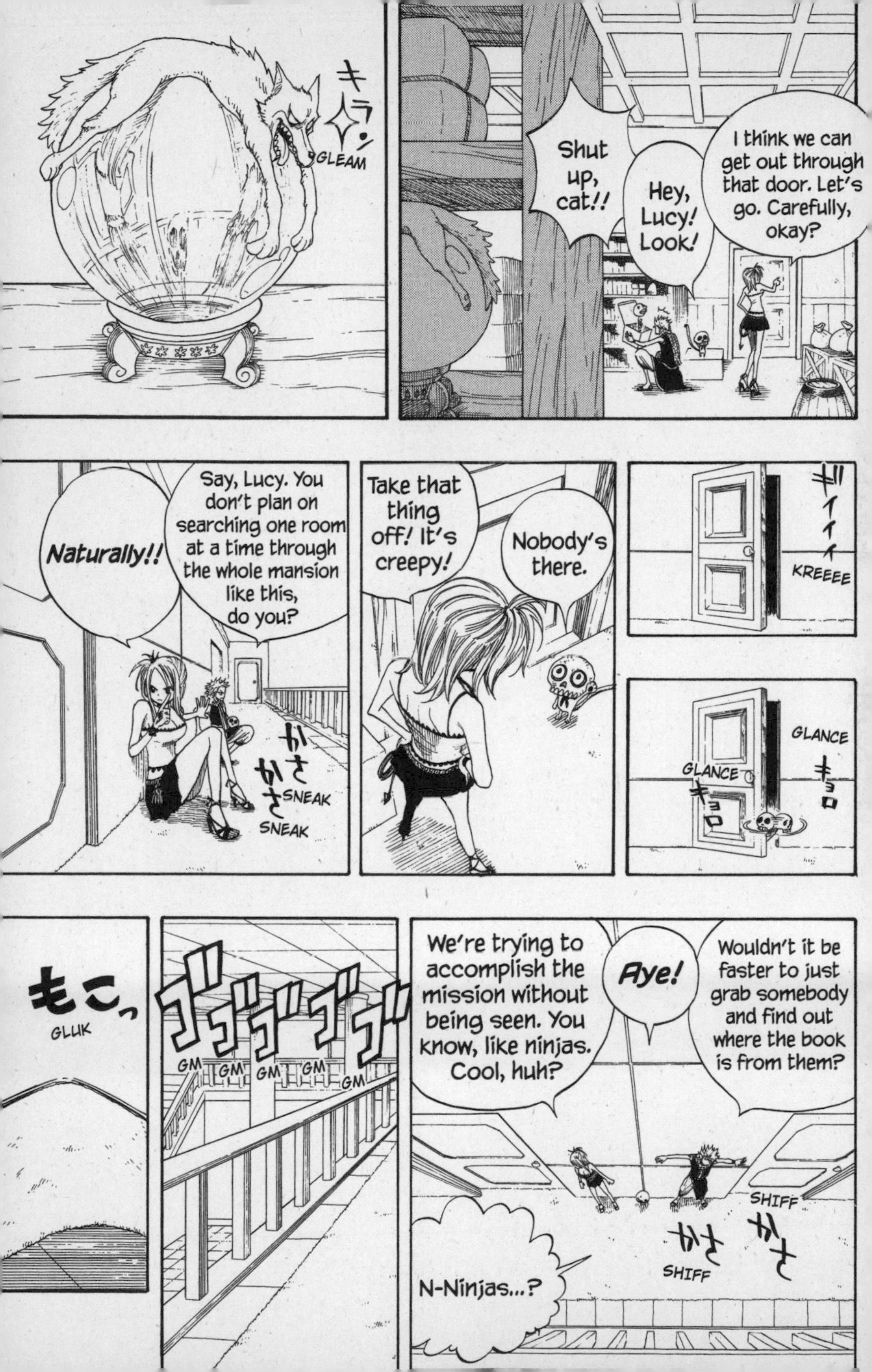
I think we can get out through that door. Let's go. Carefully, okay?
Hey, Lucy! Look!
Shut up, cat!!
キラン
GLEAM
ギイイイ
KREEEE
キョロ
GLANCE
キョロ
GLANCE
Nobody's there.
Take that thing off! It's creepy!
Say, Lucy. You don't plan on searching one room at a time through the whole mansion like this, do you?
Naturally!!
かさ かさ
SNEAK
SNEAK
Wouldn't it be faster to just grab somebody and find out where the book is from them?
Aye!
We're trying to accomplish the mission without being seen. You know, like ninjas. Cool, huh?
かさ
SHIFF
かさ
SHIFF
N-Ninjas...?
ゴゴゴゴ
GM GM GM GM GM
もこっ
GLUK

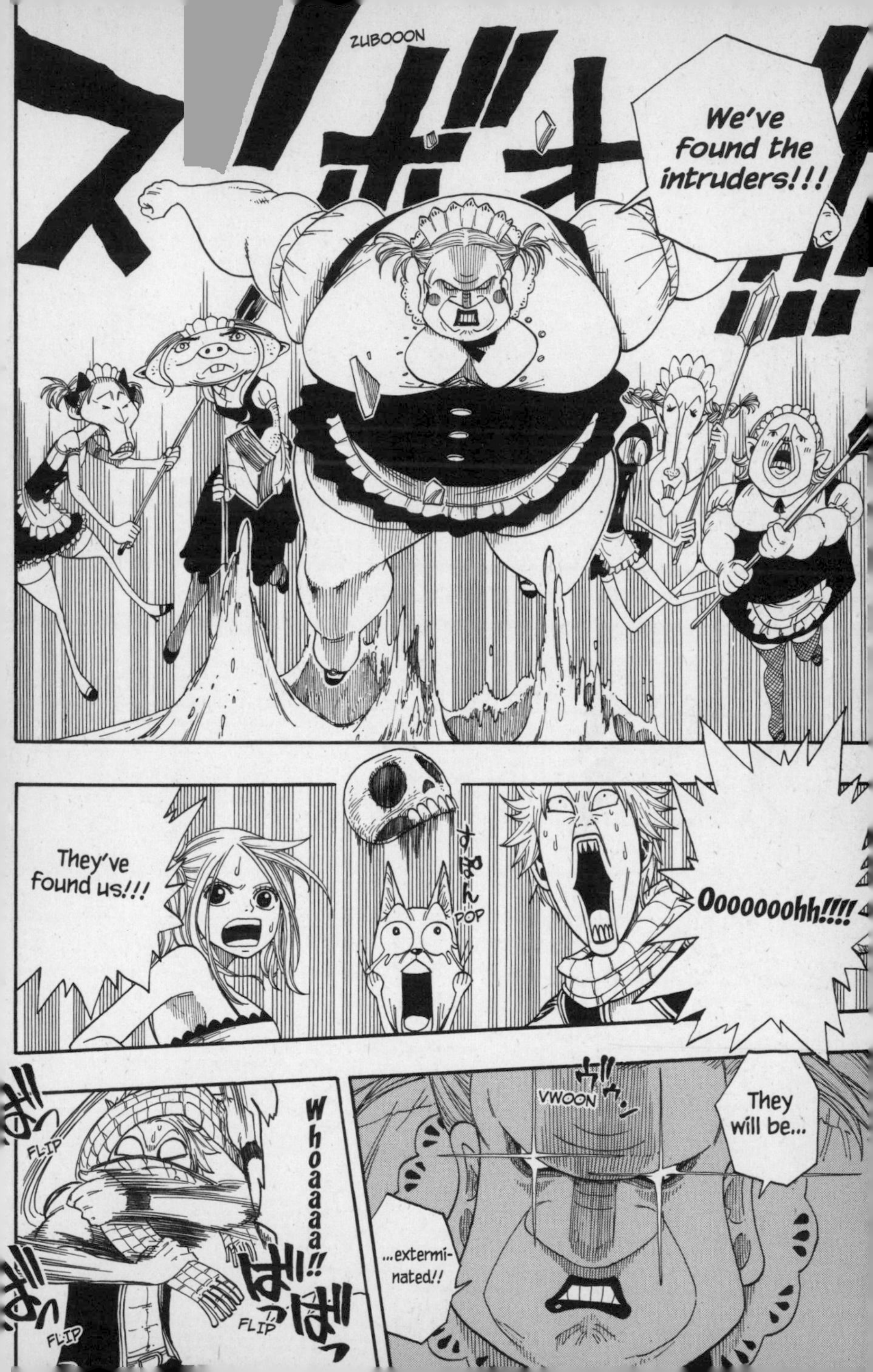
ZUBOOON
We've found the intruders!!!
Ooooooohh!!!!
POP
They've found us!!!
VWOON
They will be...
...extermi-nated!!
Whoaaaaa!!
FLIP
FLIP
FLIP

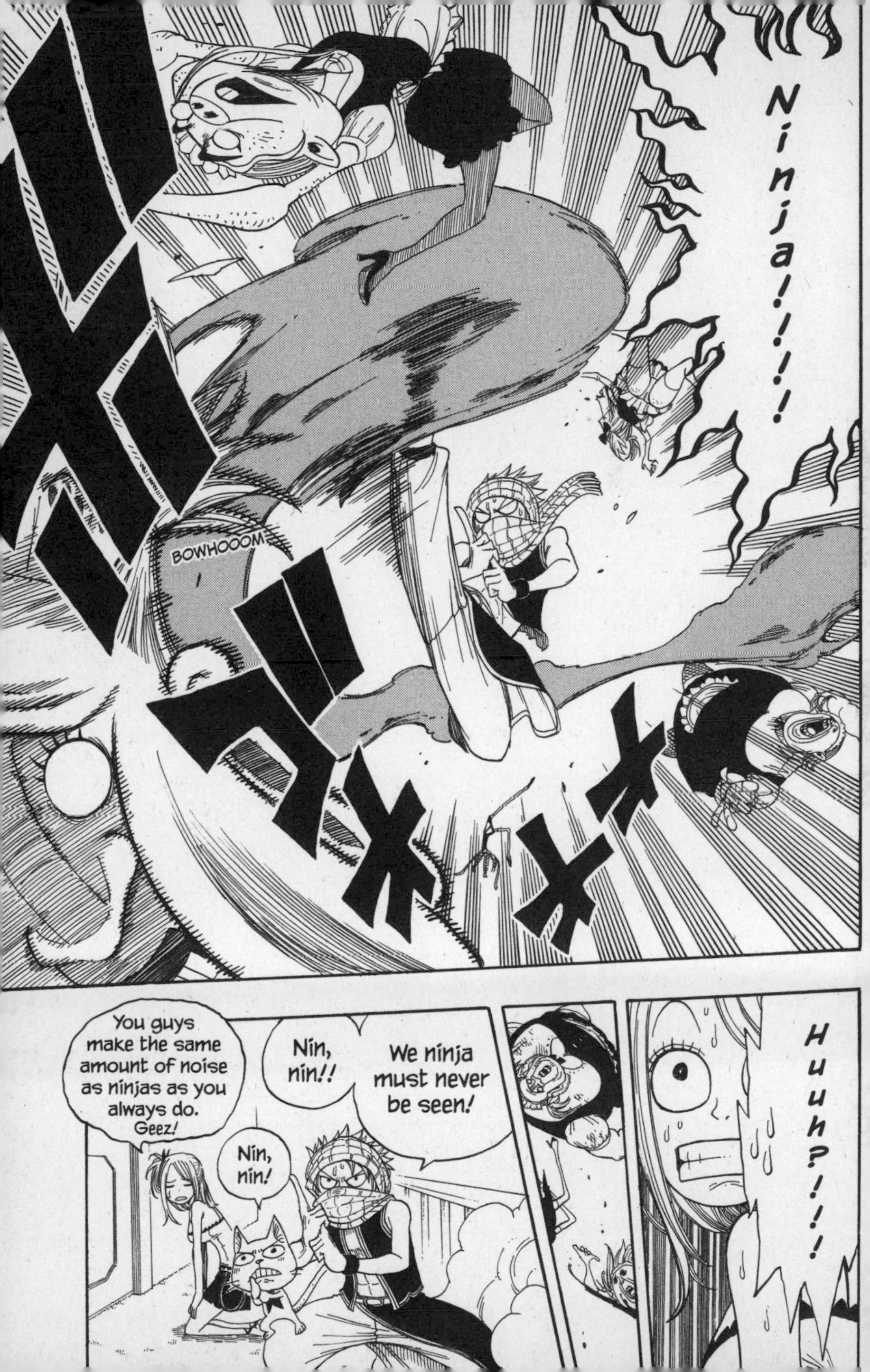
Ninja!!!!!!
BOWHOOOM
Huuh?!!!
We ninja must never be seen!
Nin, nin!!
You guys make the same amount of noise as ninjas as you always do. Geez!
Nin, nin!

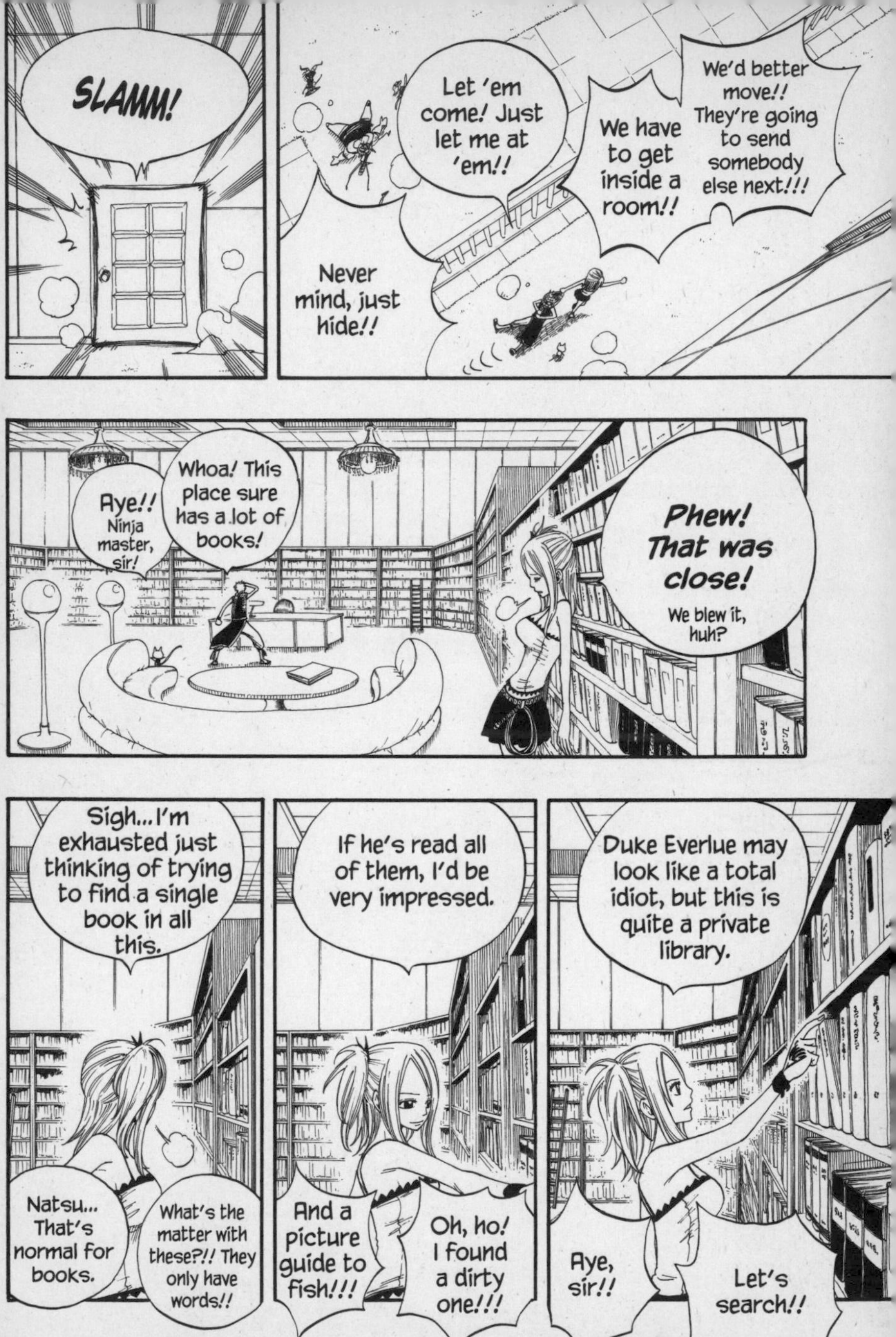

We'd better move!! They're going to send somebody else next!!!
We have to get inside a room!!
Let 'em come! Just let me at 'em!!
Never mind, just hide!!
SLAMM!
Phew! That was close!
We blew it, huh?
Whoa! This place sure has a lot of books!
Aye!! Ninja master, sir!
Duke Everlue may look like a total idiot, but this is quite a private library.
Let's search!!
Aye, sir!!
If he's read all of them, I'd be very impressed.
Oh, ho! I found a dirty one!!!
And a picture guide to fish!!!
Sigh...I'm exhausted just thinking of trying to find a single book in all this.
What's the matter with these?!! They only have words!!
Natsu... That's normal for books.

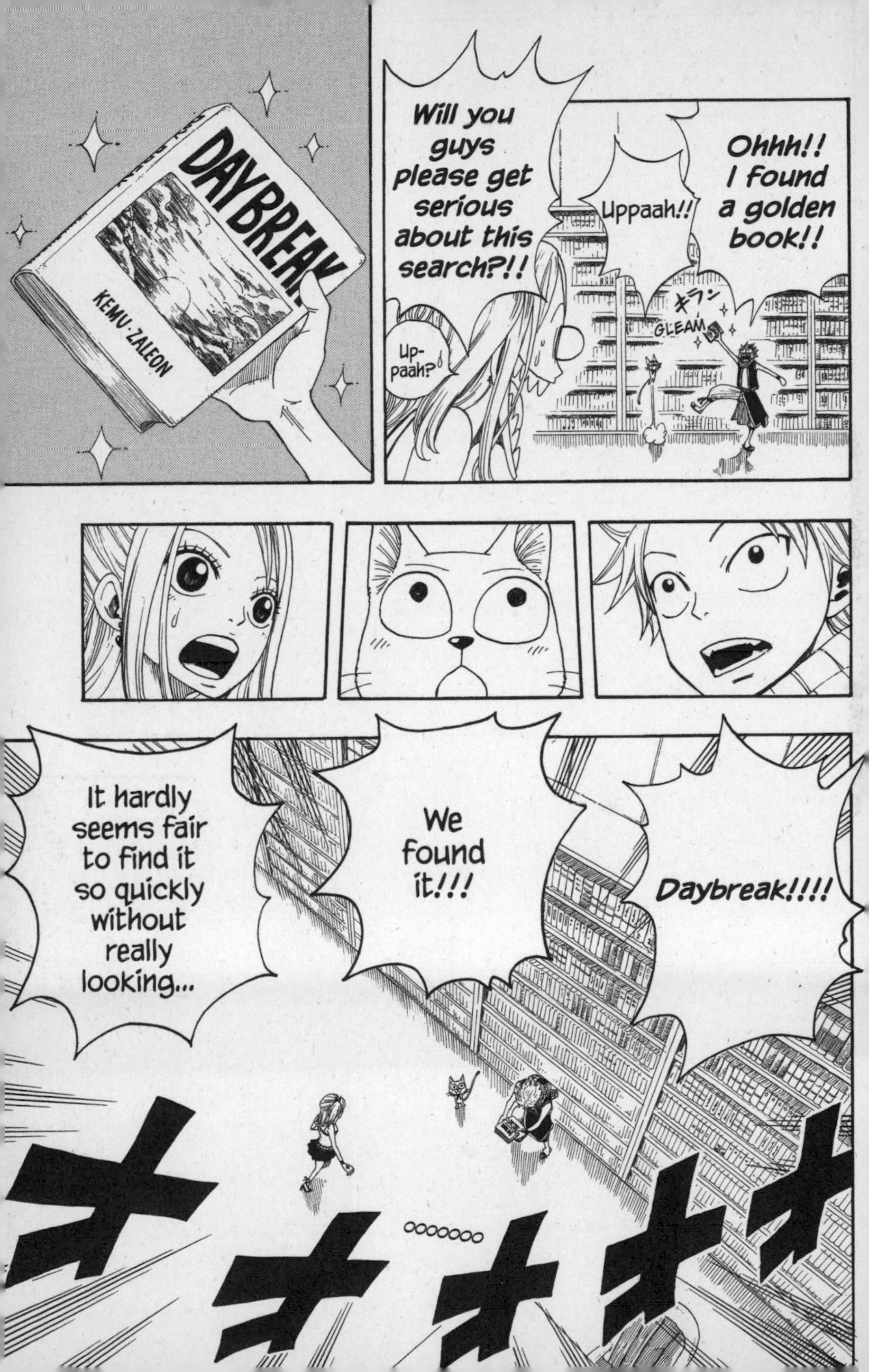
Ohhh!! I found a golden book!!
Uppaah!!
Will you guys please get serious about this search?!!
キラン
GLEAM
Up-paah?
DAYBREAK
KEMU·ZALEON
Daybreak!!!!
We found it!!!
It hardly seems fair to find it so quickly without really looking...
オオオオ
ooooooo

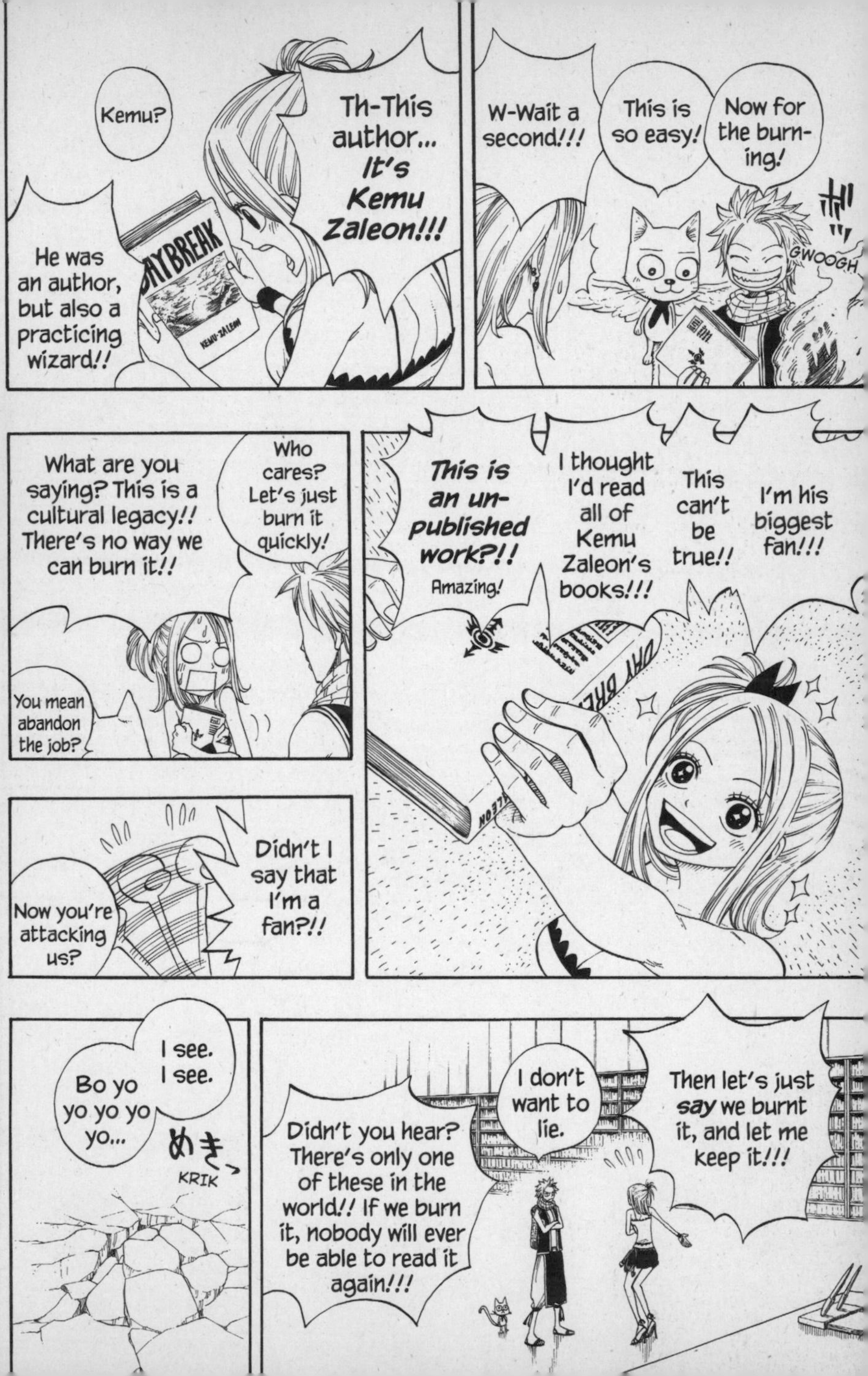
Now for the burn-ing!
This is so easy!
W-Wait a second!!!
GWOOGH
Th-This author... It's Kemu Zaleon!!!
Kemu?
He was an author, but also a practicing wizard!!
I'm his biggest fan!!!
This can't be true!!
I thought I'd read all of Kemu Zaleon's books!!!
This is an un-published work?!!
Amazing!
Who cares? Let's just burn it quickly!
What are you saying? This is a cultural legacy!! There's no way we can burn it!!
You mean abandon the job?
Didn't I say that I'm a fan?!!
Now you're attacking us?
Then let's just say we burnt it, and let me keep it!!!
I don't want to lie.
Didn't you hear? There's only one of these in the world!! If we burn it, nobody will ever be able to read it again!!!
I see. I see.
Bo yo yo yo yo yo...
めき
KRIK

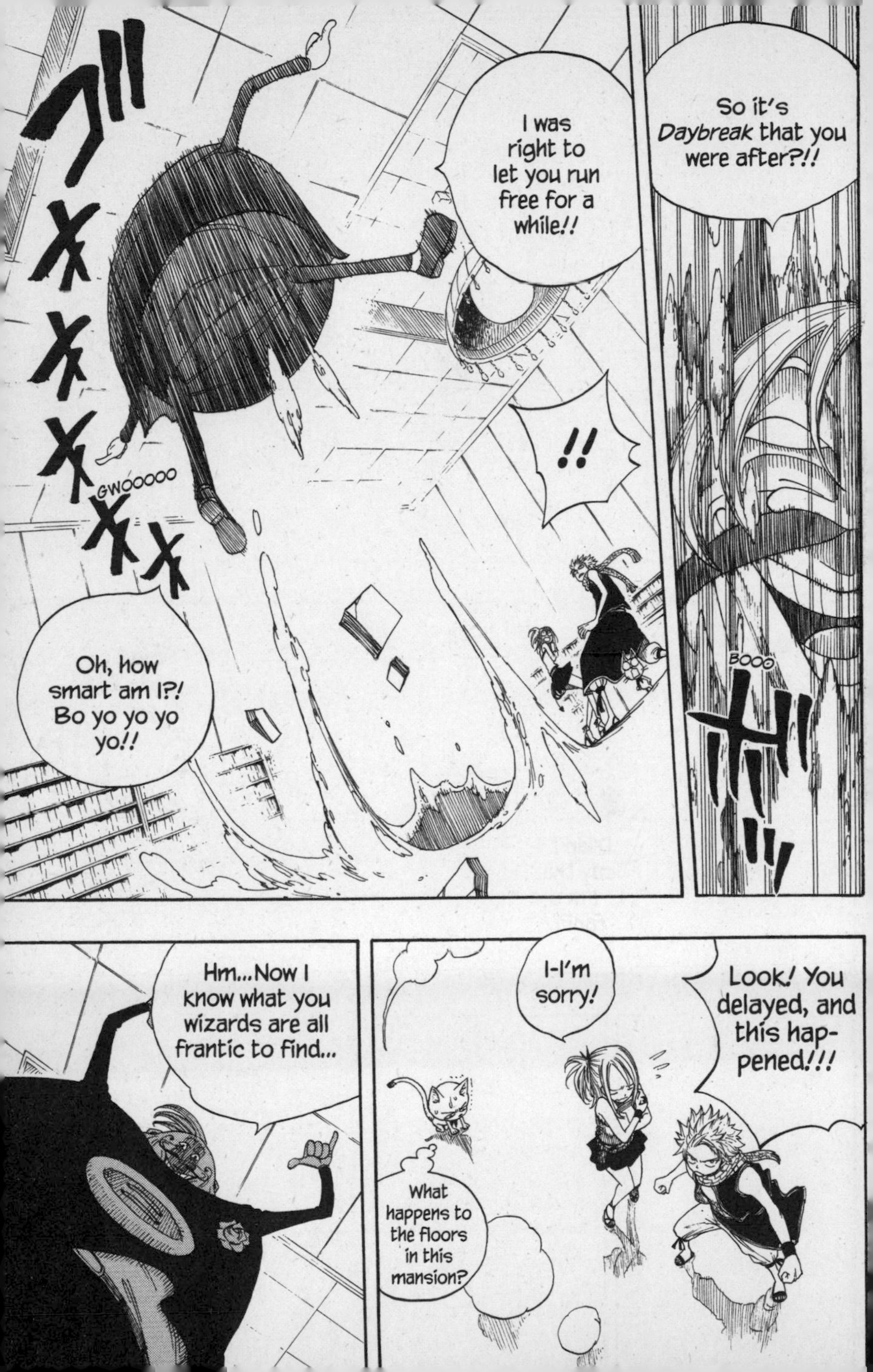
So it's *Daybreak* that you were after?!!
BOOO
I was right to let you run free for a while!!
!!
GWOOOOO
Oh, how smart am I?! Bo yo yo yo yo!!
Look! You delayed, and this hap-pened!!!
I-I'm sorry!
What happens to the floors in this mansion?
Hm...Now I know what you wizards are all frantic to find...

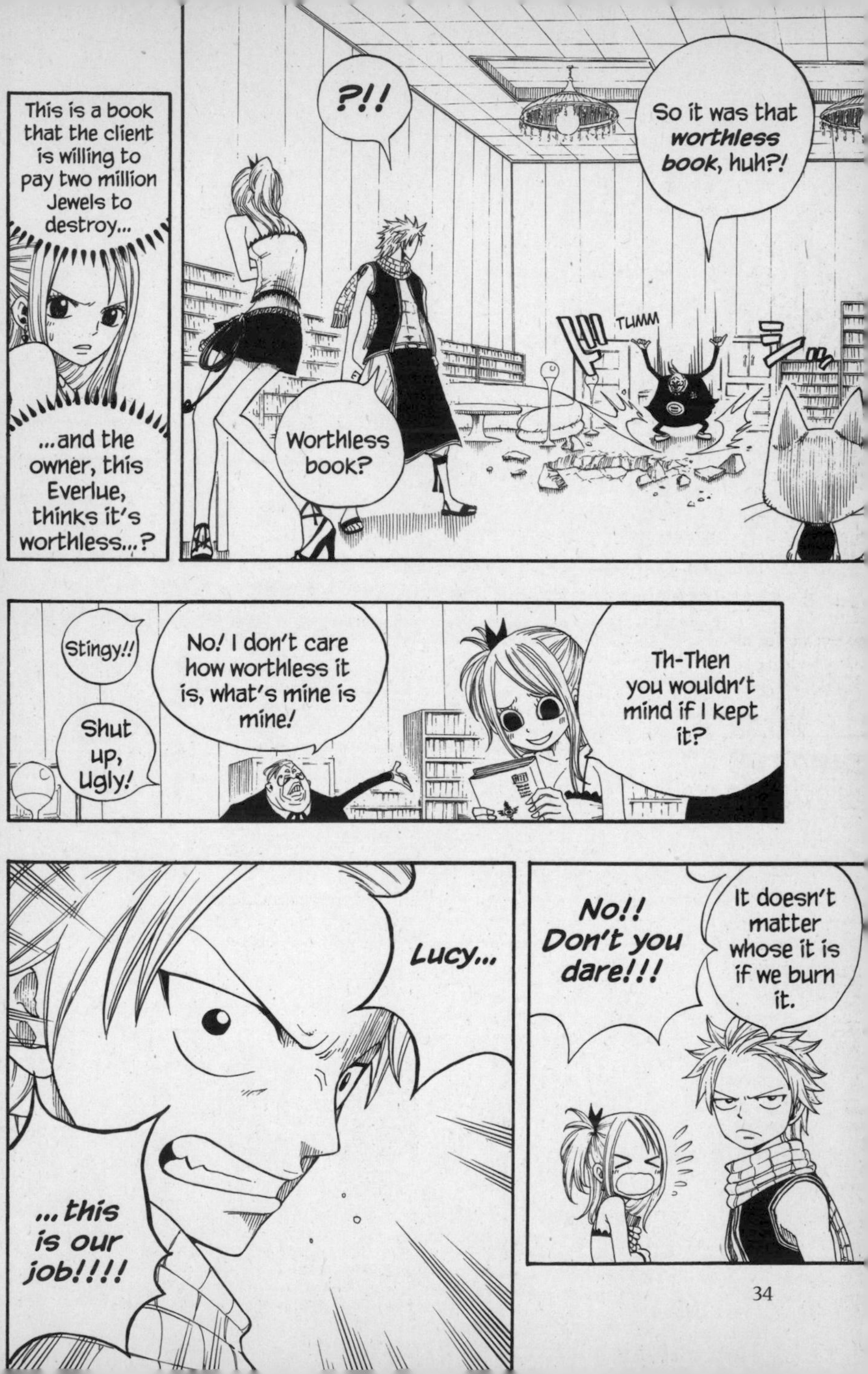
So it was that worthless book, huh?!
?!!
TUMM
Worthless book?
This is a book that the client is willing to pay two million Jewels to destroy...
...and the owner, this Everlue, thinks it's worthless...?
Th-Then you wouldn't mind if I kept it?
No! I don't care how worthless it is, what's mine is mine!
Stingy!!
Shut up, Ugly!
It doesn't matter whose it is if we burn it.
No!! Don't you dare!!!
Lucy...
...this is our job!!!!

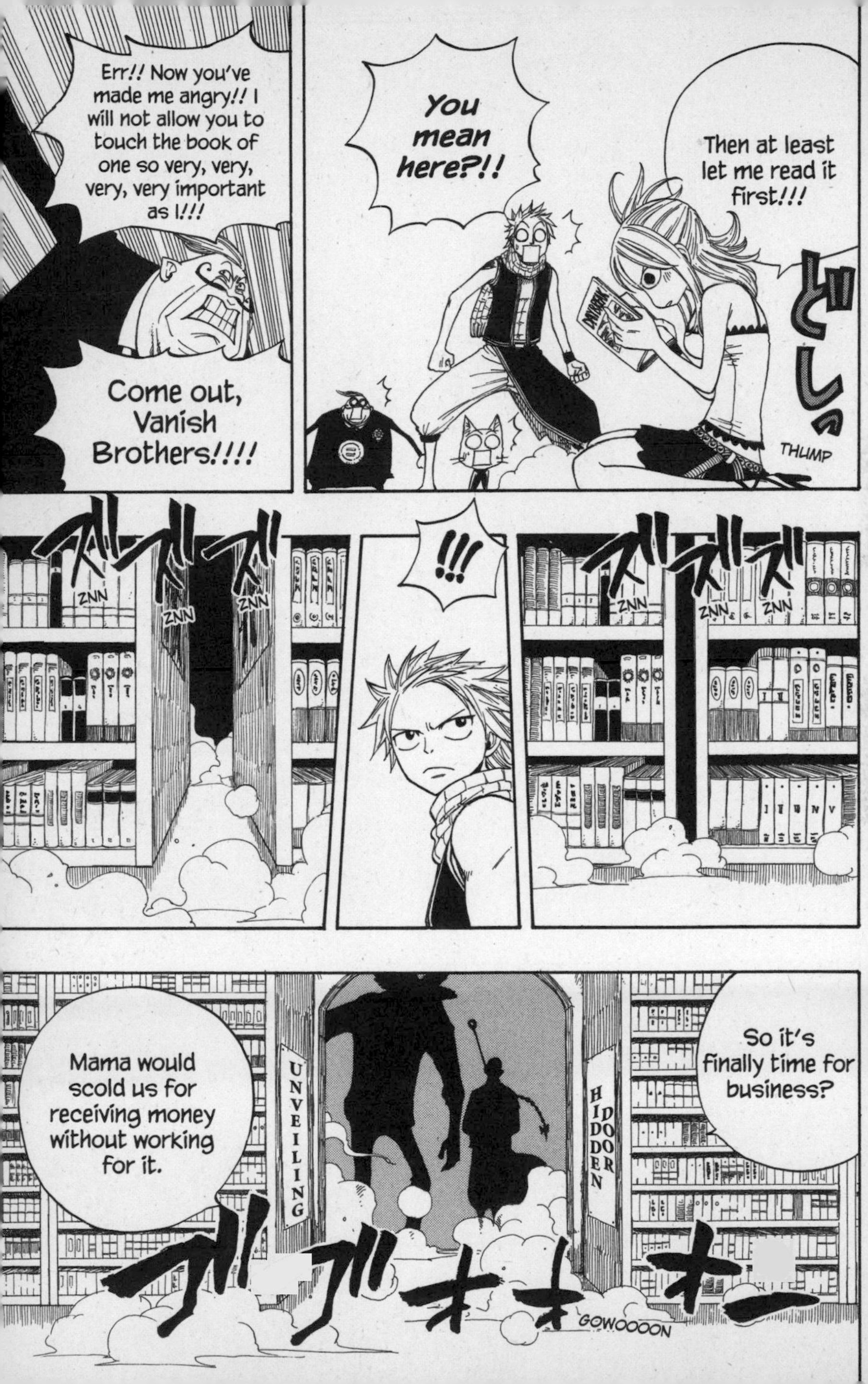
Then at least let me read it first!!!
THUMP
You mean here?!!
Err!! Now you've made me angry!! I will not allow you to touch the book of one so very, very, very, very important as I!!!
Come out, Vanish Brothers!!!!
ZNN
ZNN
ZNN
!!!
ZNN
ZNN
ZNN
So it's finally time for business?
HIDDEN DOOR
UNVEILING
Mama would scold us for receiving money without working for it.
GOWOOOON

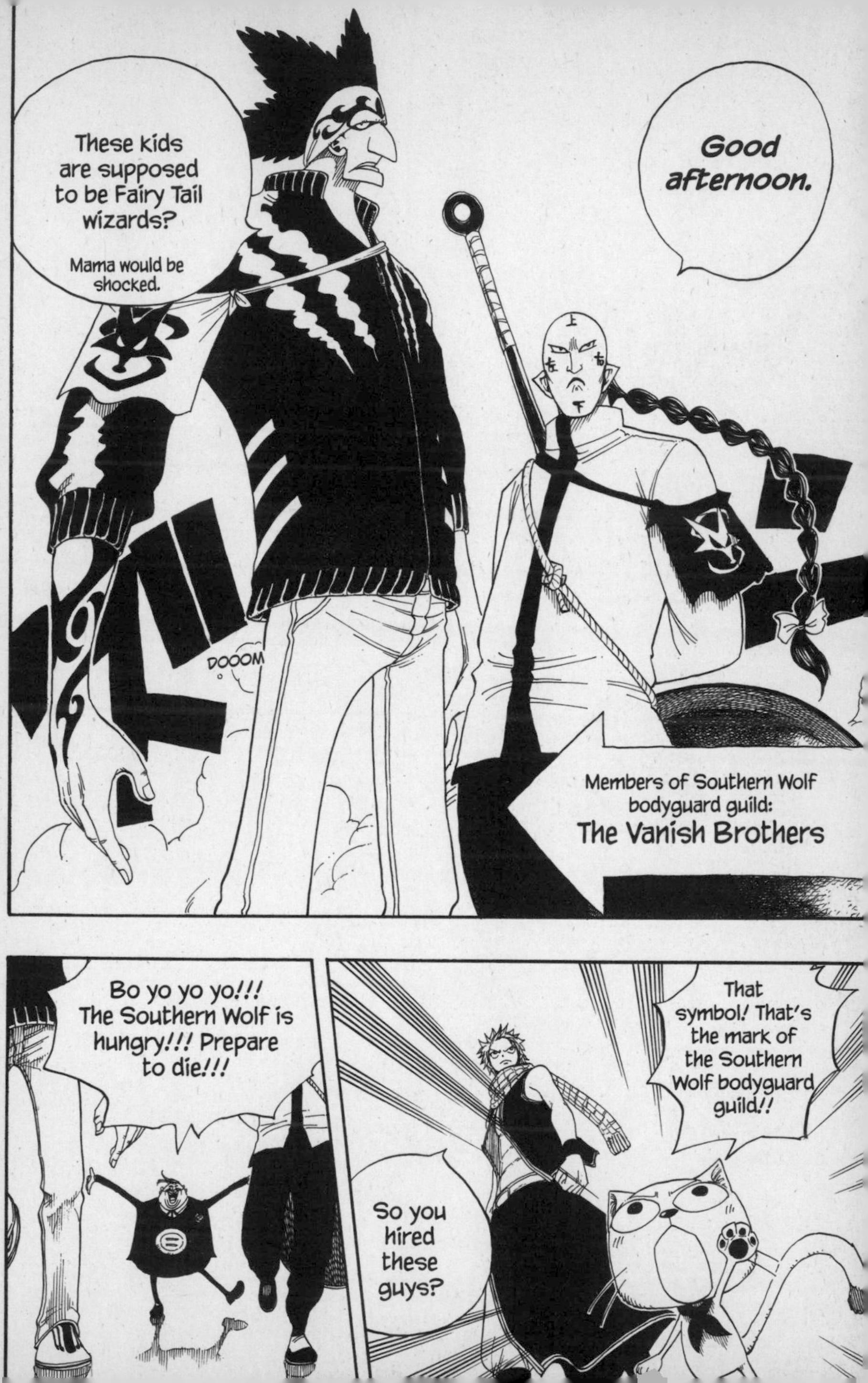
Good afternoon.
These kids are supposed to be Fairy Tail wizards?
Mama would be shocked.
DOOOM
Members of Southern Wolf bodyguard guild: The Vanish Brothers
That symbol! That's the mark of the Southern Wolf bodyguard guild!!
So you hired these guys?
Bo yo yo yo!!! The Southern Wolf is hungry!!! Prepare to die!!!

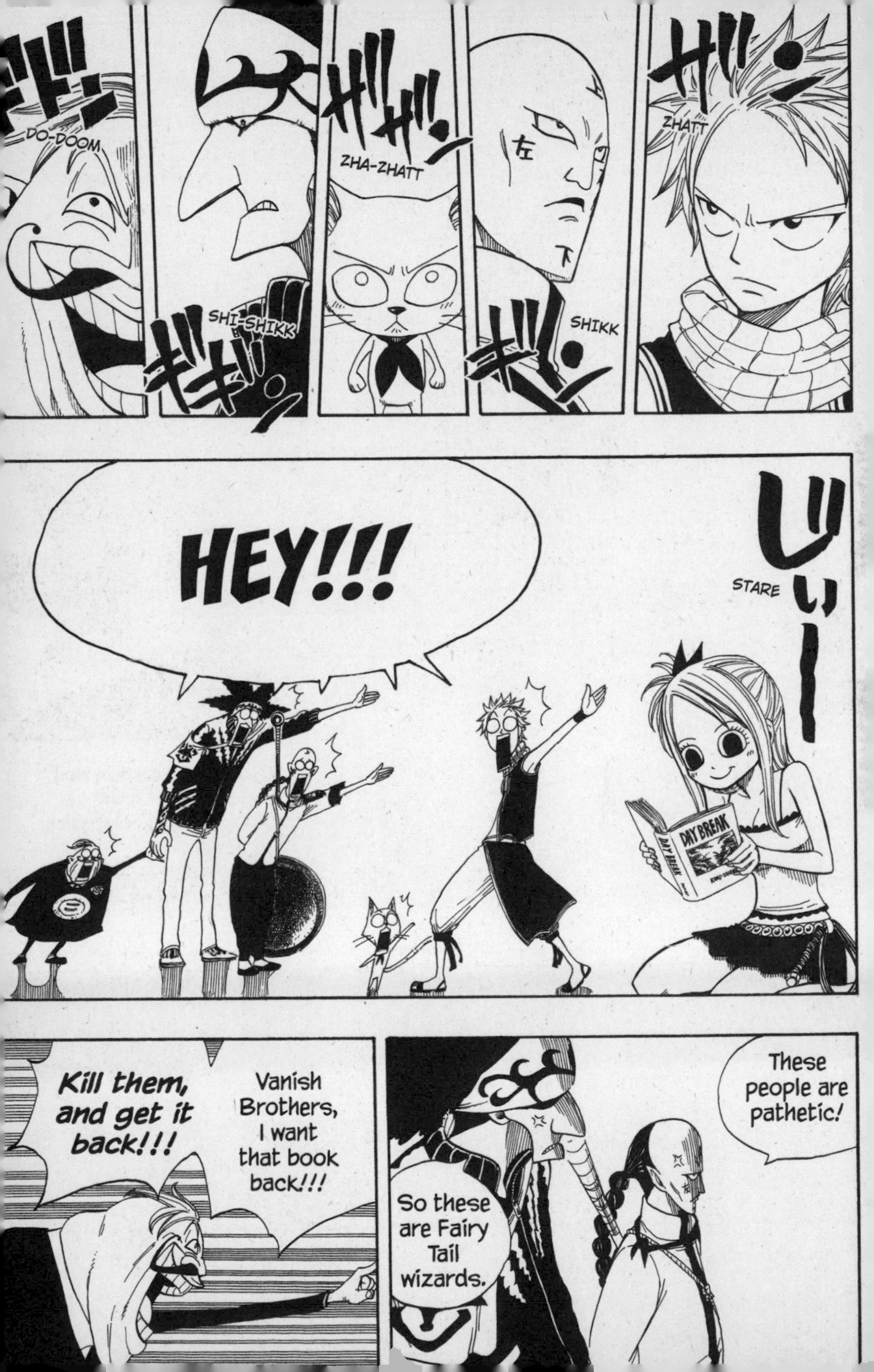
ZHATT
SHIKK
ZHA-ZHATT
SHI-SHIKK
DO-DOOM
STARE
HEY!!!
These people are pathetic!
So these are Fairy Tail wizards.
Vanish Brothers, I want that book back!!!
Kill them, and get it back!!!

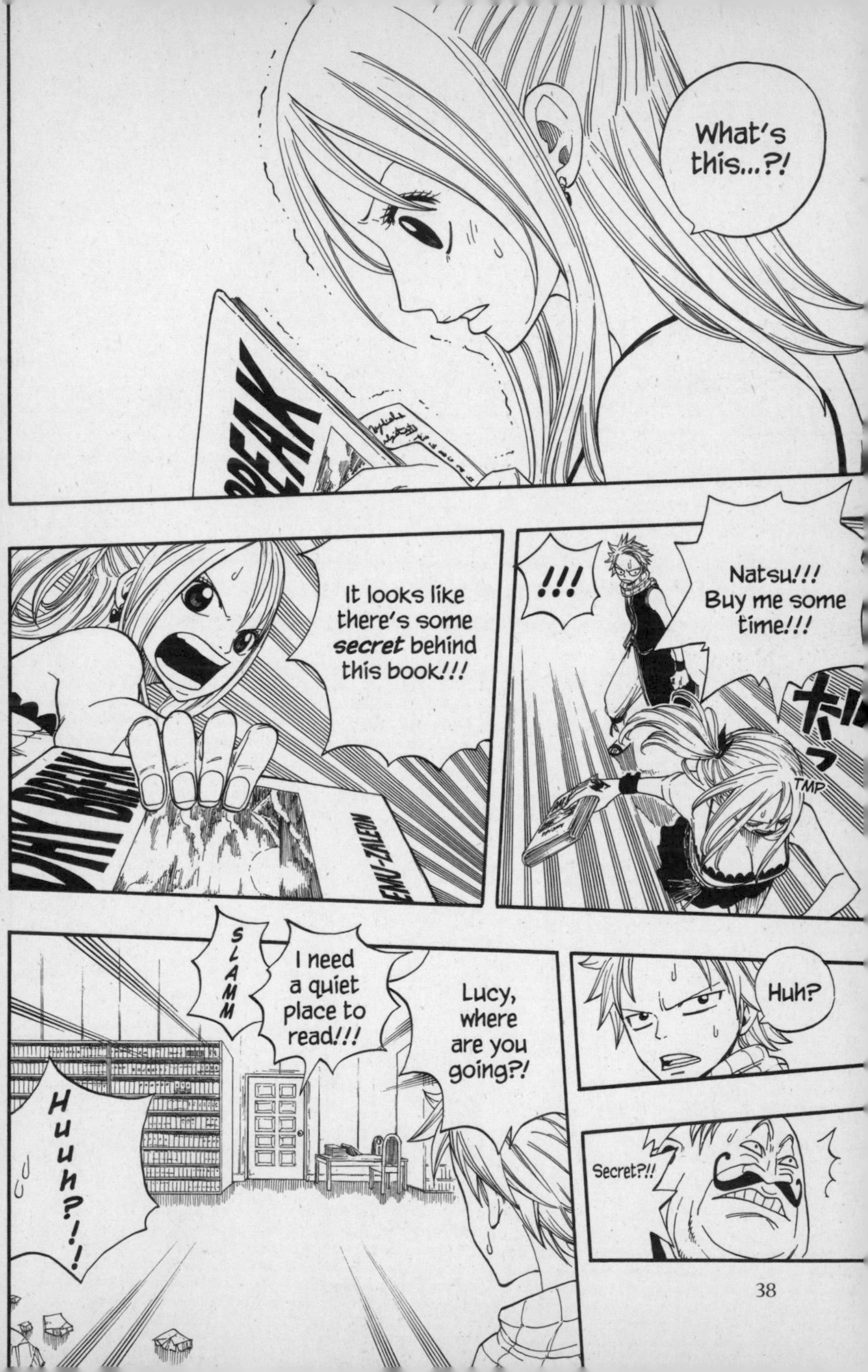
What's this...?!
Natsu!!! Buy me some time!!!
!!!
TMP
It looks like there's some *secret* behind this book!!!
DAY BREAK
KEMU-ZALEON
Huh?
Secret?!!
Lucy, where are you going?!
I need a quiet place to read!!!
SLAMM
Huuh?!!

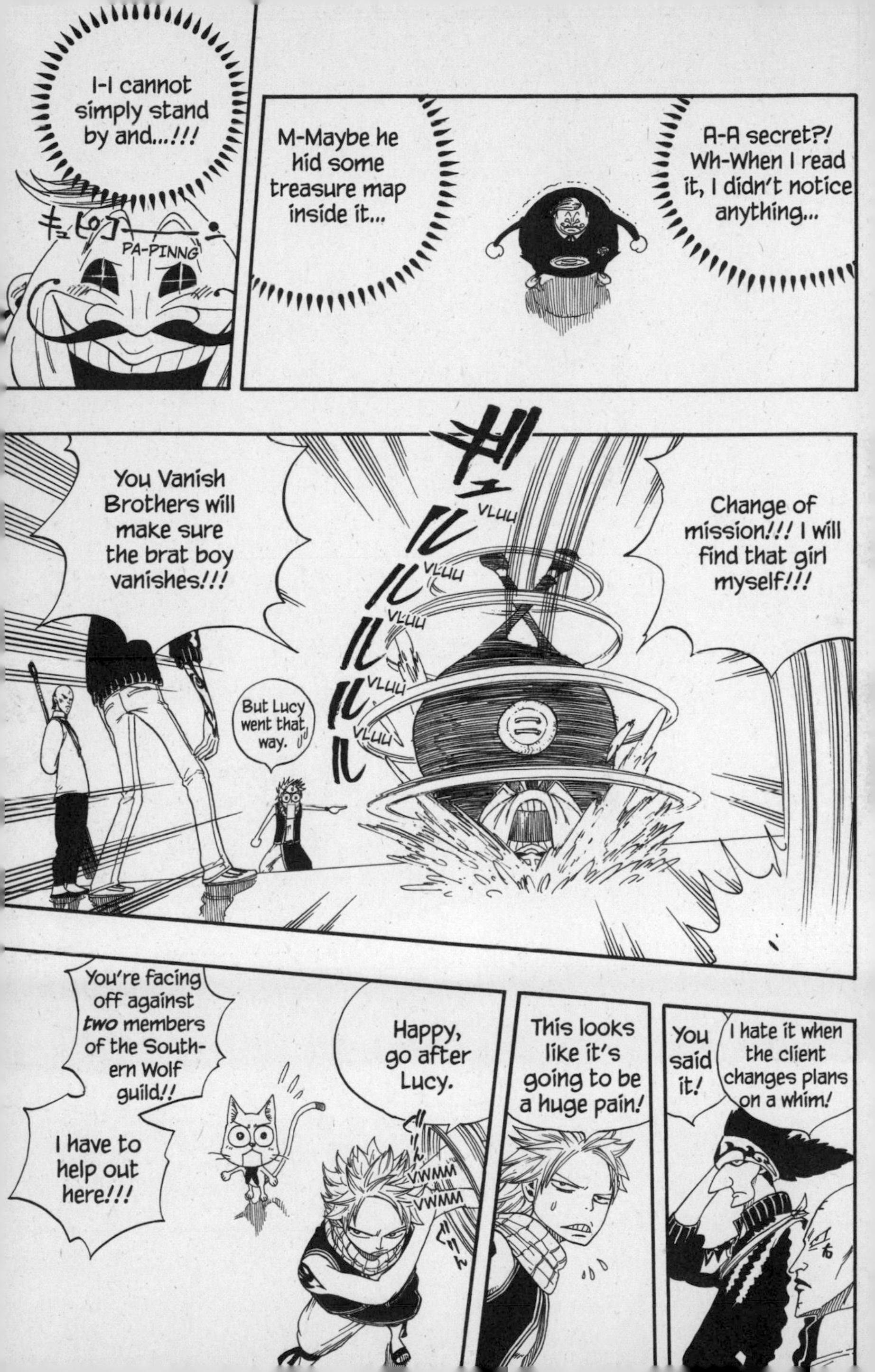
A-A secret?! Wh-When I read it, I didn't notice anything...
M-Maybe he hid some treasure map inside it...
I-I cannot simply stand by and...!!!
PA-PINNG
Change of mission!!! I will find that girl myself!!!
VLUU
VLUU
VLUU
VLUU
VLUU
You Vanish Brothers will make sure the brat boy vanishes!!!
But Lucy went that way.
I hate it when the client changes plans on a whim!
You said it!
This looks like it's going to be a huge pain!
Happy, go after Lucy.
VWMM
VWMM
You're facing off against *two* members of the Southern Wolf guild!!
I have to help out here!!!

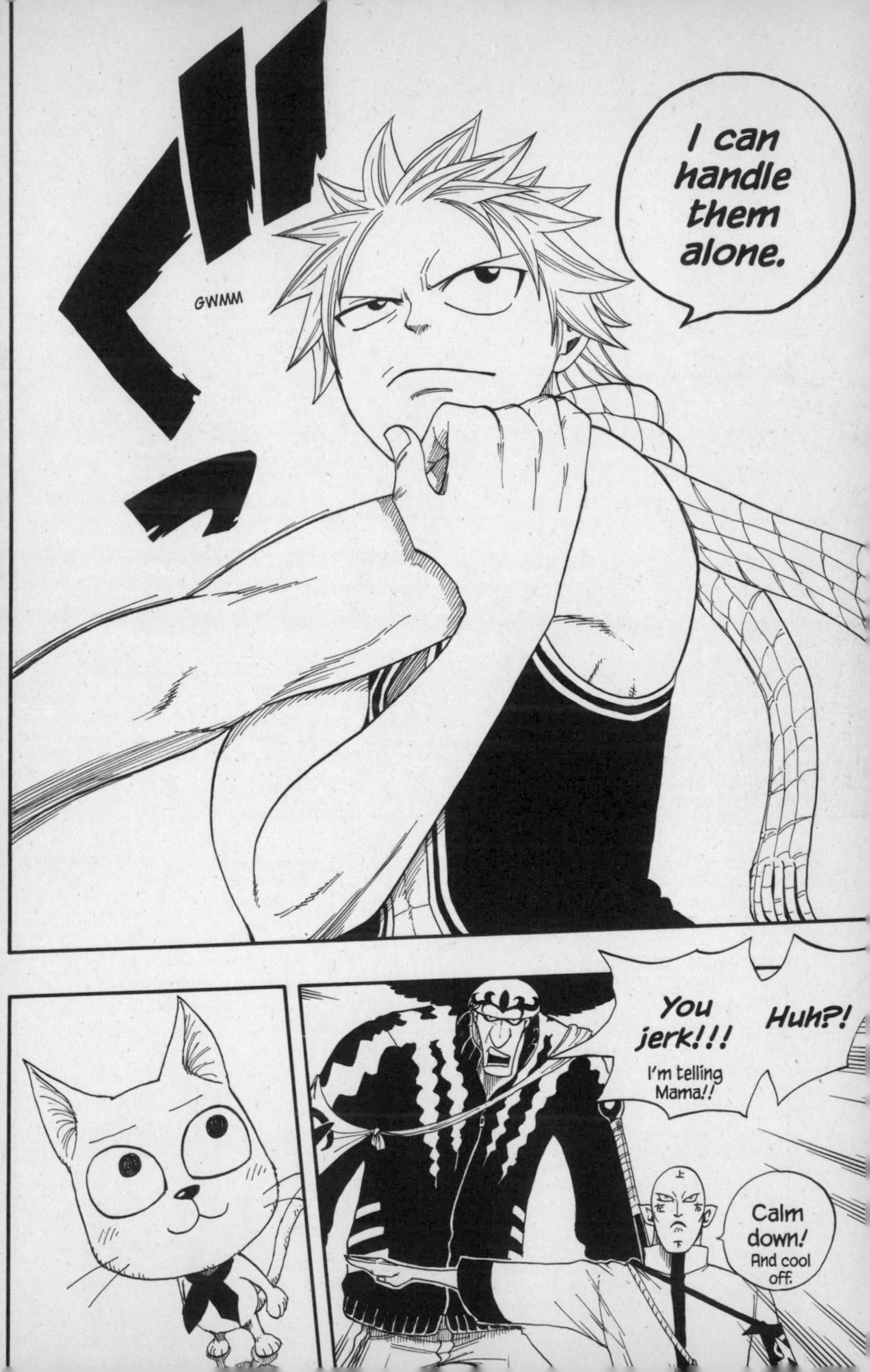
I can handle them alone.
GWMM
Huh?!
You jerk!!!
I'm telling Mama!!
Calm down!
And cool off.

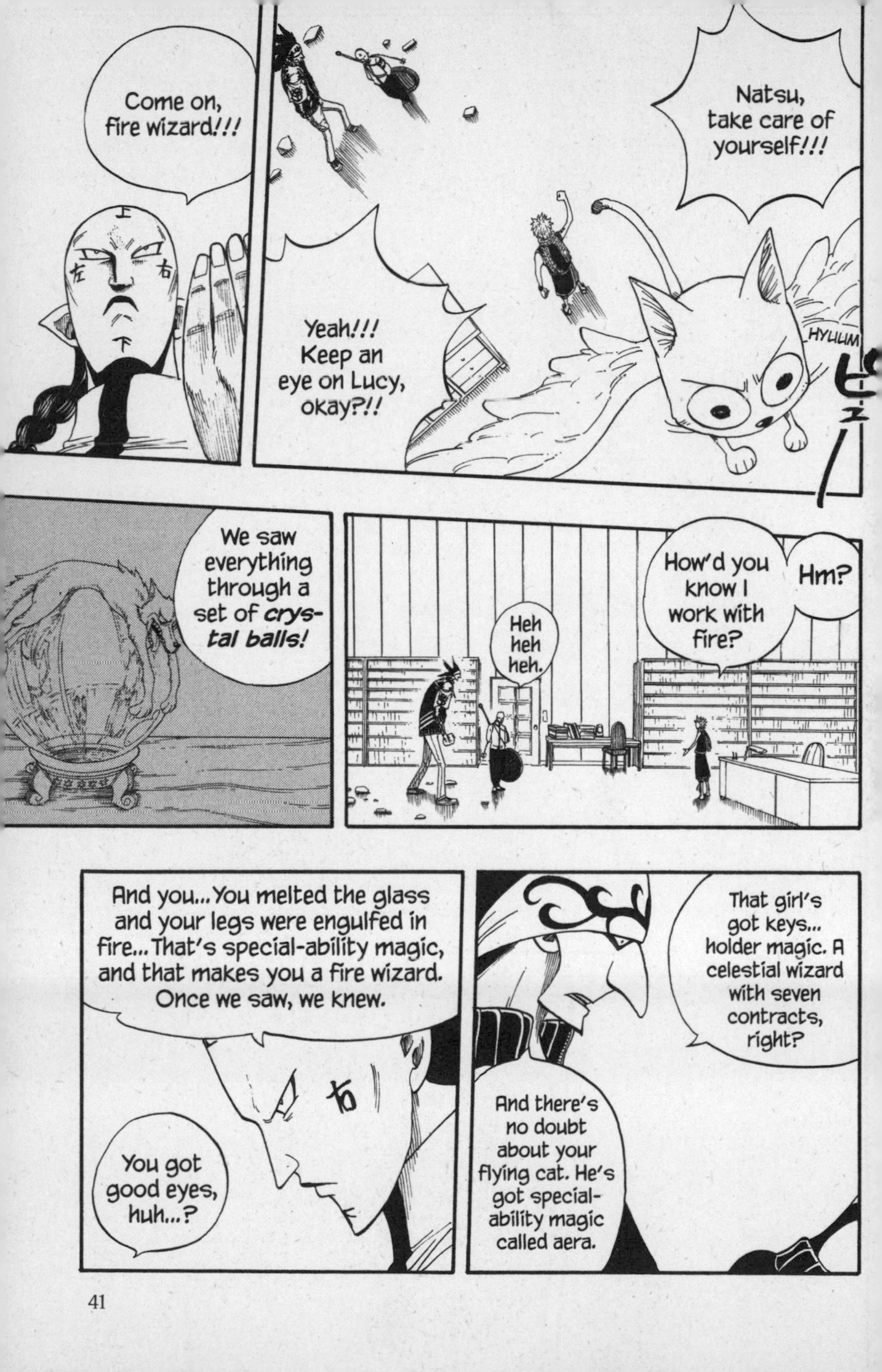
Natsu, take care of yourself!!!
Yeah!!! Keep an eye on Lucy, okay?!!
HYUUM
Come on, fire wizard!!!
Hm?
How'd you know I work with fire?
Heh heh heh.
We saw everything through a set of *crystal balls!*
That girl's got keys... holder magic. A celestial wizard with seven contracts, right?
And there's no doubt about your flying cat. He's got special-ability magic called aera.
And you... You melted the glass and your legs were engulfed in fire... That's special-ability magic, and that makes you a fire wizard. Once we saw, we knew.
You got good eyes, huh...?

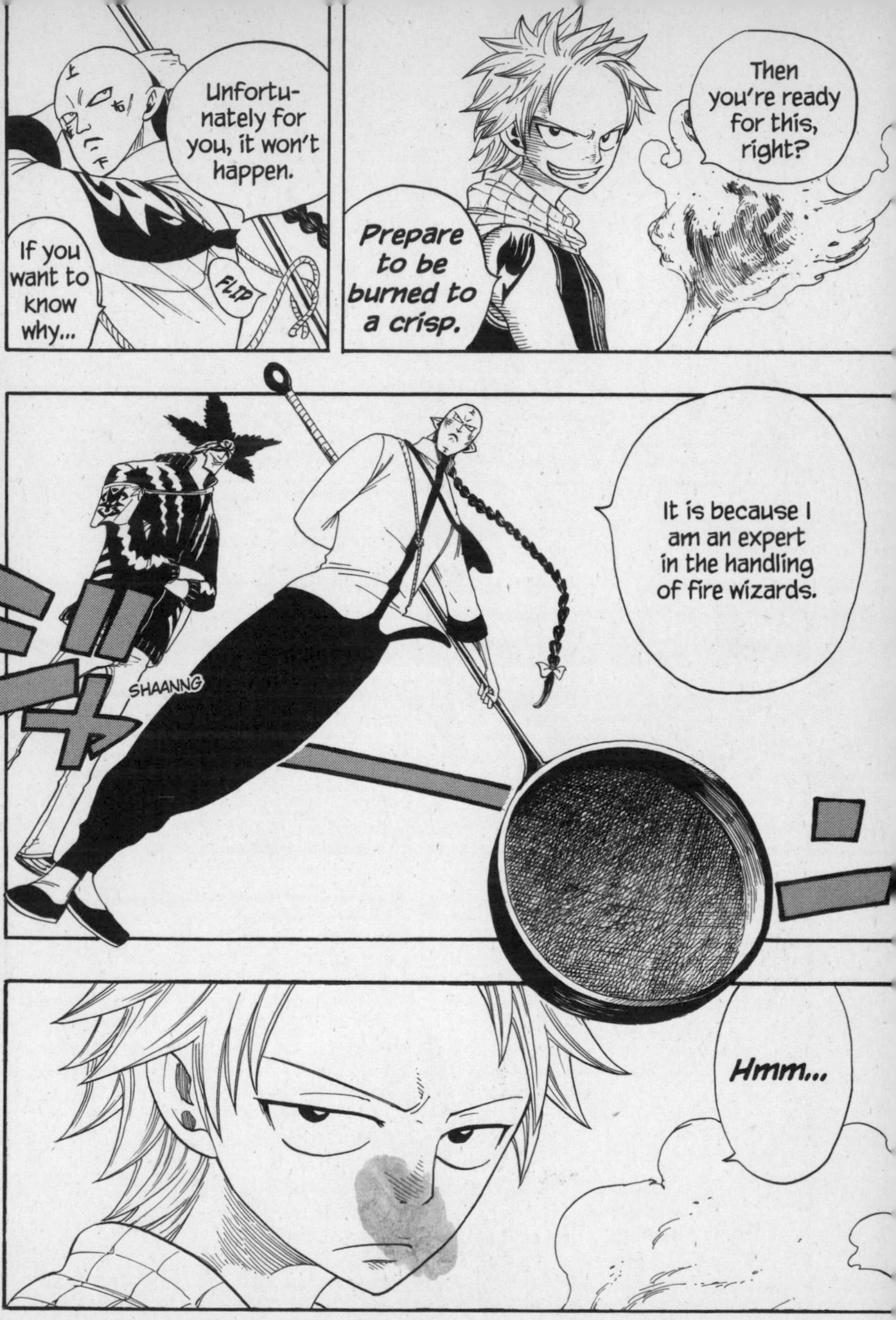
Then you're ready for this, right?
Prepare to be burned to a crisp.
Unfortu-nately for you, it won't happen.
If you want to know why...
FLIP
It is because I am an expert in the handling of fire wizards.
SHAANNG
Hmm...

FAIRY TAIL

Chapter 7: The Wizard's Weakness

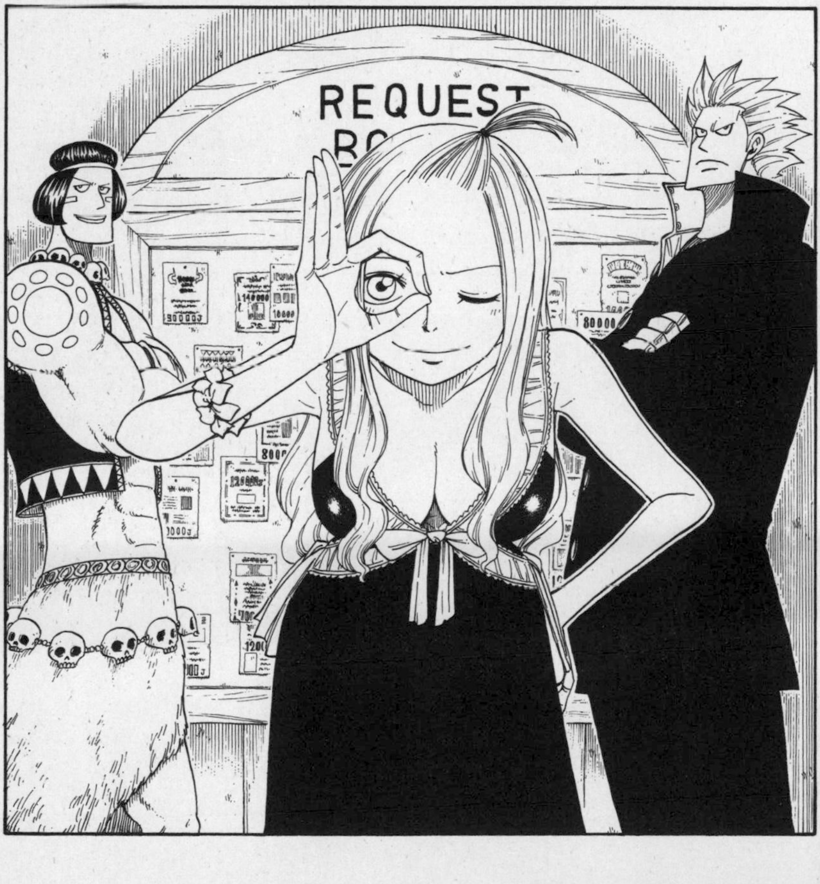
REQUEST

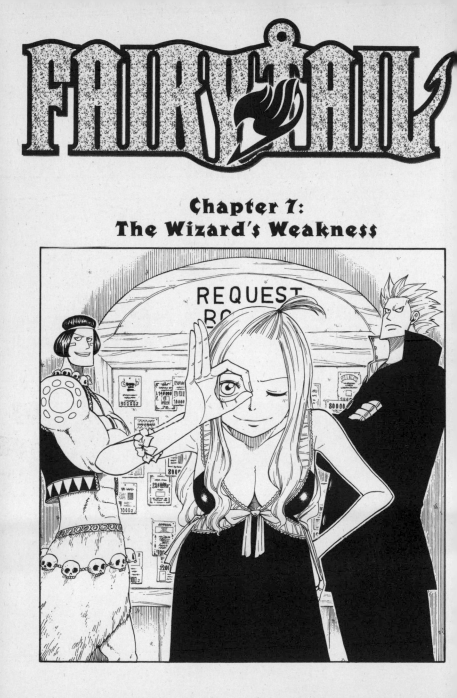

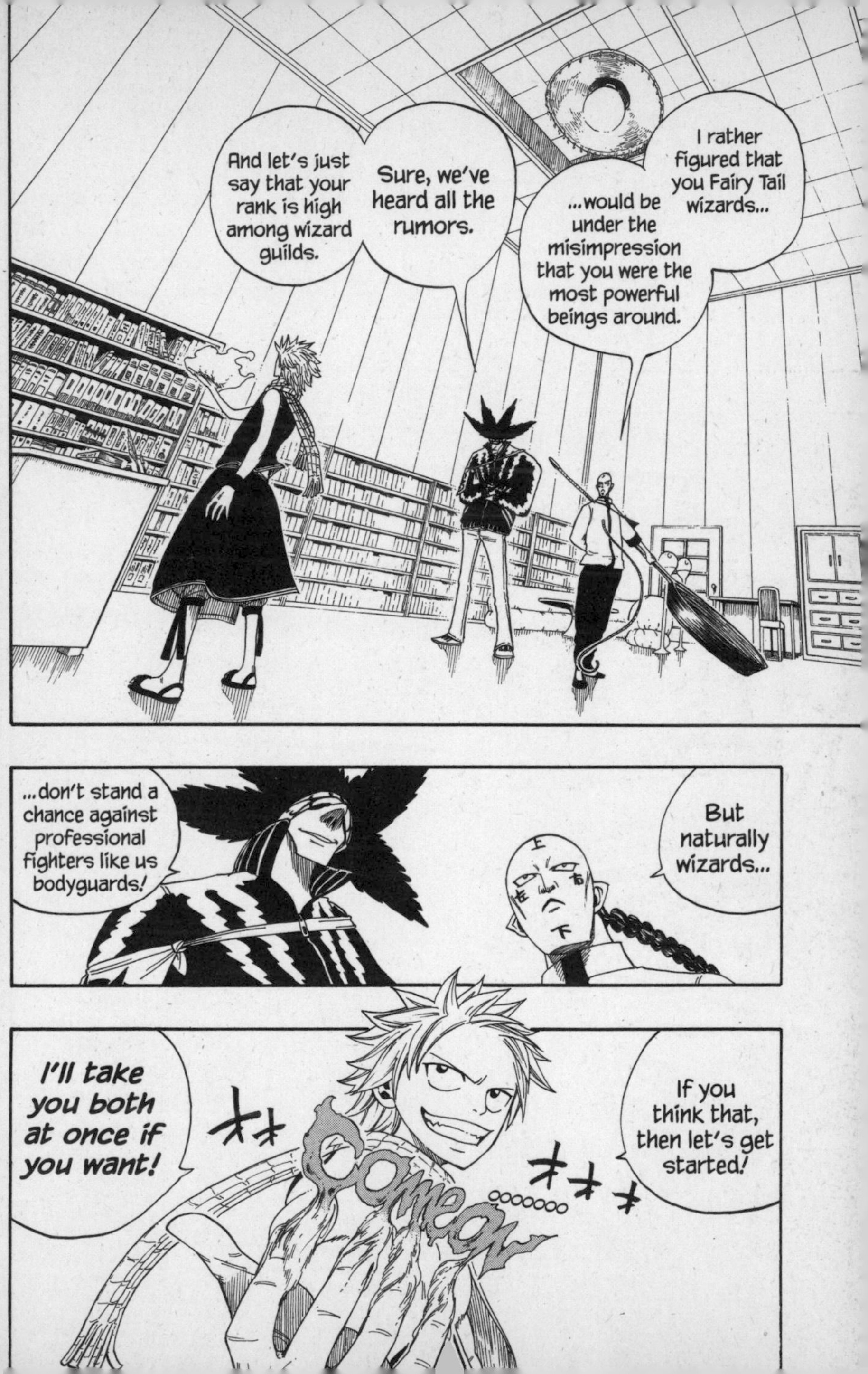
I rather figured that you Fairy Tail wizards...
...would be under the misimpression that you were the most powerful beings around.
Sure, we've heard all the rumors.
And let's just say that your rank is high among wizard guilds.
But naturally wizards...
...don't stand a chance against professional fighters like us bodyguards!
If you think that, then let's get started!
I'll take you both at once if you want!

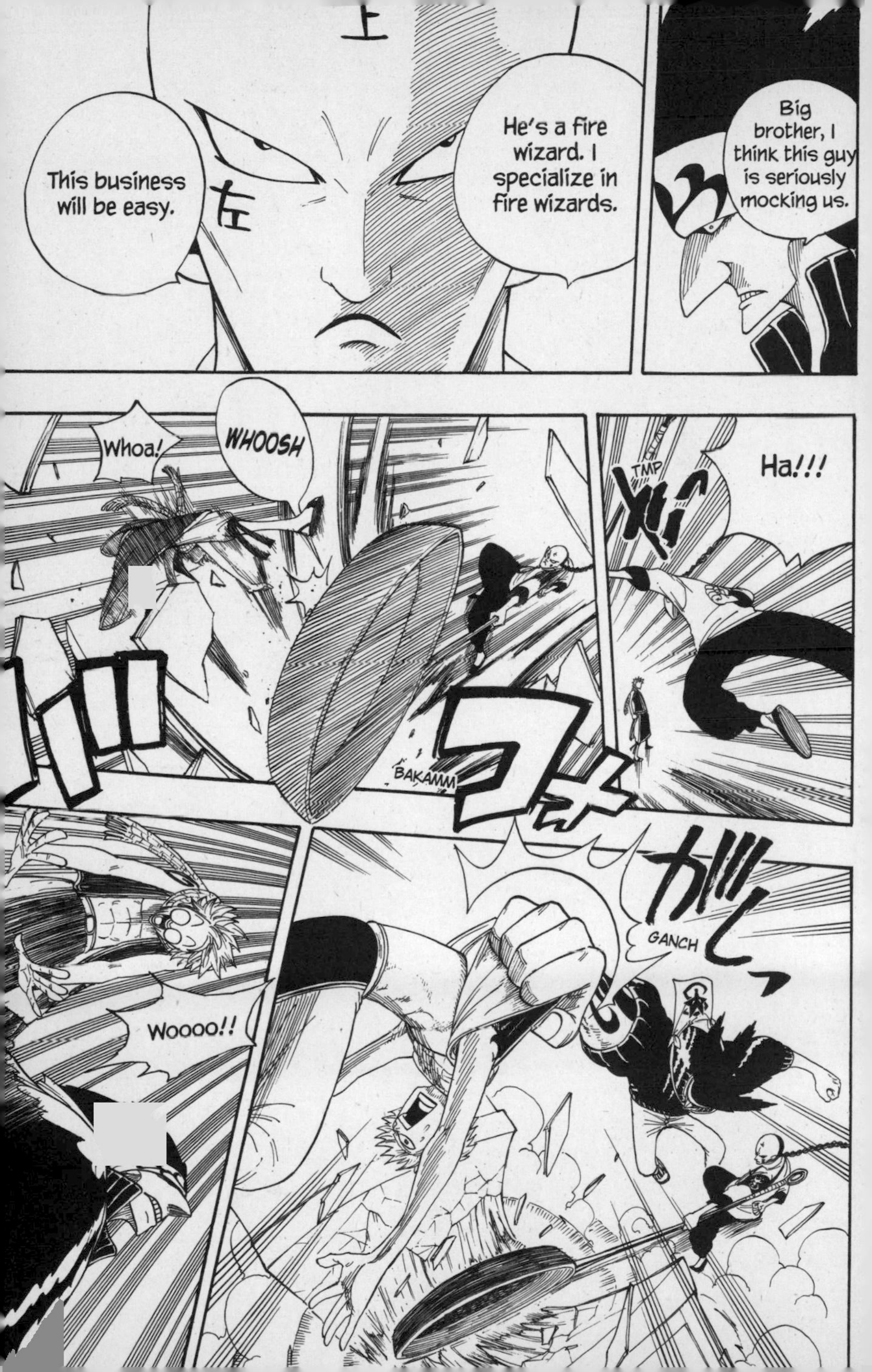
Big brother, I think this guy is seriously mocking us.
He's a fire wizard. I specialize in fire wizards.
This business will be easy.
Ha!!!
TMP
WHOOSH
Whoa!
BAKAMM
GANCH
Woooo!!

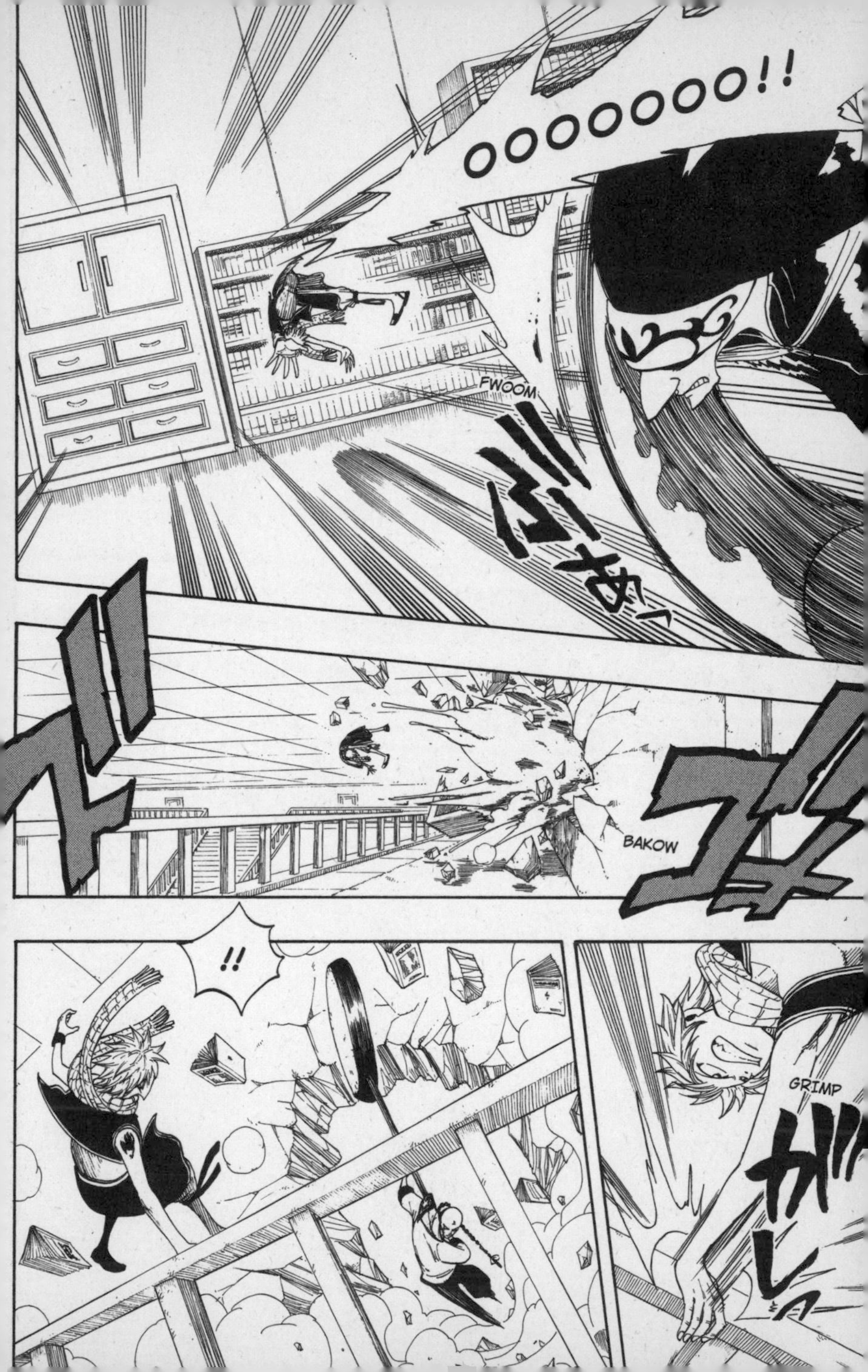
OOOOOOOO!!
FWOOM
BAKOW
!!
GRIMP

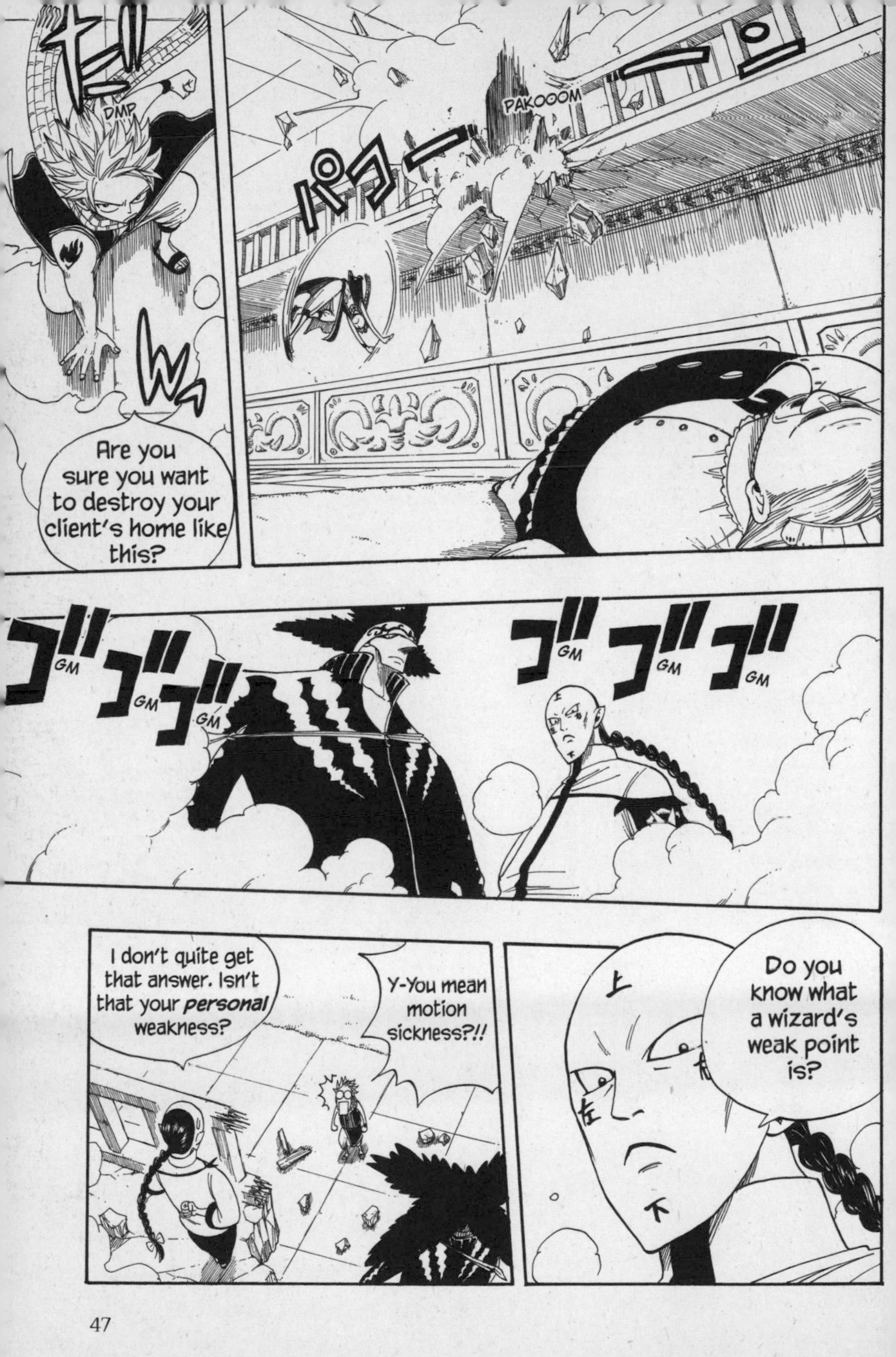
PAKOOOM
DMP
Are you sure you want to destroy your client's home like this?
GM GM GM
GM GM GM GM
Do you know what a wizard's weak point is?
Y-You mean motion sickness?!!
I don't quite get that answer. Isn't that your *personal* weakness?

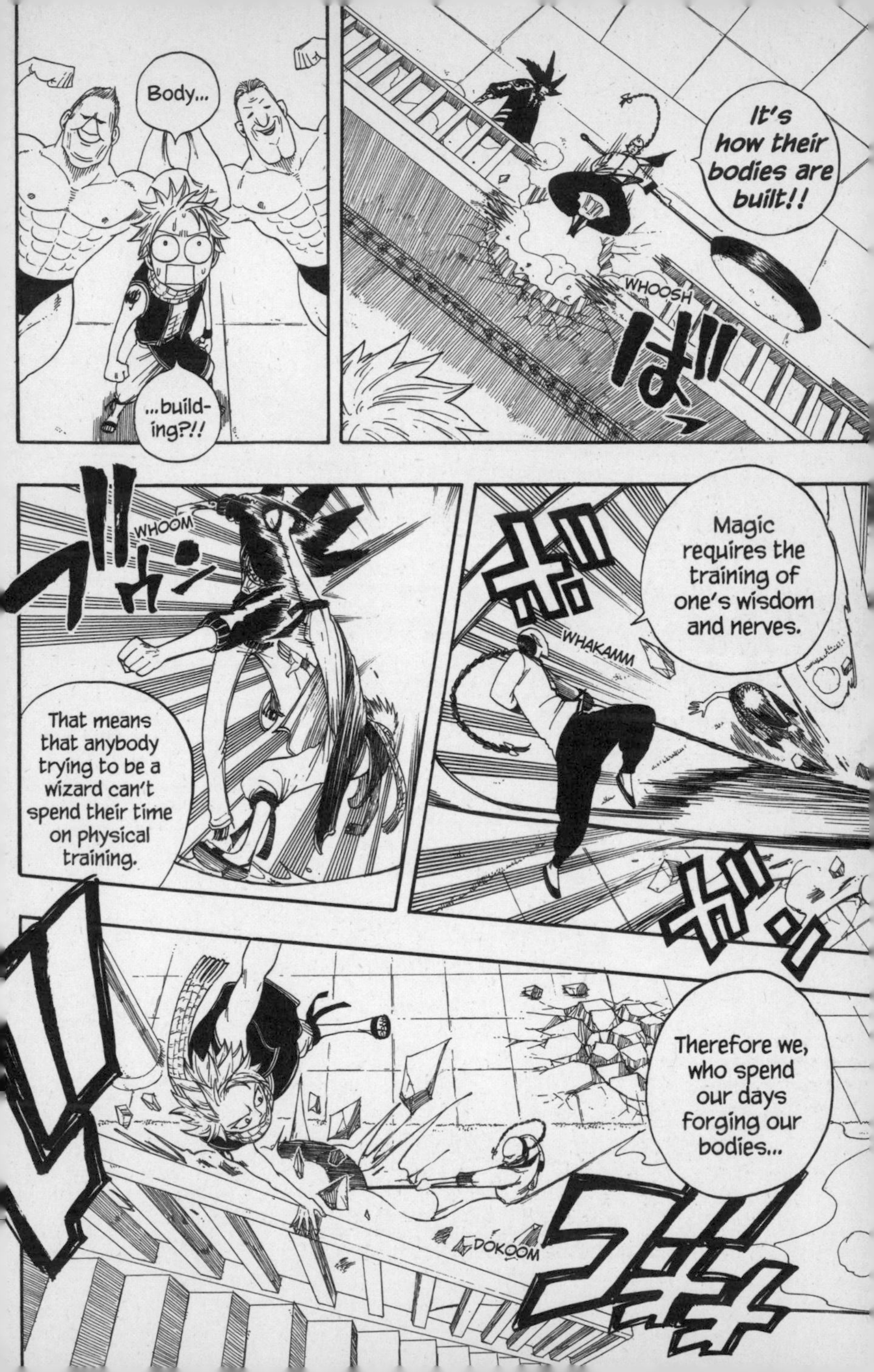
It's how their bodies are built!!
WHOOSH
Body...
...building?!!
Magic requires the training of one's wisdom and nerves.
WHAKAMM
WHOOM
That means that anybody trying to be a wizard can't spend their time on physical training.
Therefore we, who spend our days forging our bodies...
DOKOOM

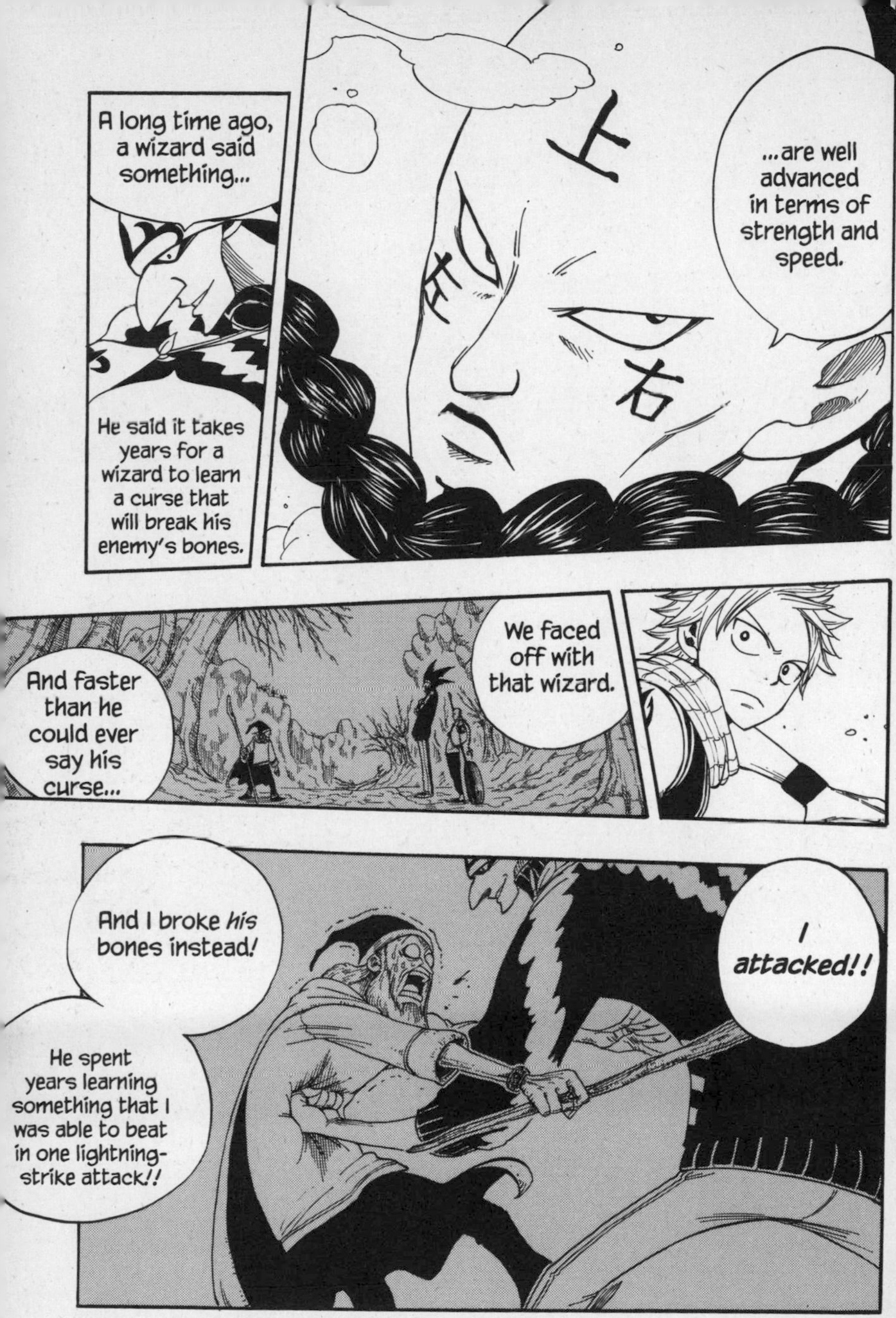
...are well advanced in terms of strength and speed.
A long time ago, a wizard said something...
He said it takes years for a wizard to learn a curse that will break his enemy's bones.
We faced off with that wizard.
And faster than he could ever say his curse...
I attacked!!
And I broke *his* bones instead!
He spent years learning something that I was able to beat in one lightning-strike attack!!

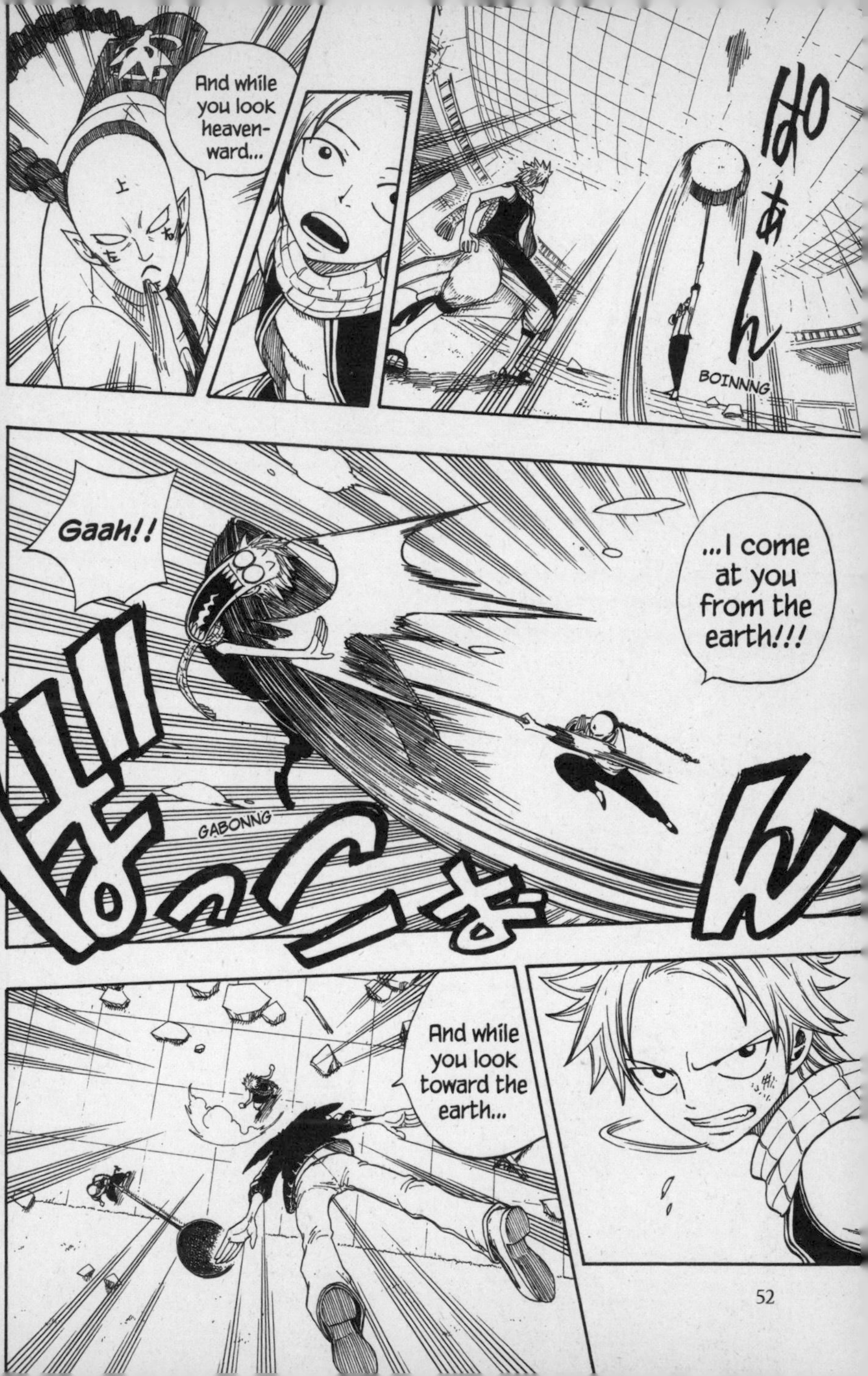
BOINNNG
And while you look heavenward...
...I come at you from the earth!!!
Gaah!!
GABONNG
And while you look toward the earth...

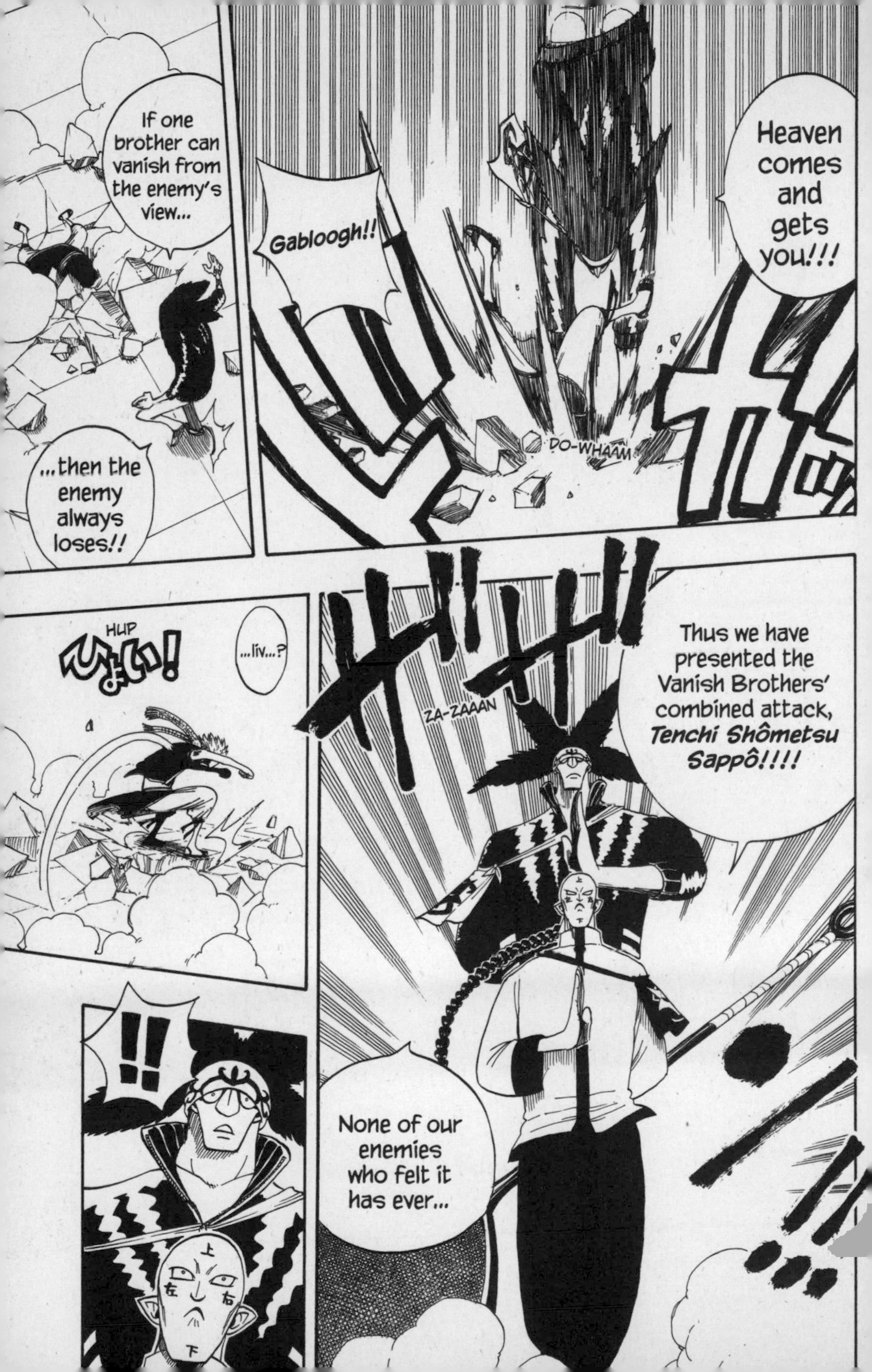

Heaven comes and gets you!!!
Gabloogh!!
DO-WHAAM
If one brother can vanish from the enemy's view...
...then the enemy always loses!!
ZA-ZAAAN
Thus we have presented the Vanish Brothers' combined attack, *Tenchi Shômetsu Sappô!!!!*
None of our enemies who felt it has ever...
HUP
...liv...?
!!

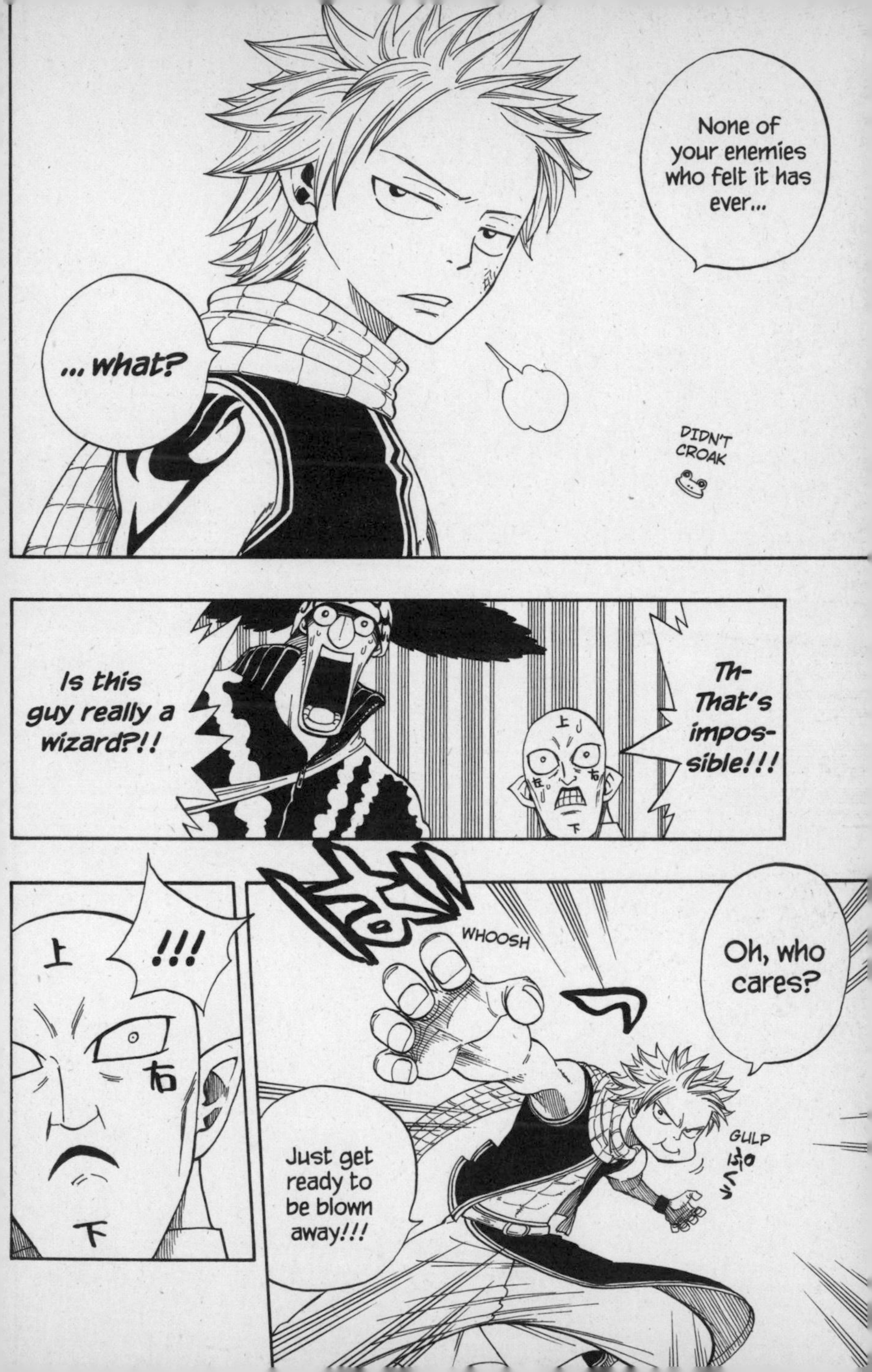
None of your enemies who felt it has ever...
DIDN'T CROAK
... what?
Th- That's impos- sible!!!
Is this guy really a wizard?!!
Oh, who cares?
WHOOSH
GULP
Just get ready to be blown away!!!
!!!

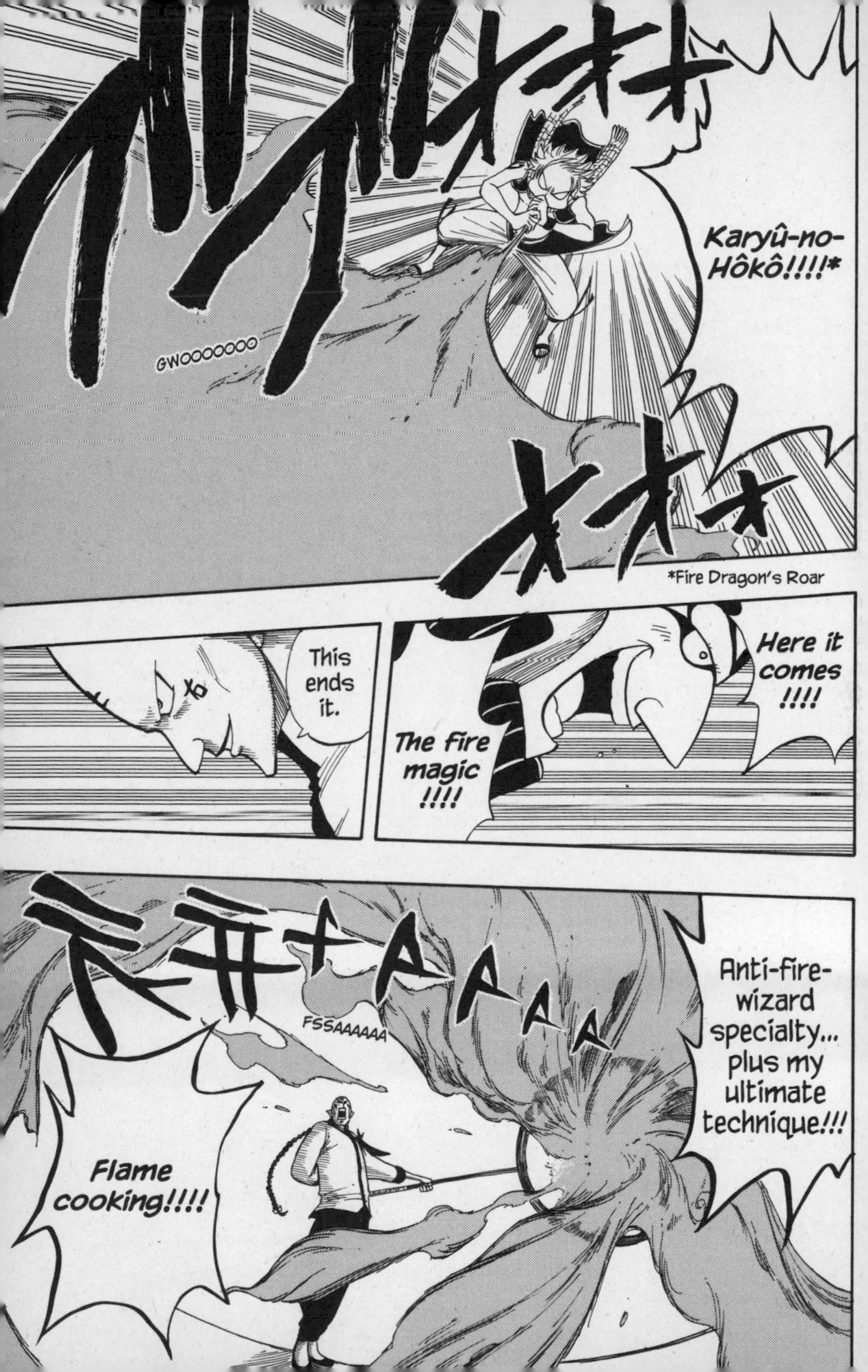
Karyû-no-Hôkô!!!!*
GWOOOOOOO
*Fire Dragon's Roar
Here it comes!!!!
The fire magic!!!!
This ends it.
Anti-fire-wizard specialty... plus my ultimate technique!!!
FSSAAAAAA
Flame cooking!!!!

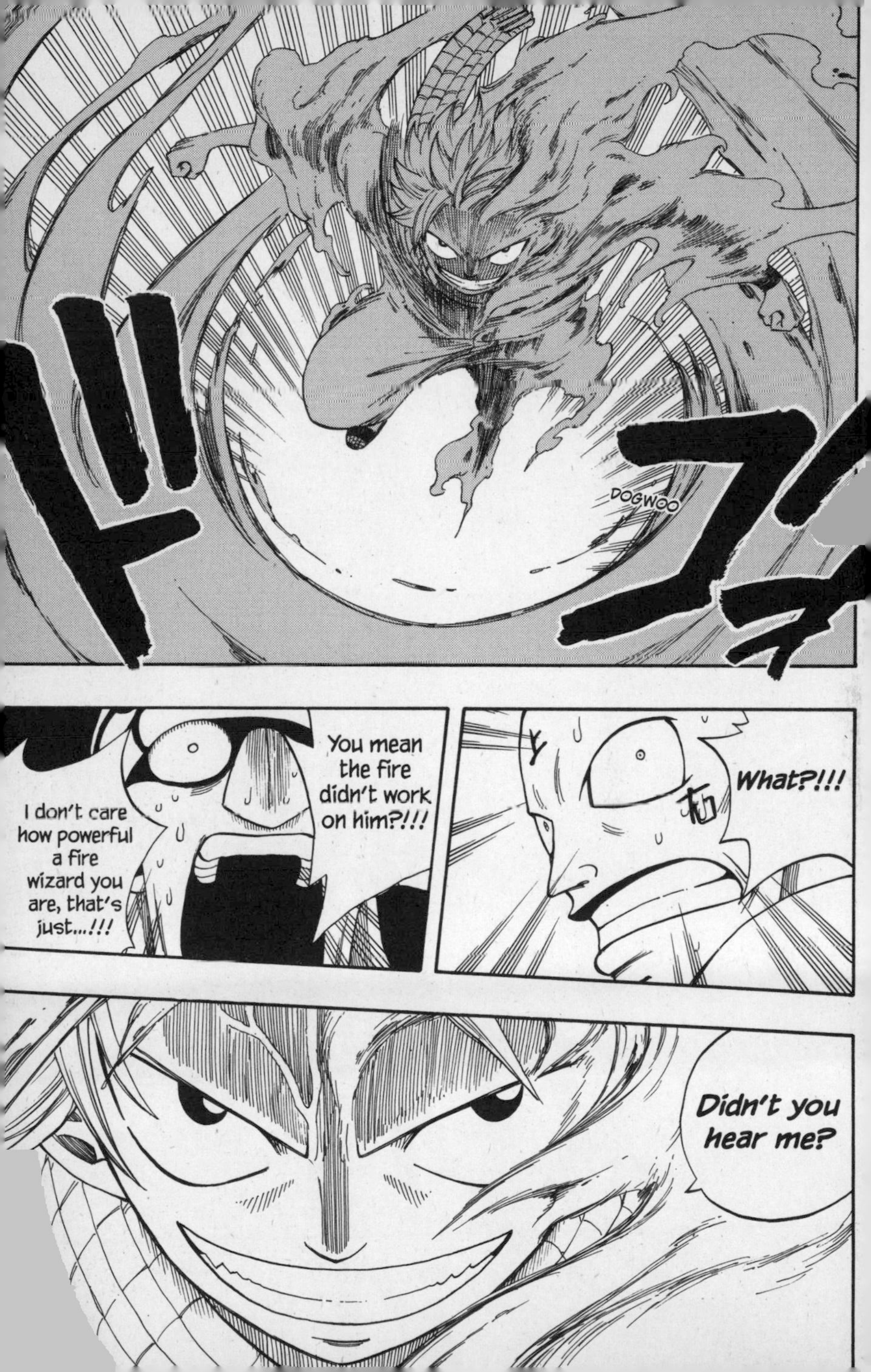
DOGWOO
What?!!!
You mean the fire didn't work on him?!!!
I don't care how powerful a fire wizard you are, that's just...!!!
Didn't you hear me?

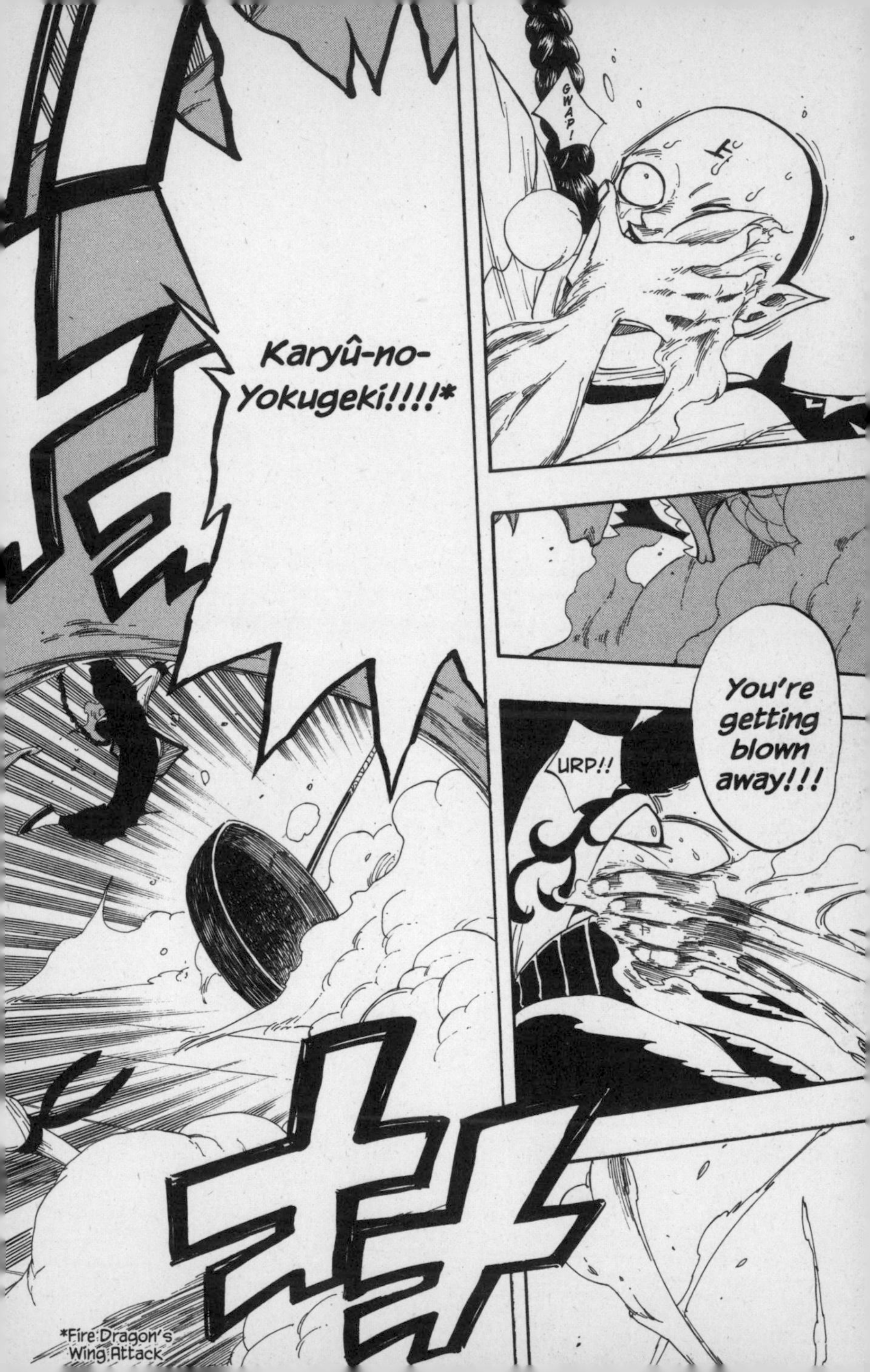
GWAP!
URP!!
You're getting blown away!!!
Karyû-no-Yokugeki!!!!!*

*Fire Dragon's Wing Attack

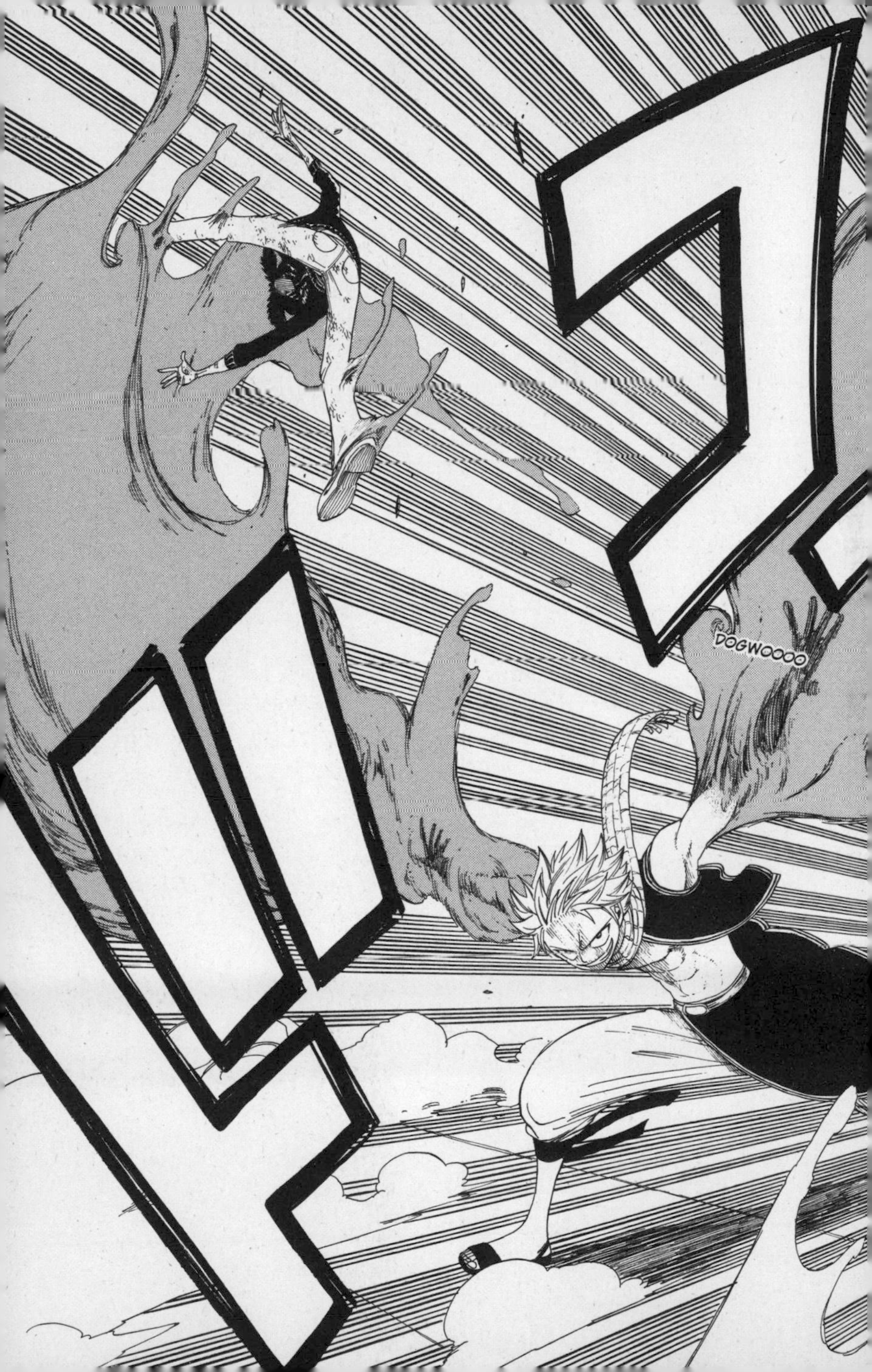
DOGWOOOO

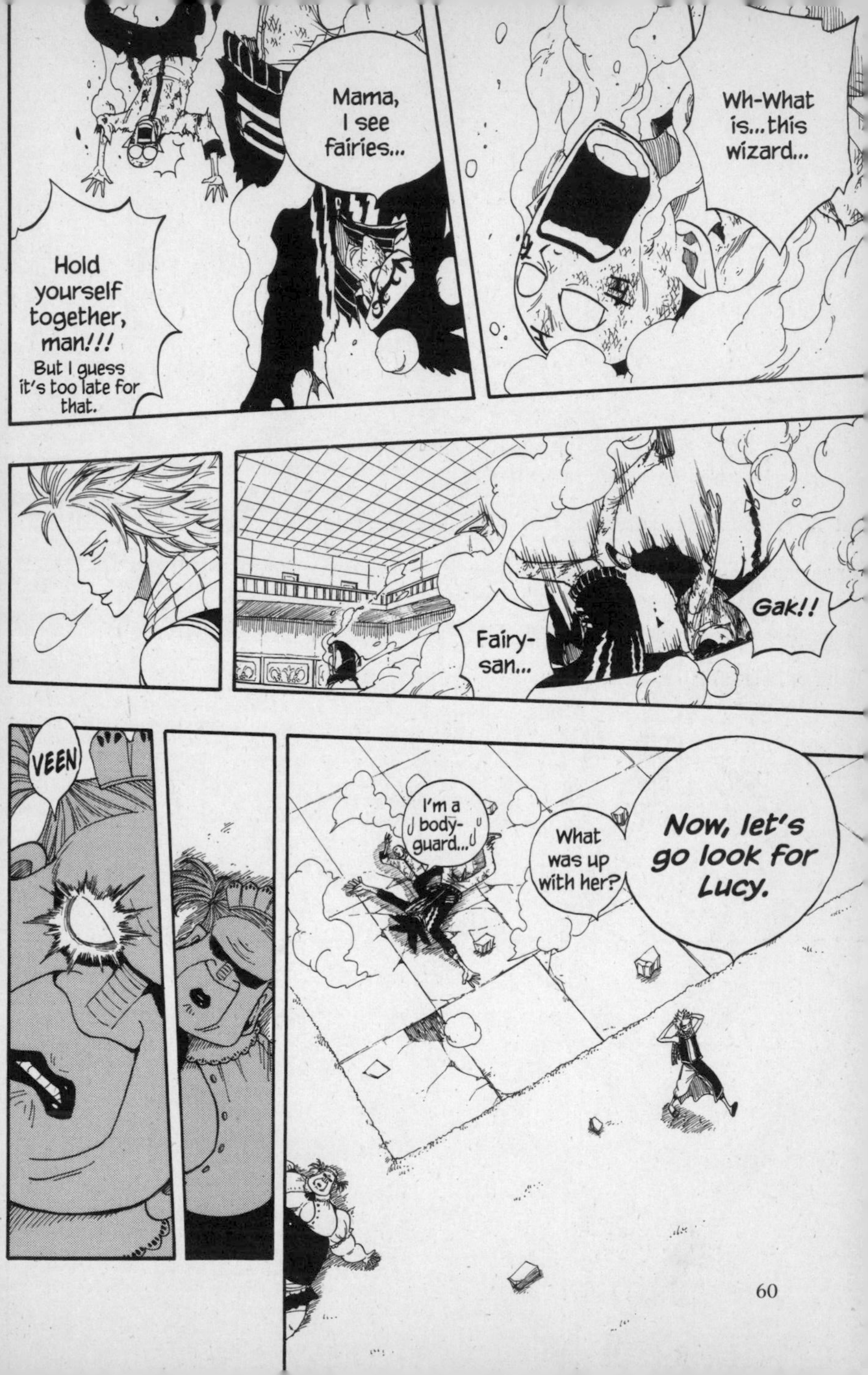
Wh-What is...this wizard...
Mama, I see fairies...
Hold yourself together, man!!!
But I guess it's too late for that.
Gak!!
Fairy-san...
Now, let's go look for Lucy.
What was up with her?
I'm a bodyguard...
VEEN

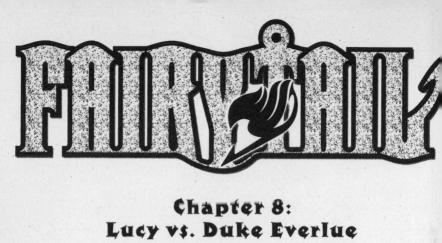

Chapter 8:
Lucy vs. Duke Everlue

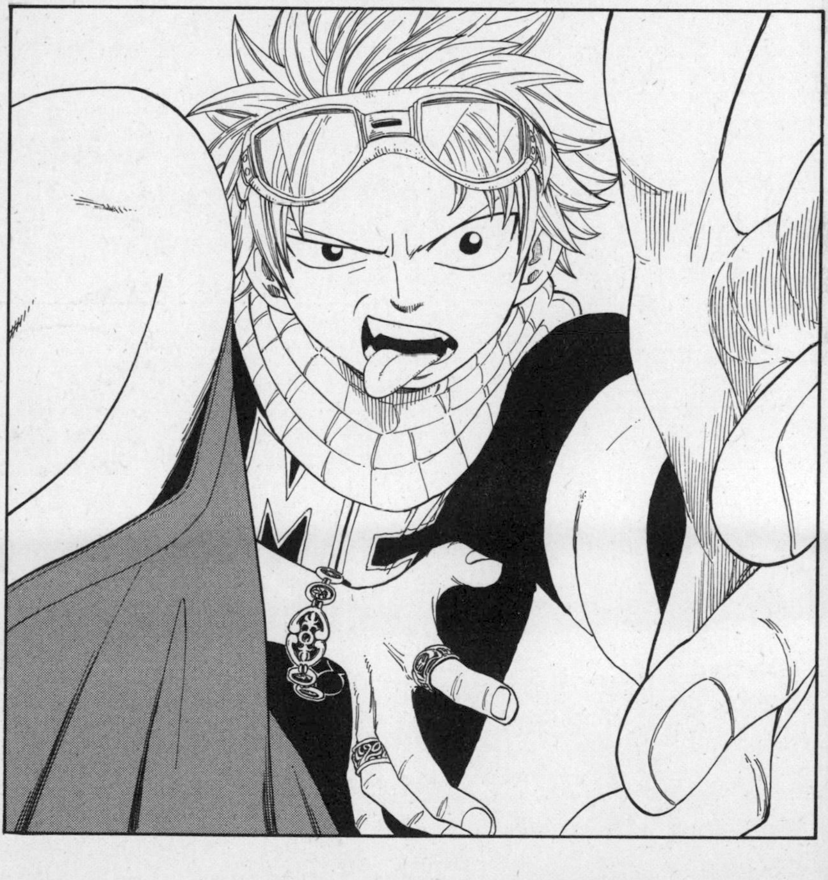

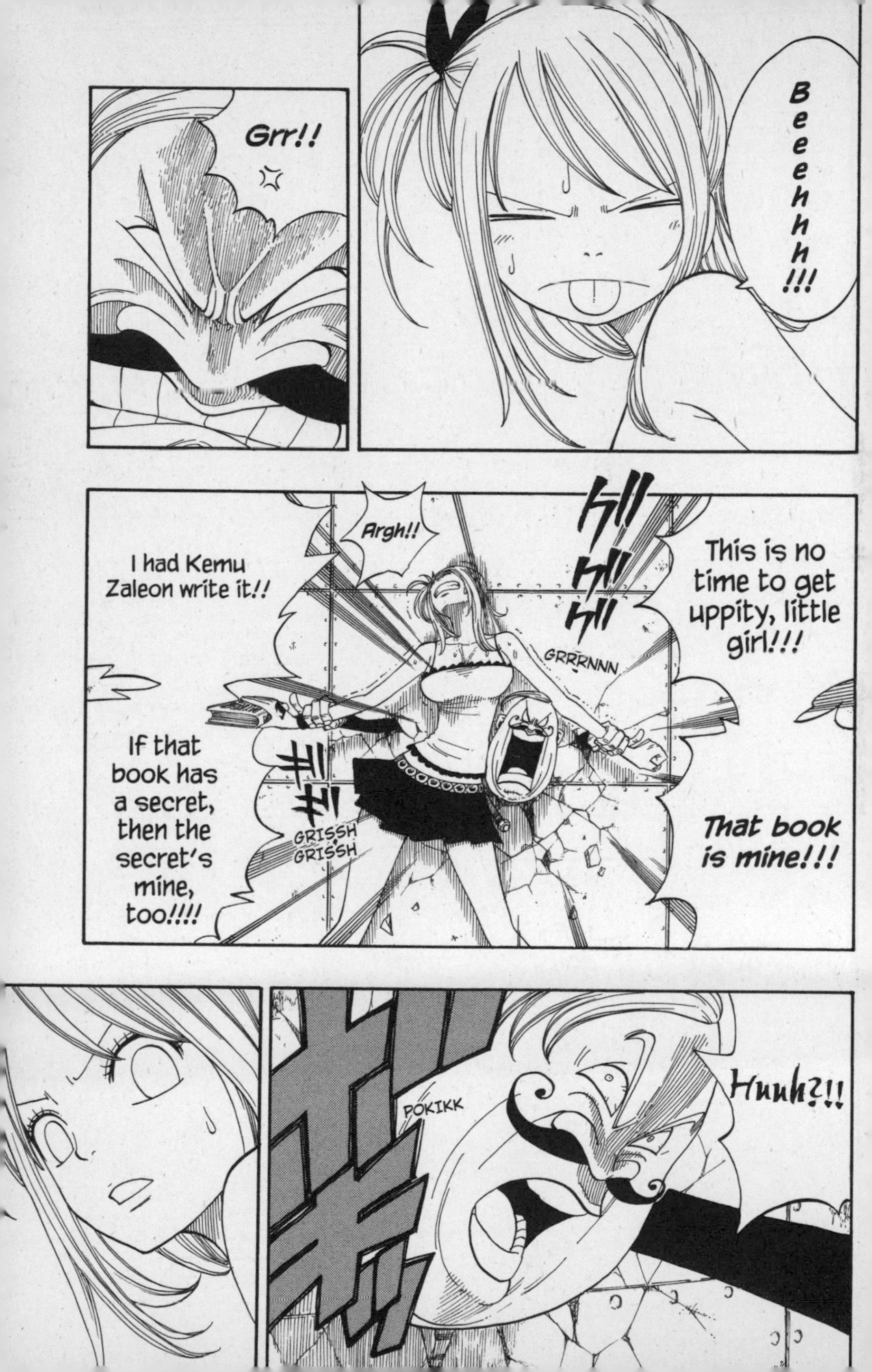
Beeehhh!!!
Grr!!
This is no time to get uppity, little girl!!!
Argh!!
I had Kemu Zaleon write it!!
GRRRNNN
That book is mine!!!
If that book has a secret, then the secret's mine, too!!!!
GRISSH GRISSH
Hnuh?!!
POKIKK

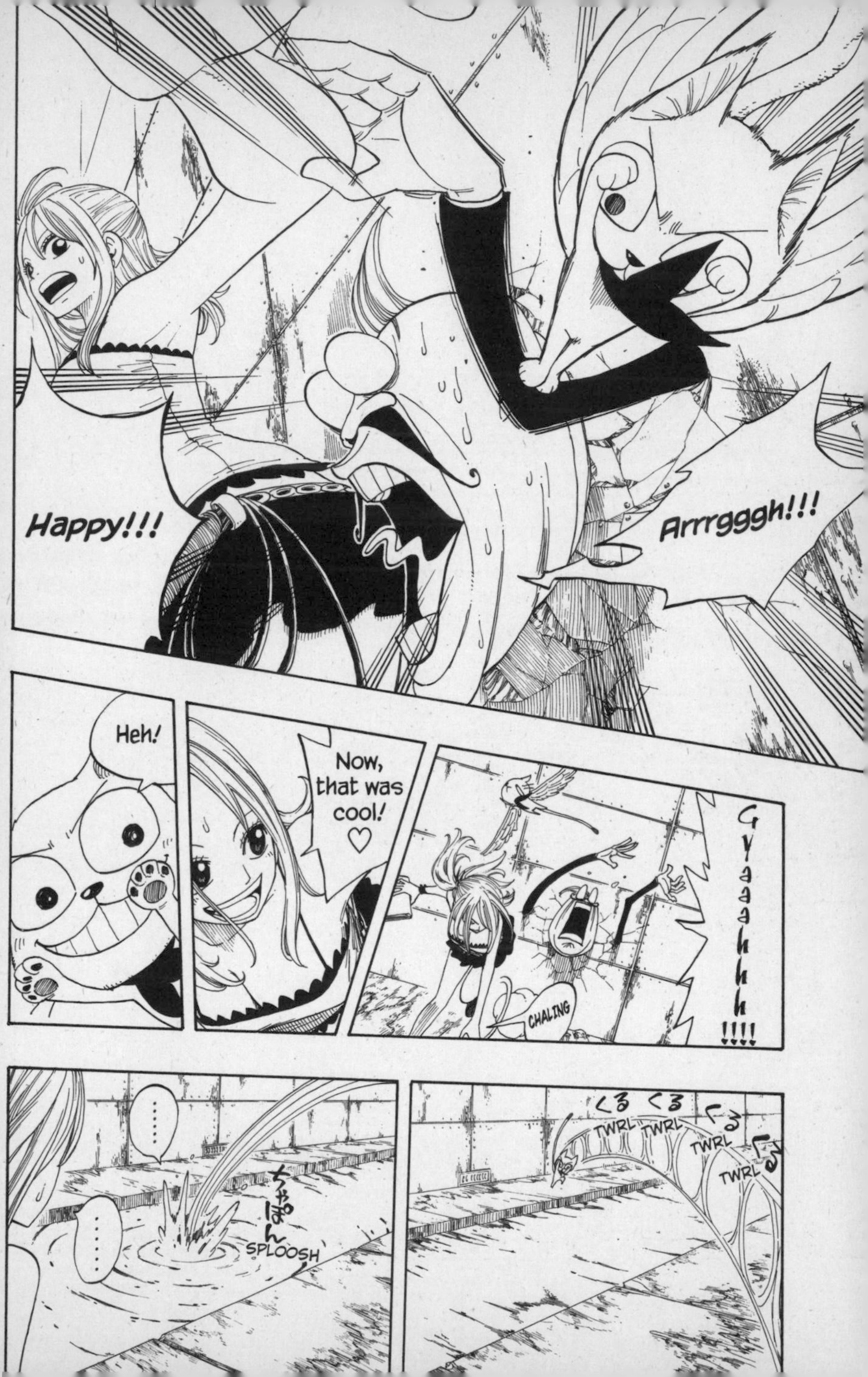
Arrrgggh!!!
Happy!!!
Gyaaaahhhh!!!!
CHALING
Now, that was cool! ♡
Heh!
くる くる
TWRL TWRL
くる
TWRL
くる
TWRL
ちゃぽん
SPLOOSH
......
......

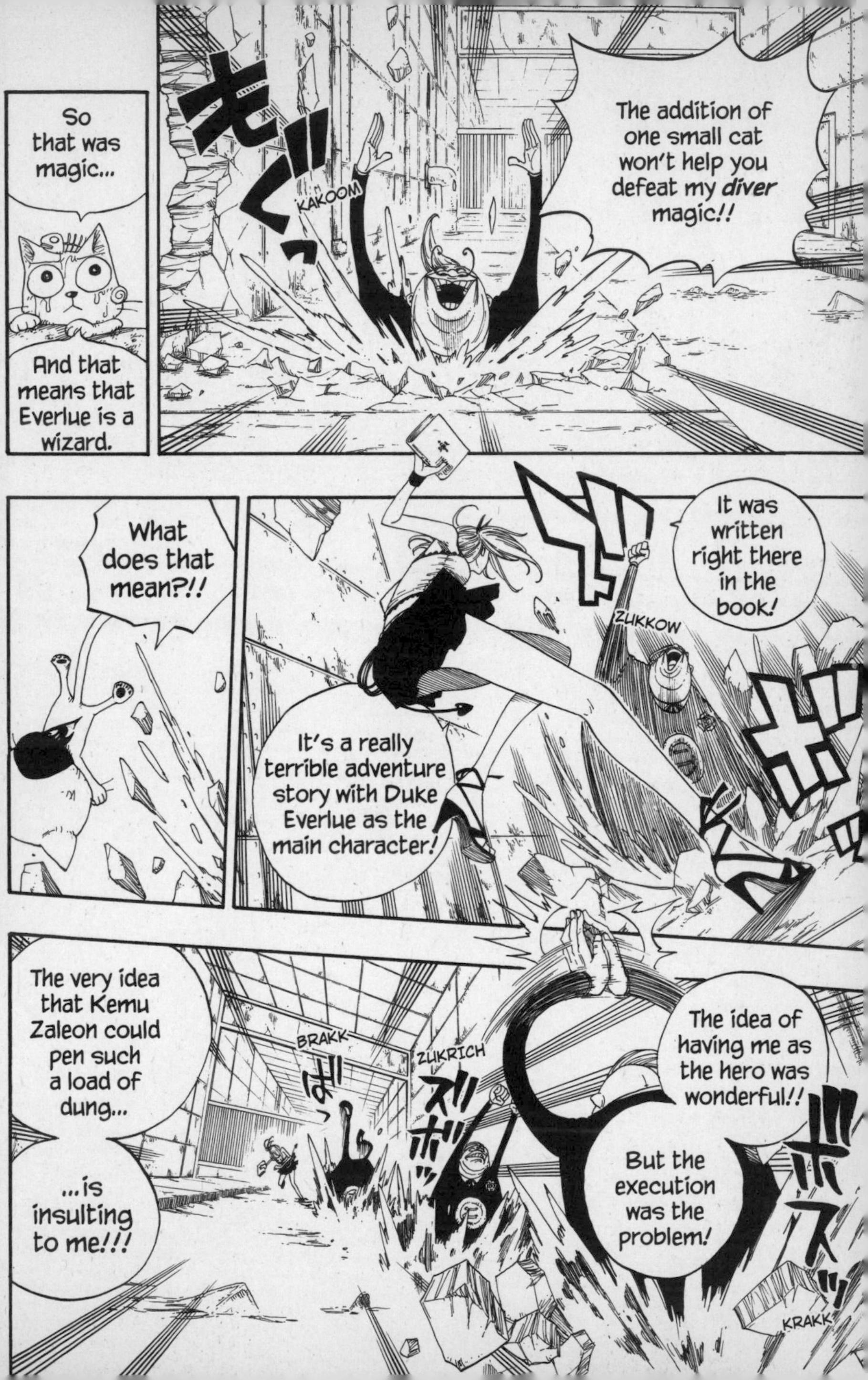
KAKOOM
The addition of one small cat won't help you defeat my *diver* magic!!
So that was magic...
And that means that Everlue is a wizard.
ZUKKOW
It was written right there in the book!
It's a really terrible adventure story with Duke Everlue as the main character!
What does that mean?!!
KRAKK
The idea of having me as the hero was wonderful!!
But the execution was the problem!
ZUKRICH
BRAKK
The very idea that Kemu Zaleon could pen such a load of dung...
...is insulting to me!!!

A very, very, very, very important person like me ordered him to write a book with me as the hero!

And the idiot refused!!!

WHOOSH

What kind of reasoning is that?

...that if he didn't write it, I'd simply *revoke the rights of citizenship for him and every relative connected to his family.*

So I was kind enough to inform him...

ZUBLUSH

And in the end, the upstart did write it*!!!*

Does he have the power to do that?

But that would mean that they couldn't join any trade guilds or work guilds at all!

Revoke his rights of citizenship?

GATCH

That would mean that this jerk has complete autocratic authority over the entire area.

There are still areas under feudal rule.

GLANCE

GLANCE

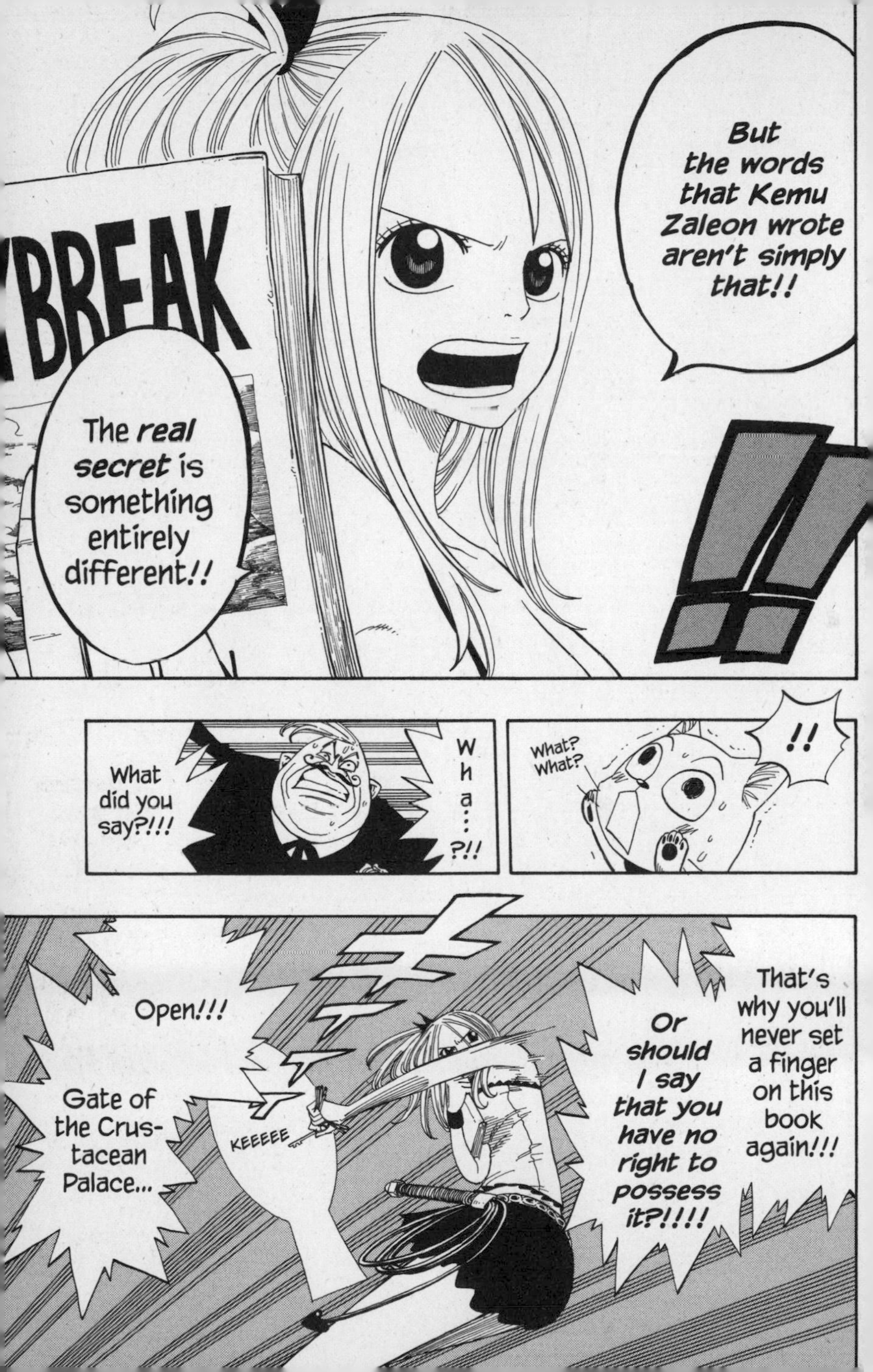
But the words that Kemu Zaleon wrote aren't simply that!!
BREAK
The *real secret* is something entirely different!!
!!
!!
What? What?
Wha…?!!
What did you say?!!!
That's why you'll never set a finger on this book again!!!
Or should I say that you have no right to possess it?!!!!
Gate of the Crus-tacean Palace...
Open!!!
KEEEEE

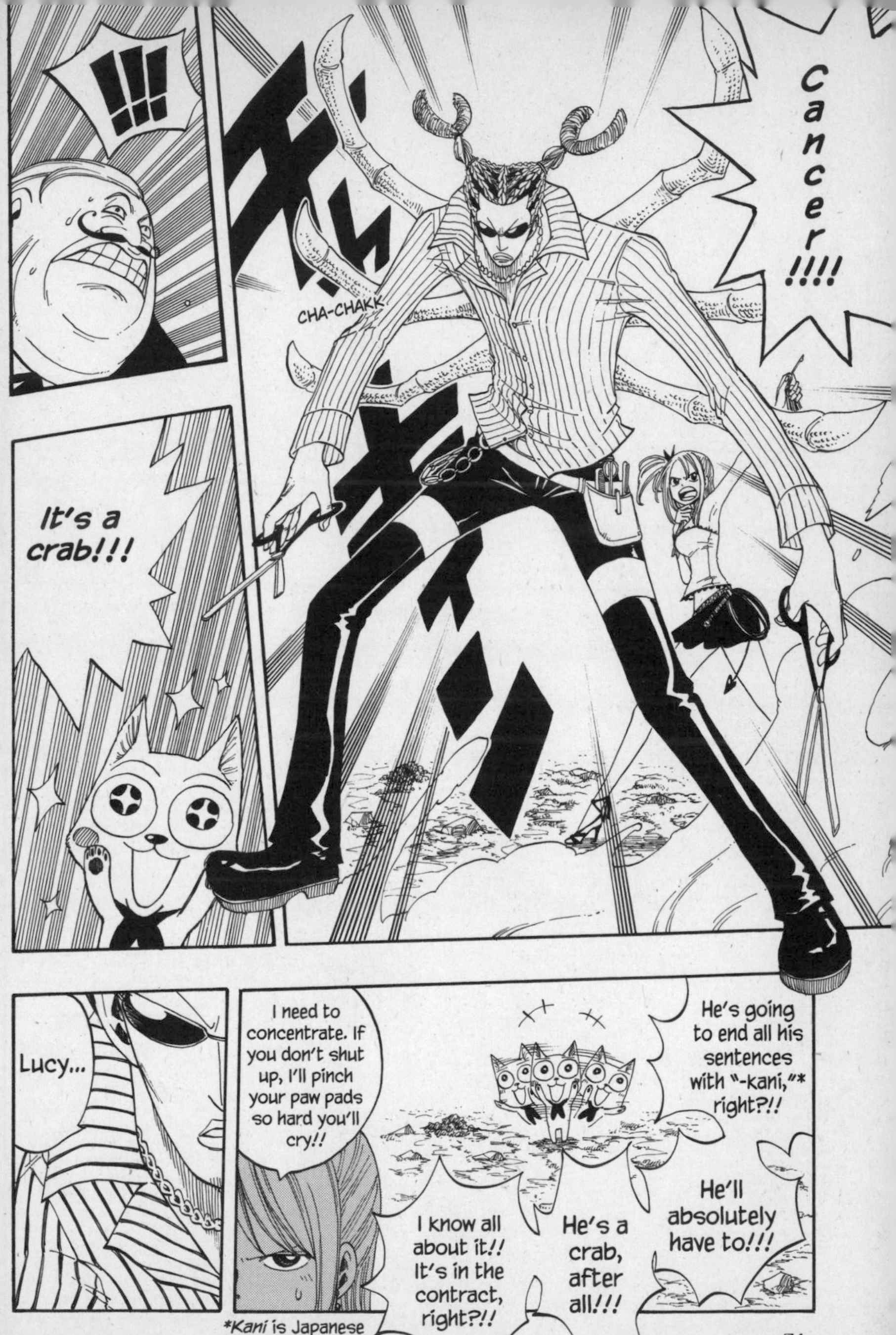
Cancer!!!!
CHA-CHAKK
!!!
It's a crab!!!
He's going to end all his sentences with "-kani,"* right?!!
He'll absolutely have to!!!
He's a crab, after all!!!
I know all about it!! It's in the contract, right?!!
I need to concentrate. If you don't shut up, I'll pinch your paw pads so hard you'll cry!!
Lucy...

*Kani is Japanese for "crab."

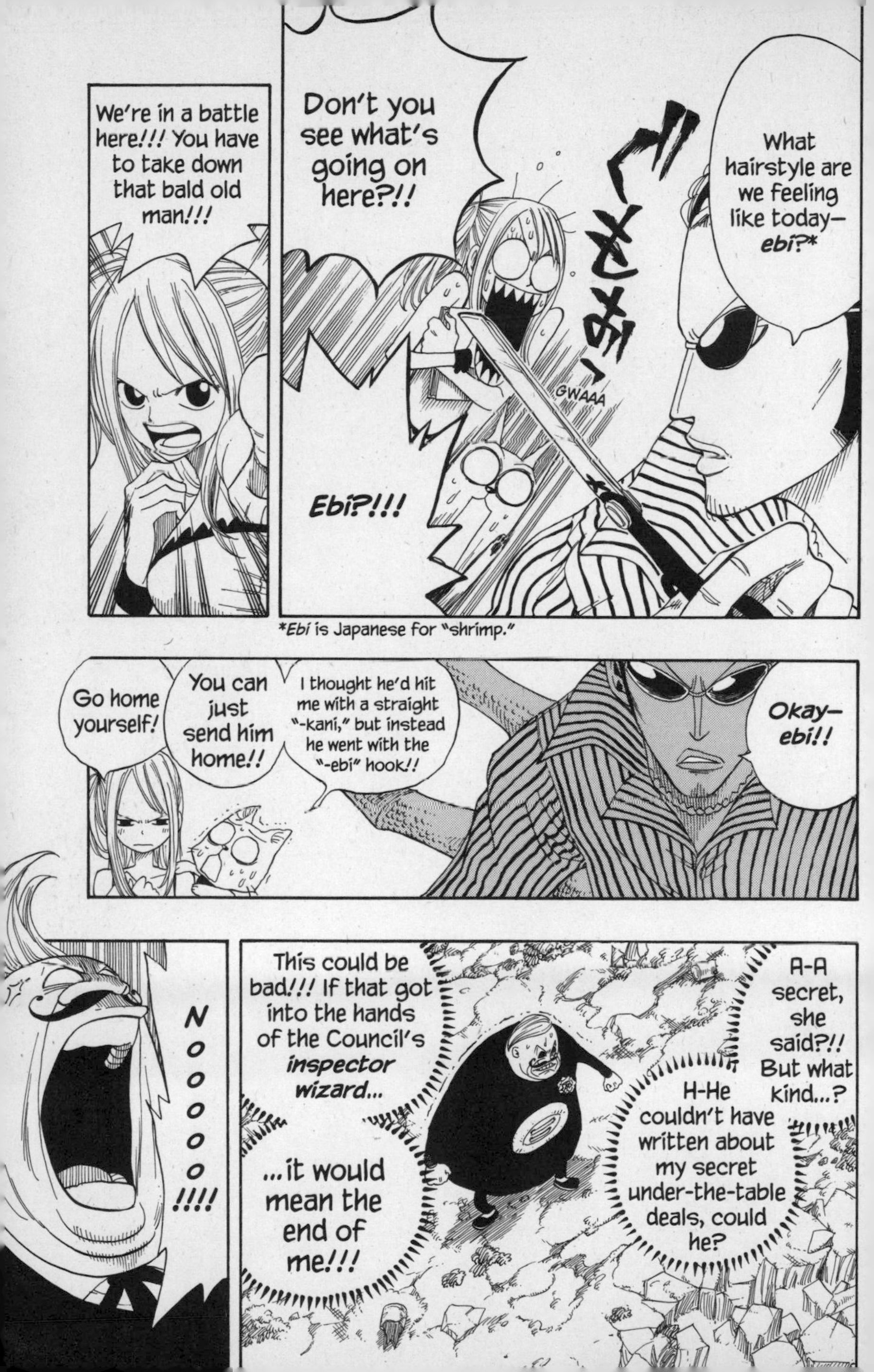
What hairstyle are we feeling like today—*ebi*?*
Don't you see what's going on here?!!
GWAAA
Ebi?!!!
We're in a battle here!!! You have to take down that bald old man!!!
Okay—*ebi*!!
I thought he'd hit me with a straight "-kani," but instead he went with the "-ebi" hook!!
You can just send him home!!
Go home yourself!
A-A secret, she said?!! But what kind...?
H-He couldn't have written about my secret under-the-table deals, could he?
This could be bad!!! If that got into the hands of the Council's *inspector wizard*...
...it would mean the end of me!!!
NOOOOOO!!!!

**Ebi* is Japanese for "shrimp."

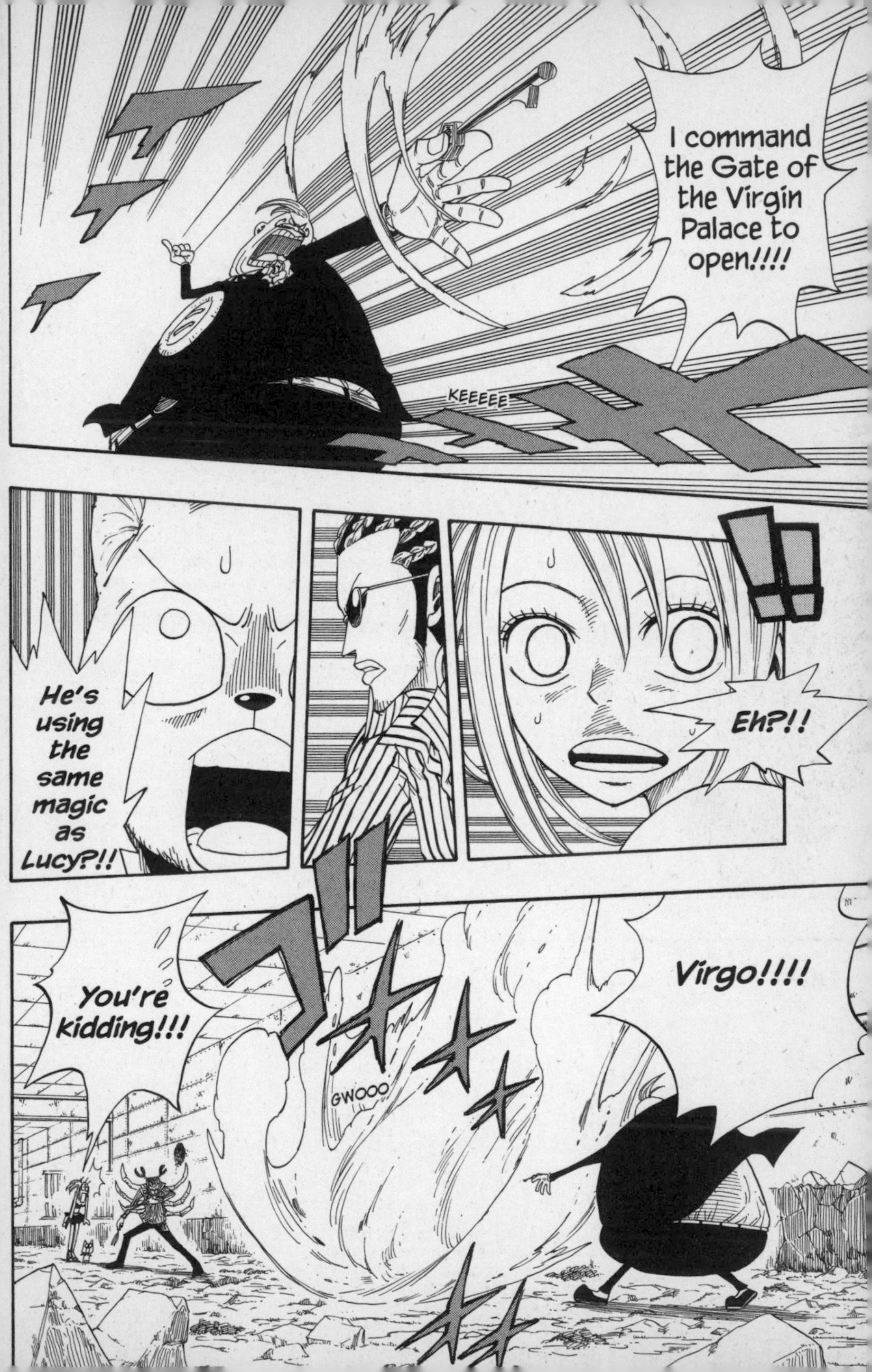
I command the Gate of the Virgin Palace to open!!!!
KEEEEE
Eh?!!
He's using the same magic as Lucy?!!
Virgo!!!!
GWOOO
You're kidding!!!

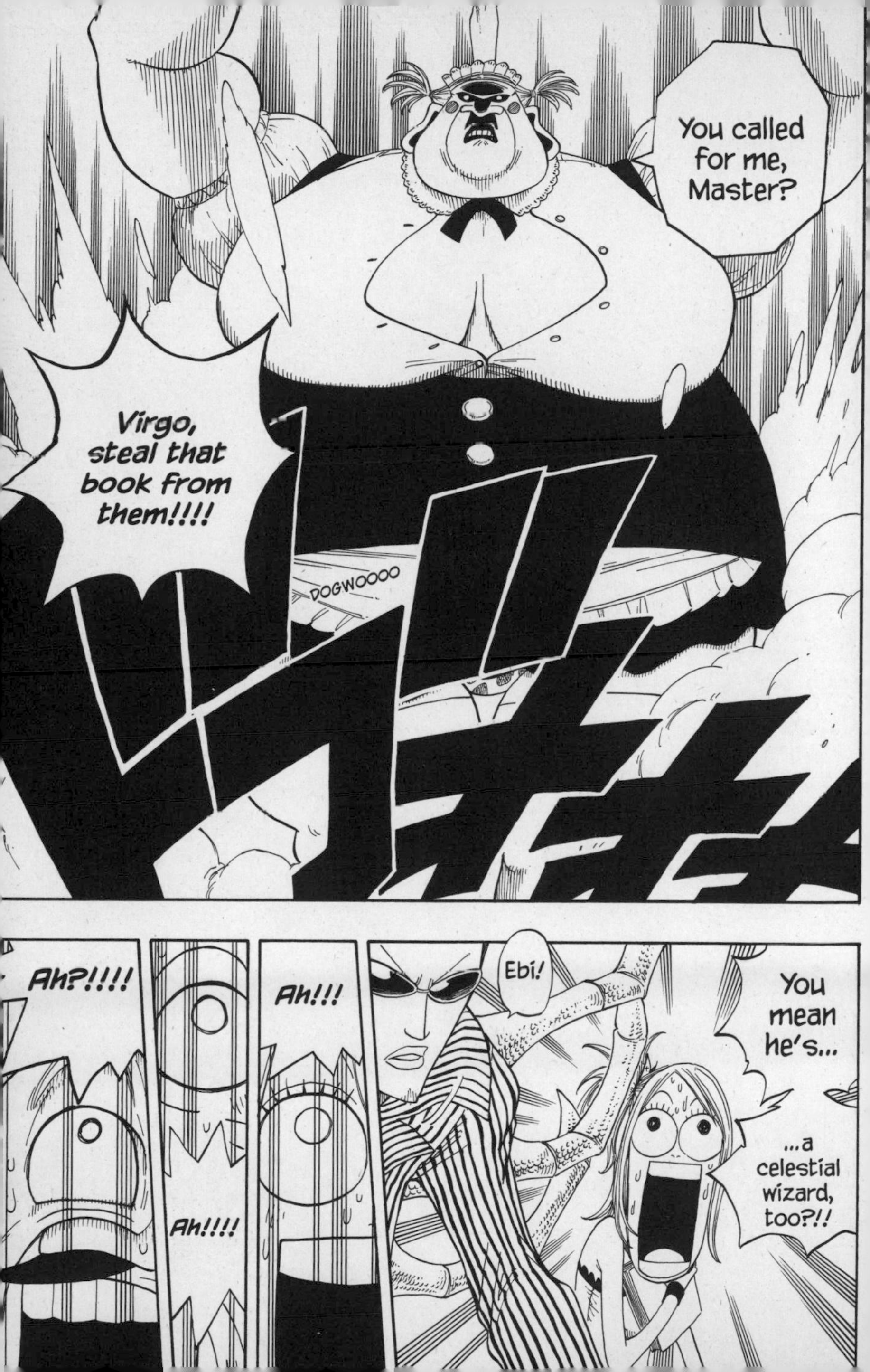
You called for me, Master?
Virgo, steal that book from them!!!!
DOGWOOOO
Ebi!
You mean he's...
...a celestial wizard, too?!!
Ah!!!
Ah!!!!
Ah?!!!!

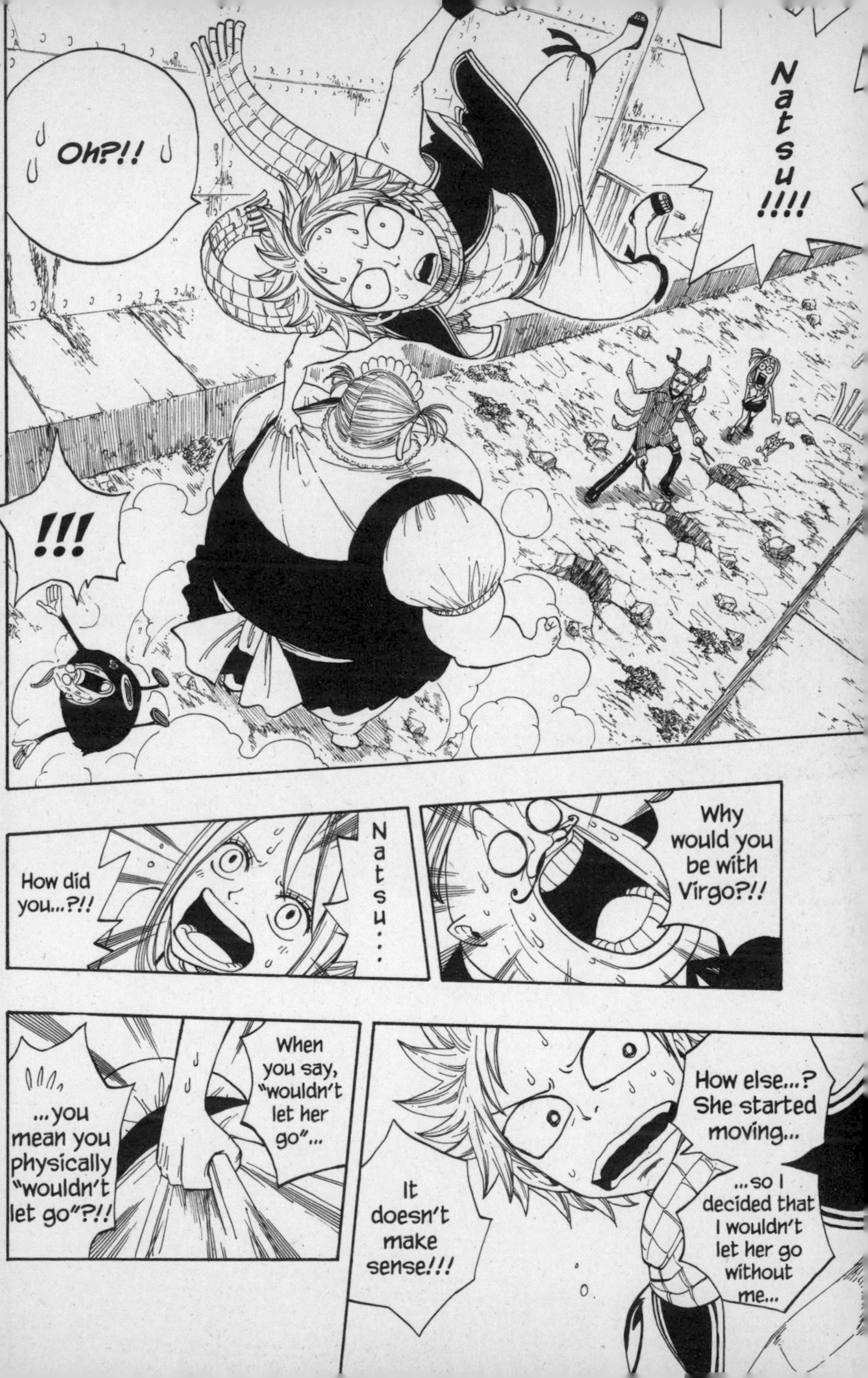
Natsu!!!!
Oh?!!
!!!
Why would you be with Virgo?!!
Natsu...
How did you...?!!
How else...? She started moving...
...so I decided that I wouldn't let her go without me...
It doesn't make sense!!!
When you say, "wouldn't let her go"...
...you mean you physically "wouldn't let go"?!!

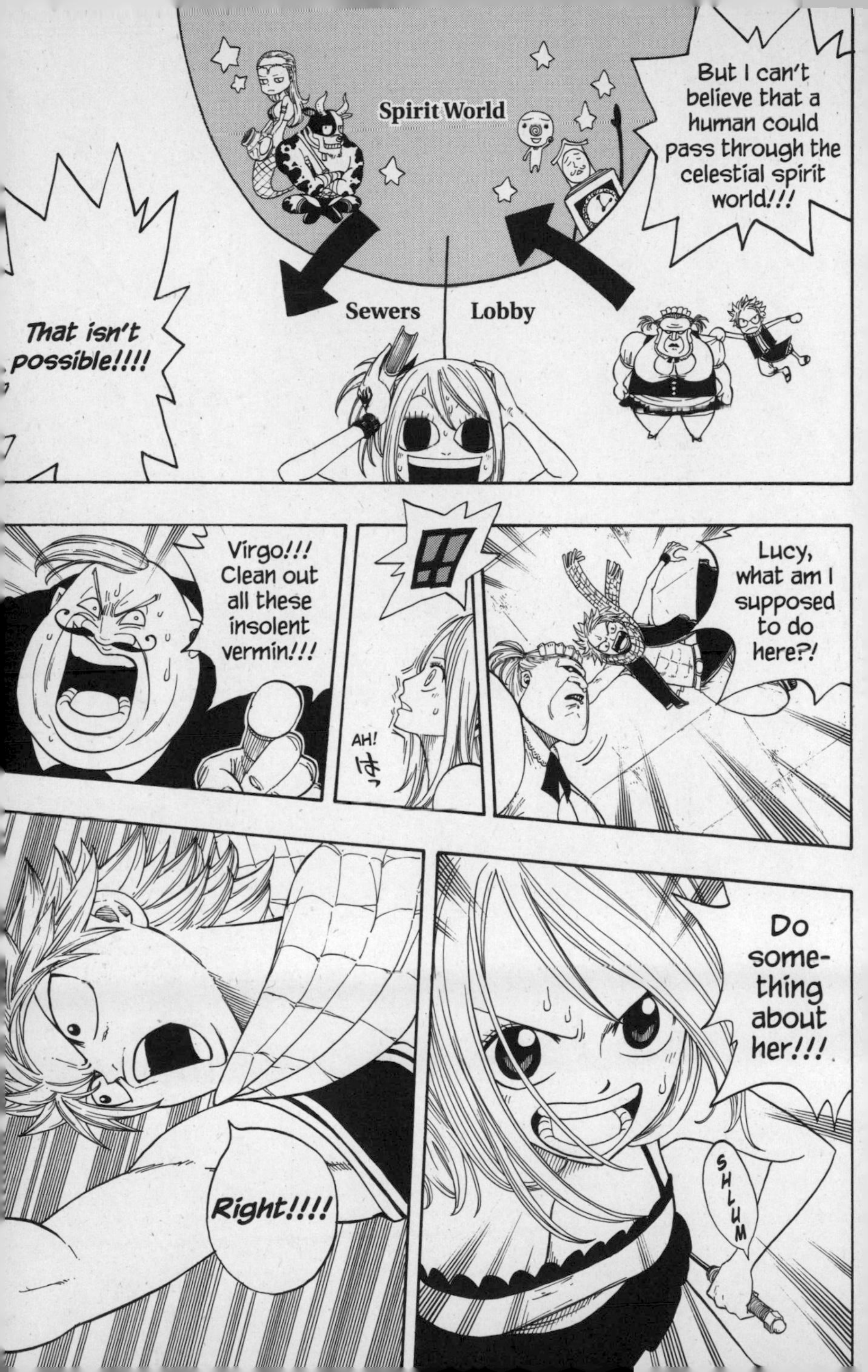
But I can't believe that a human could pass through the celestial spirit world!!!
Spirit World
Lobby
Sewers
That isn't possible!!!!
Lucy, what am I supposed to do here?!
AH!
はっ
Virgo!!! Clean out all these insolent vermin!!!
Do some-thing about her!!!
SHLUM
Right!!!!

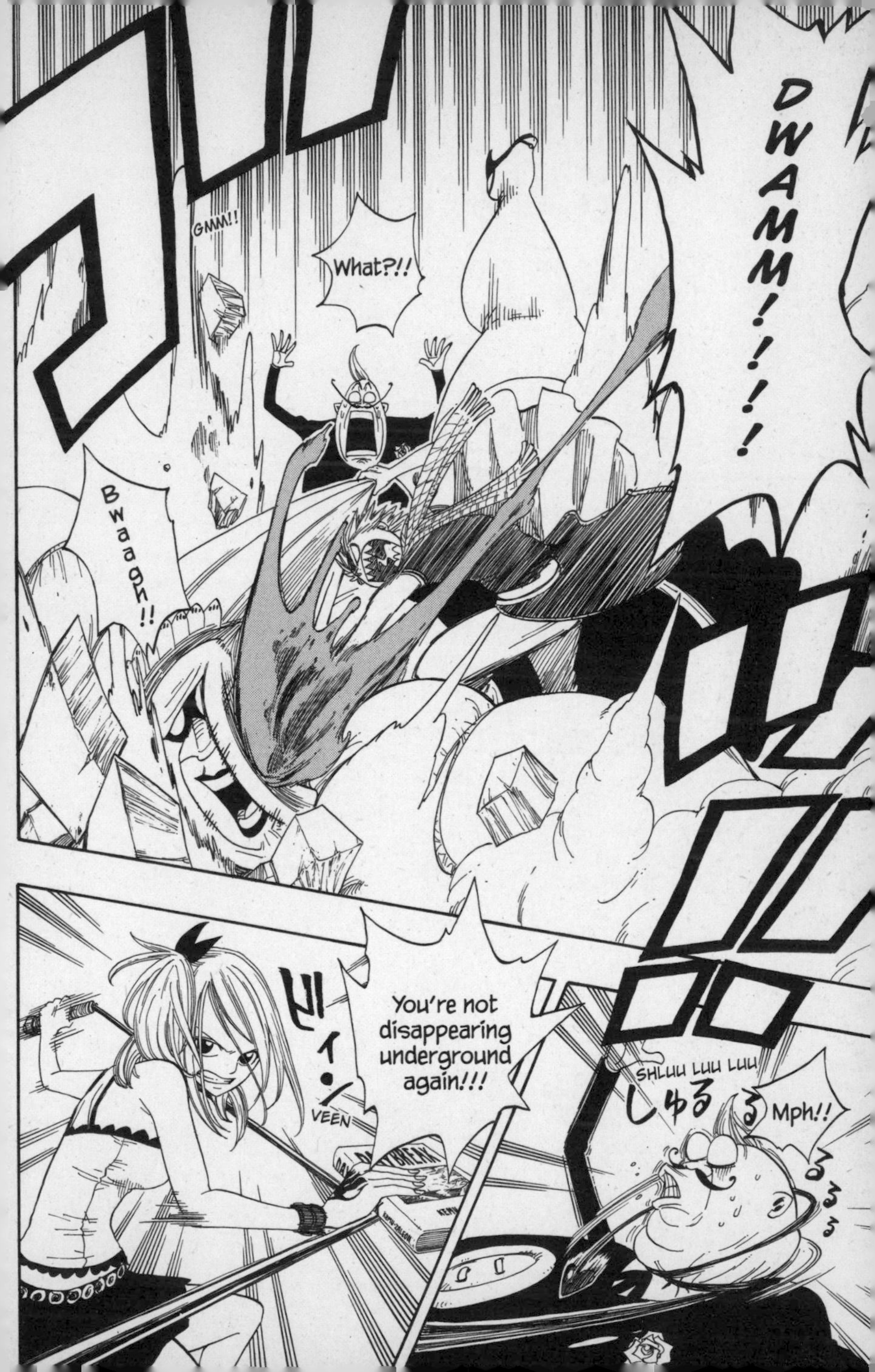
DWAMM!!!!!
What?!!
GMM!!
Bwaagh!!
You're not disappearing underground again!!!
SHLUU LUU LUU
しゅるる
Mph!!
ビィ・ン
VEEN

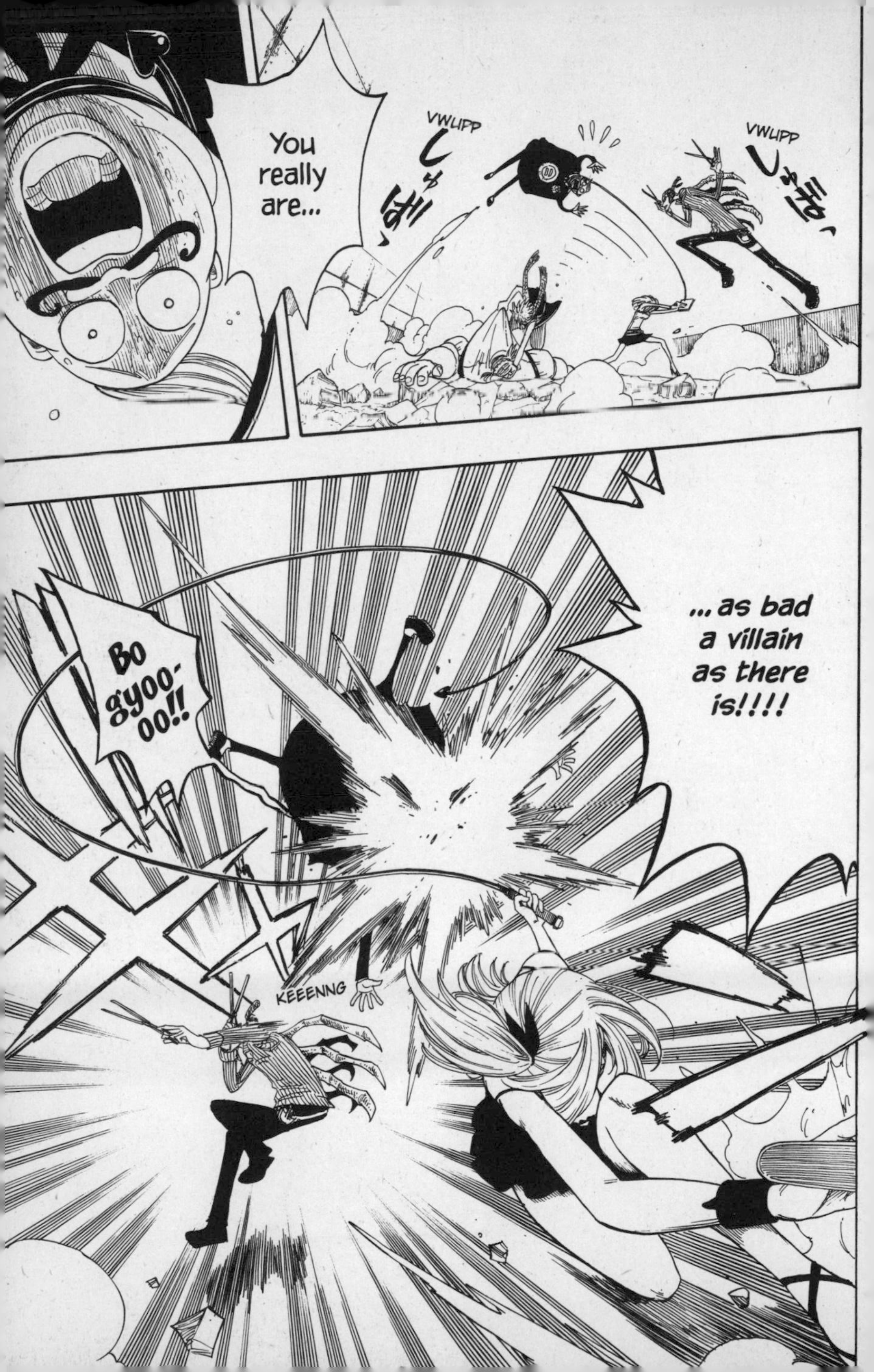
VWUPP
VWUPP
You really are...
...as bad a villain as there is!!!!
Bo gyoo-oo!!
KEEENNG

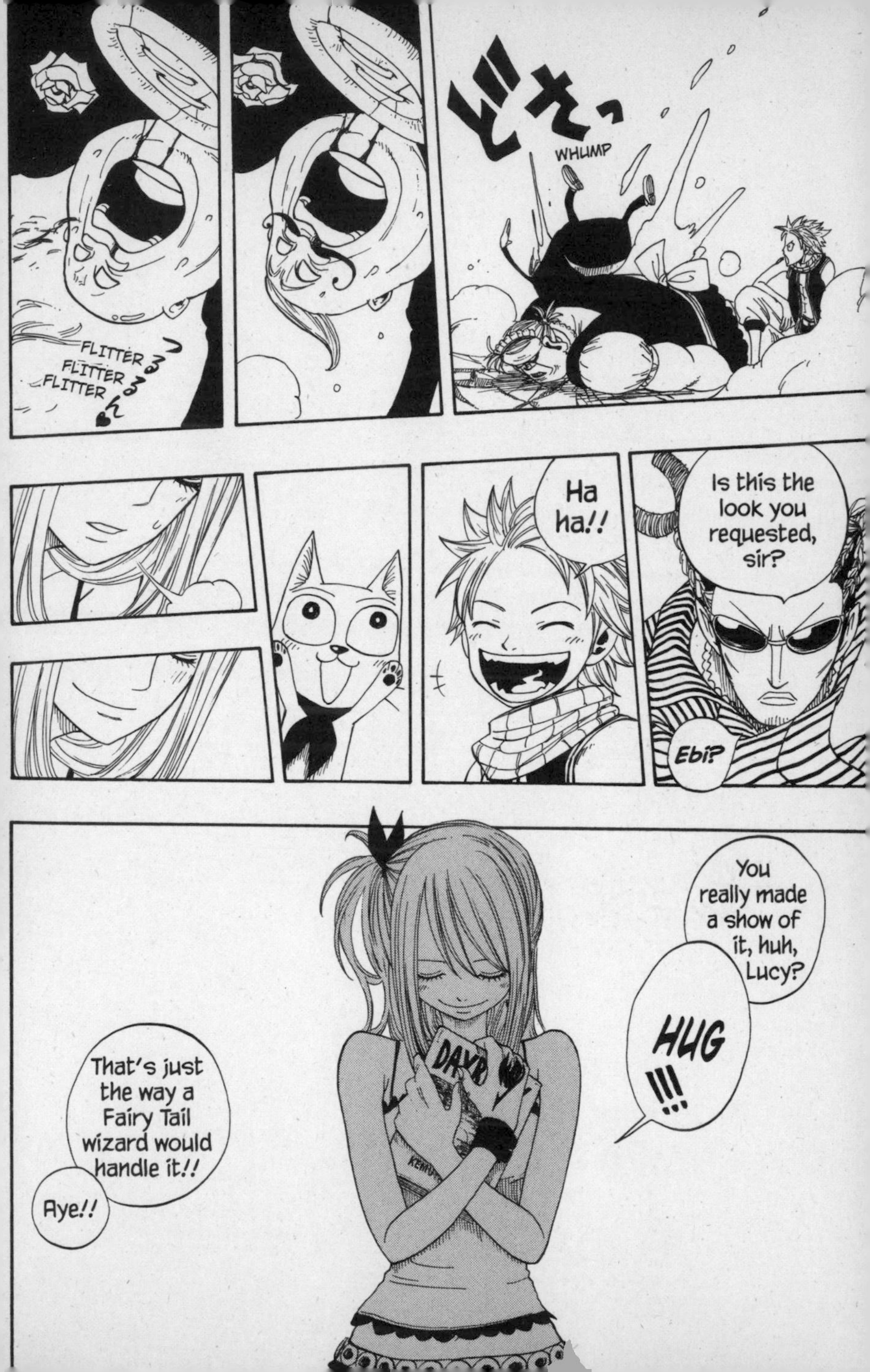
どさっ
WHUMP
FLITTER
FLITTER
FLITTER
Is this the look you requested, sir?
Ebi?
Ha ha!!
You really made a show of it, huh, Lucy?
HUG !!!
That's just the way a Fairy Tail wizard would handle it!!
Aye!!

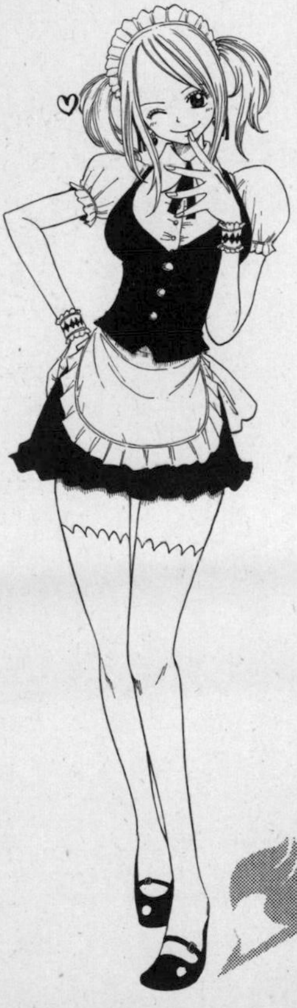

FAIRY TAIL

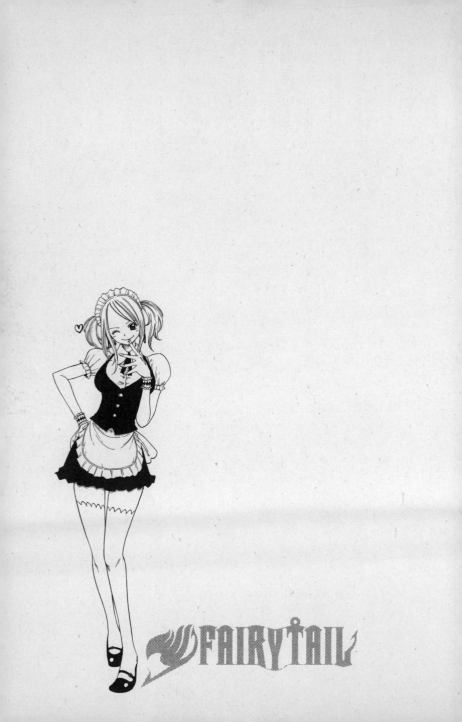

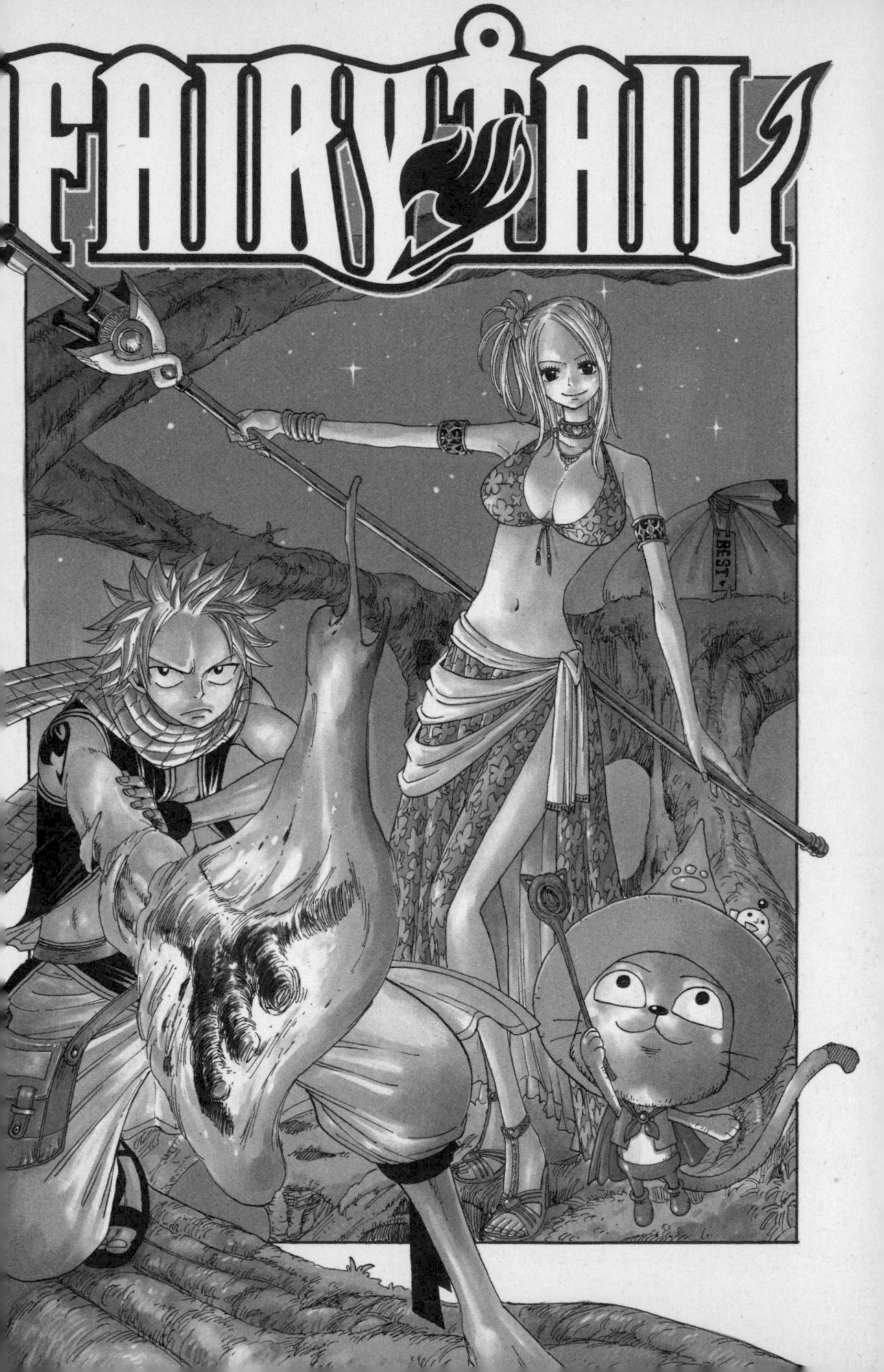
FAIRY TAIL
BEST

Chapter 9: Dear Kaby

It's an adventure novel with Duke Everlue as the hero.

This is the book that Duke Everlue forced Kemu Zaleon to write.

...nobody would think that these are words written by Kemu Zaleon.

Its plotting and word usage are terrible. Not a complete loss, but...

?

...right inside this book!

DAYBREAK

KEMU · ZALEON

That's how I came up with the idea that there's a *secret* hidden...

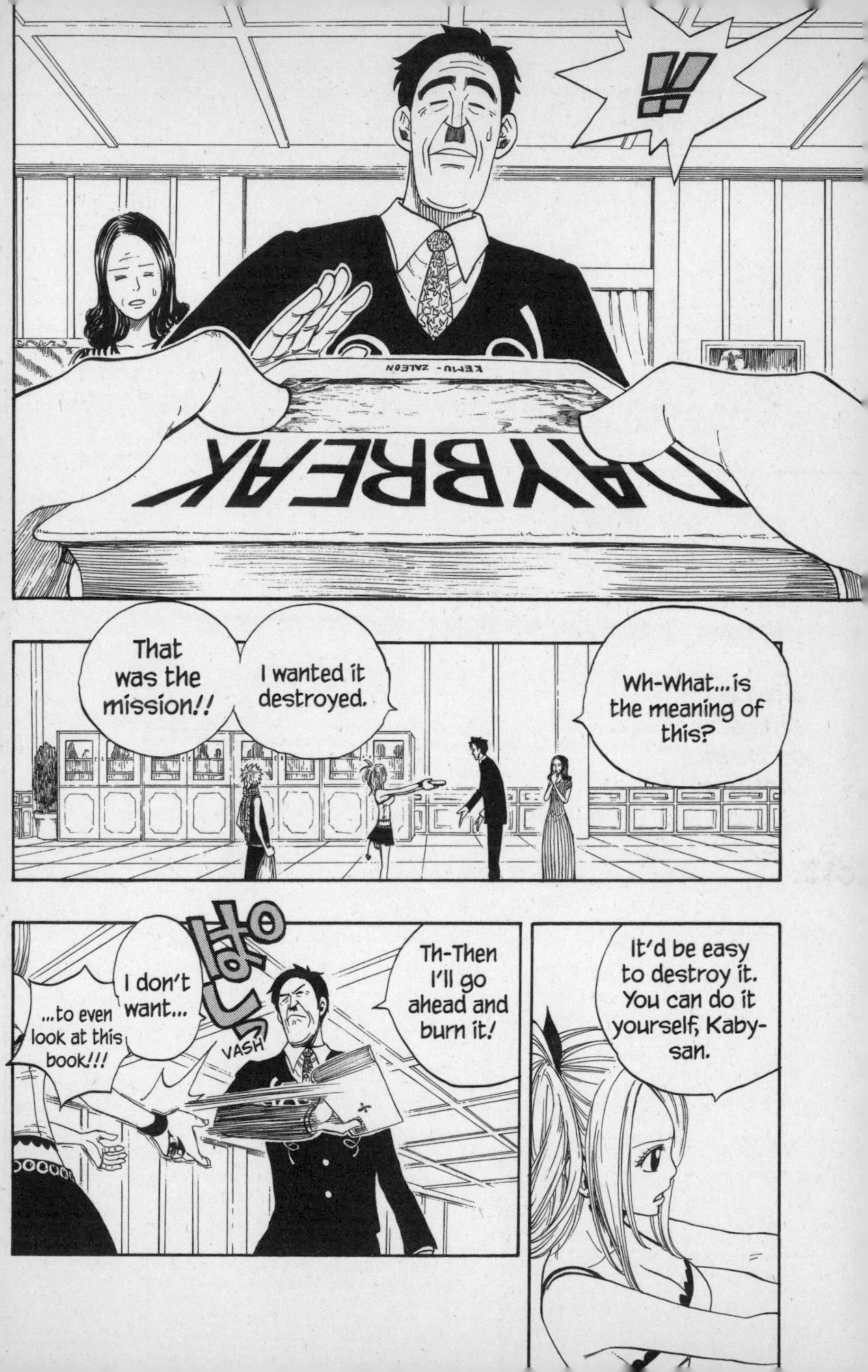

DAYBREAK
Wh-What...is the meaning of this?
I wanted it destroyed.
That was the mission!!
It'd be easy to destroy it. You can do it yourself, Kaby-san.
Th-Then I'll go ahead and burn it!
ぱしっ
VASH
I don't want...
...to even look at this book!!!

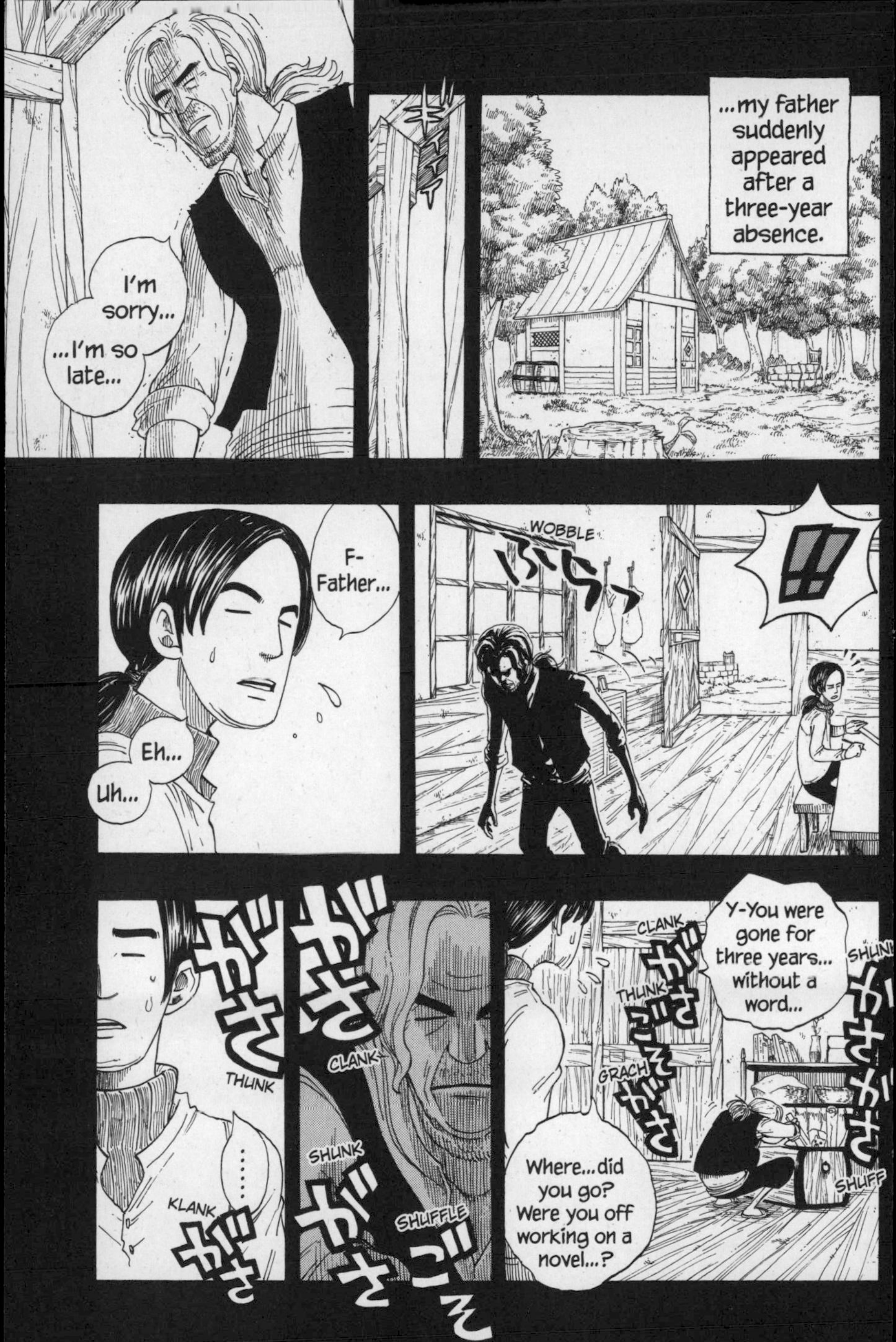
...my father suddenly appeared after a three-year absence.
I'm sorry... ...I'm so late...
!!
WOBBLE
ふらっ
F-Father...
Eh...
uh...
Y-You were gone for three years... without a word...
SHUNK
SHUFF
CLANK
THUNK
GRACH
Where...did you go? Were you off working on a novel...?
CLANK
SHUNK
SHUFFLE
THUNK
......
KLANK

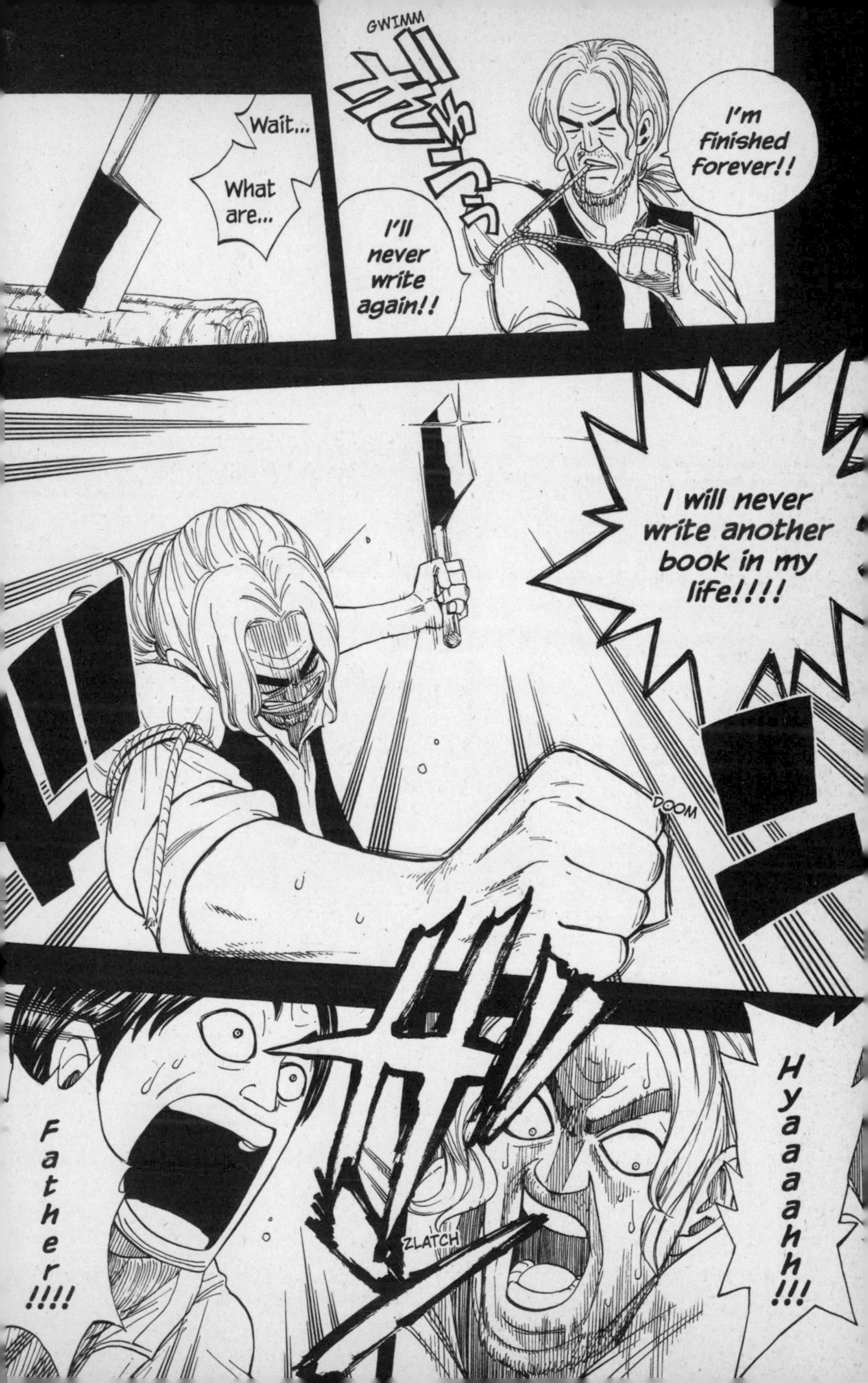
I'm finished forever!!
GWIMM
I'll never write again!!
Wait...
What are...
I will never write another book in my life!!!!
DOOM
Hyaaaahh!!!
ZLATCH
Father!!!!

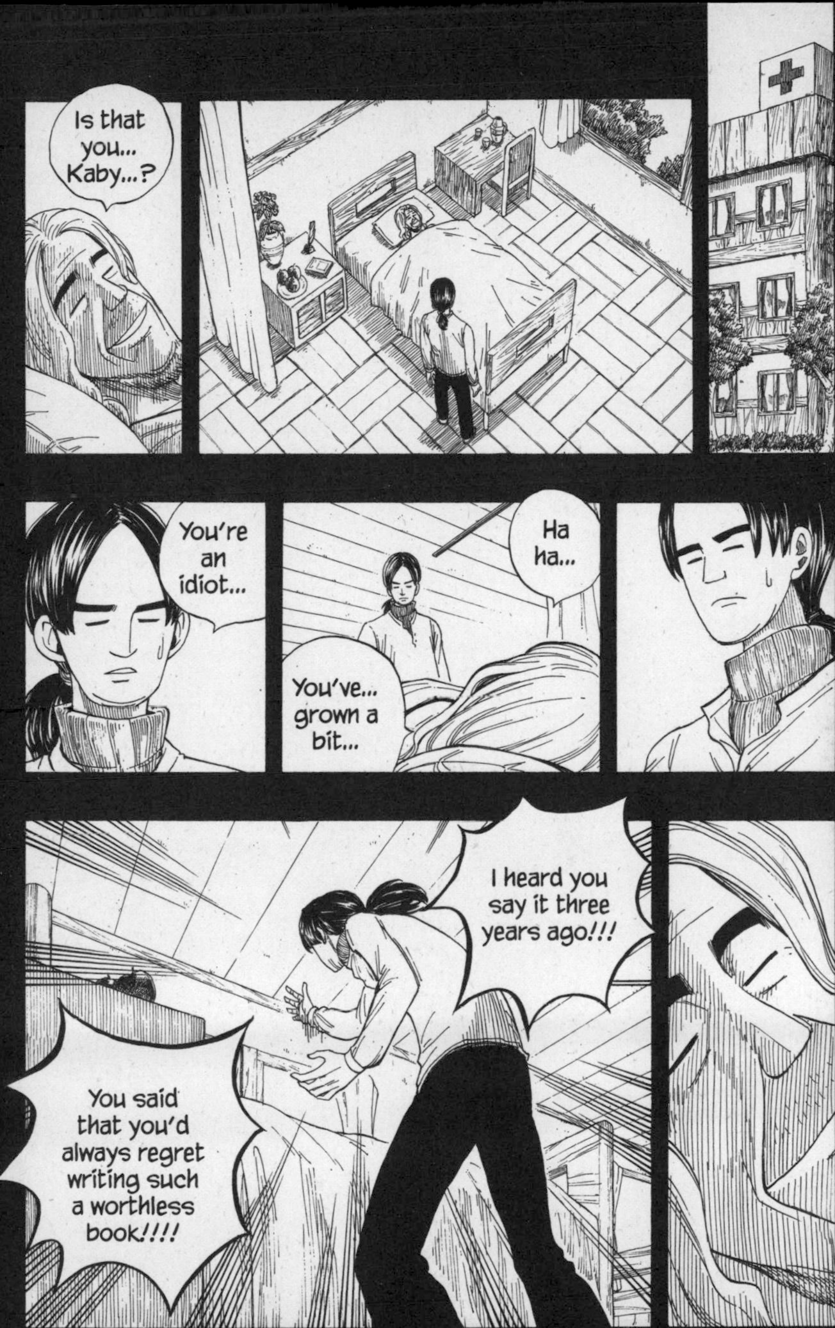
Is that you... Kaby...?
Ha ha...
You've... grown a bit...
You're an idiot...
I heard you say it three years ago!!!
You said that you'd always regret writing such a worthless book!!!!

If I hadn't said those hurtful things, my father might never have killed himself.

But as the months turned to years, the hate gradually changed to regret.

FSSH

...and destroy it to protect the honor of my father's name in the world.

So to atone at least a little, I wanted to find the embarrassing final work of his life...

SHFFL

FASH

DAYBREAK

KRAKLE KRAKLE

I'm sure Father would want this, too.

Wait!!

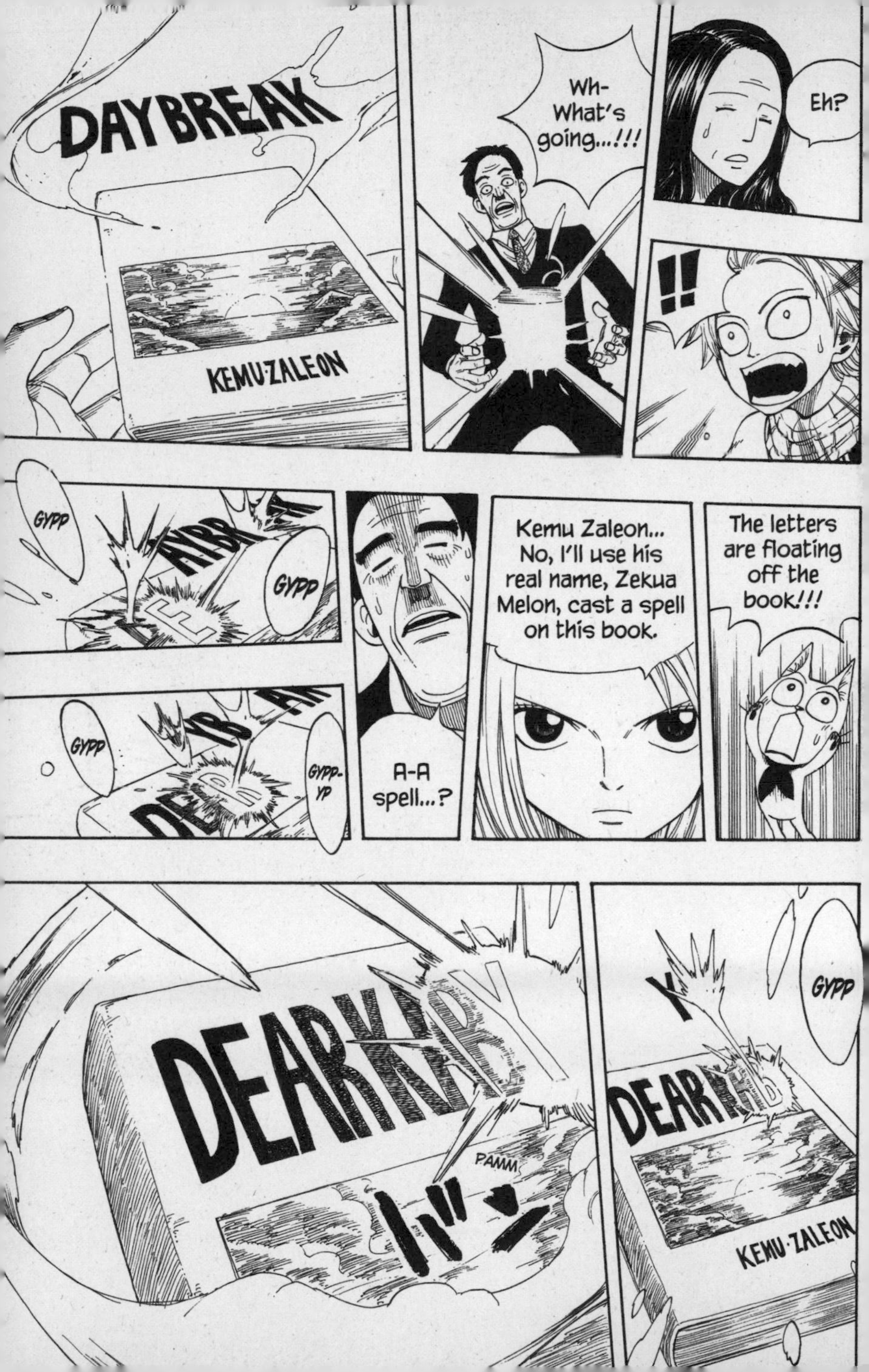
Eh?
!!
Wh- What's going...!!!
DAYBREAK
KEMU·ZALEON
The letters are floating off the book!!!
Kemu Zaleon... No, I'll use his real name, Zekua Melon, cast a spell on this book.
A-A spell...?
GYPP
GYPP
GYPP-YP
GYPP
GYPP
Y
KEMU·ZALEON
PAMM

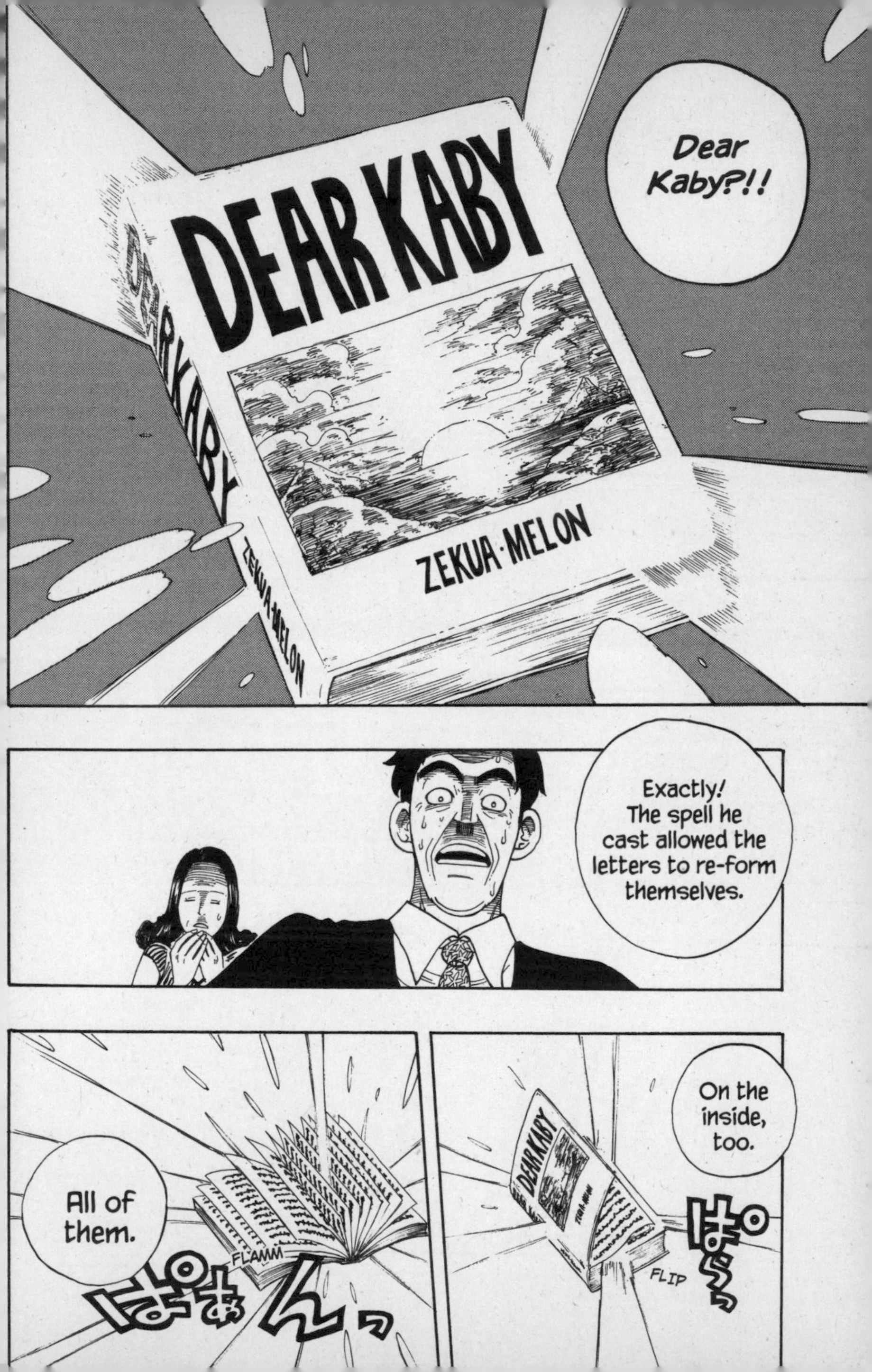
Dear Kaby?!!
DEAR KABY
ZEKUA·MELON
Exactly! The spell he cast allowed the letters to re-form themselves.
On the inside, too.
DEAR KABY
FLIP
All of them.
FLAMM

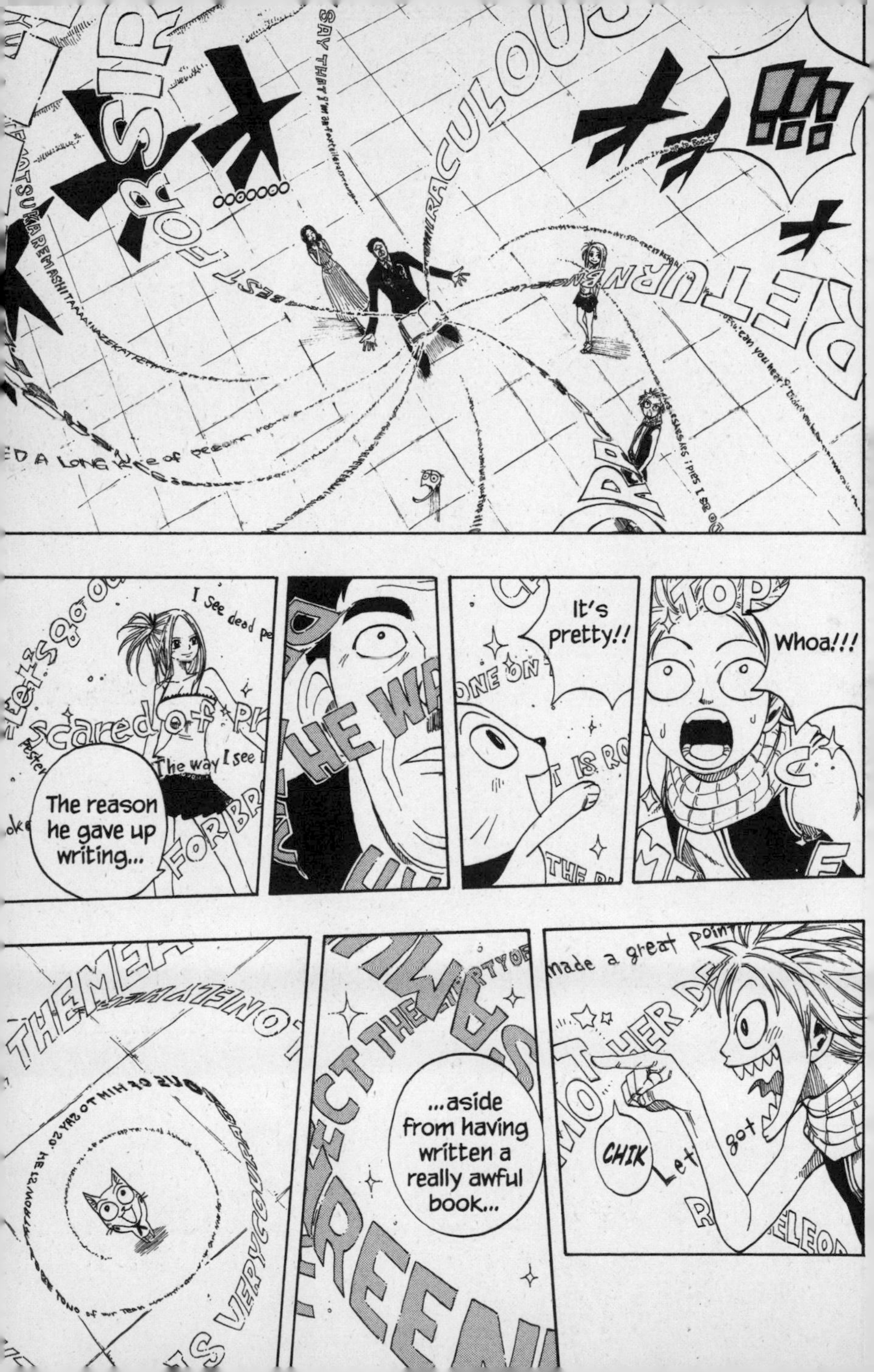
Whoa!!!
It's pretty!!
The reason he gave up writing...
CHIK
...aside from having written a really awful book...

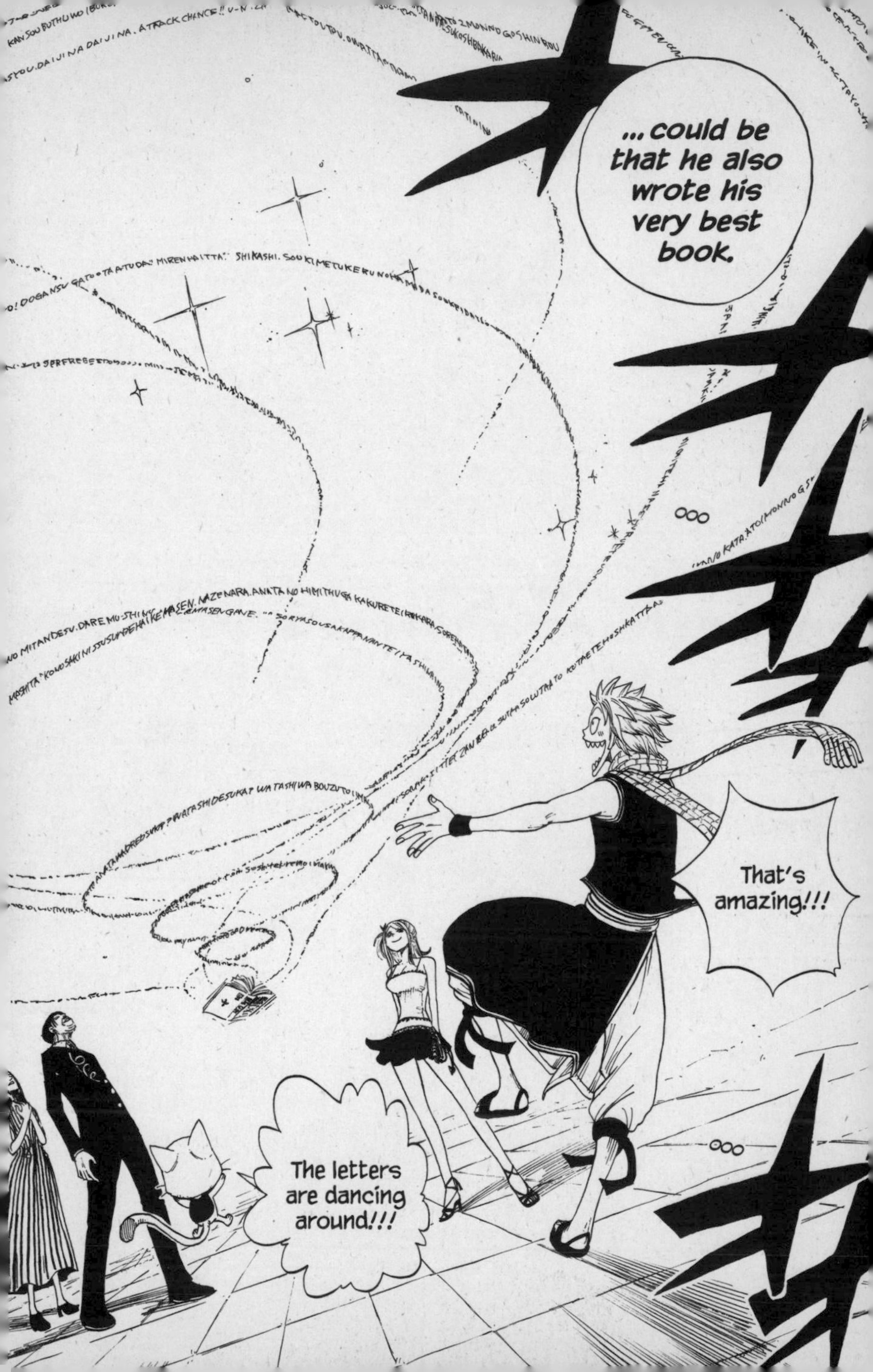
...could be that he also wrote his very best book.
That's amazing!!!
The letters are dancing around!!!

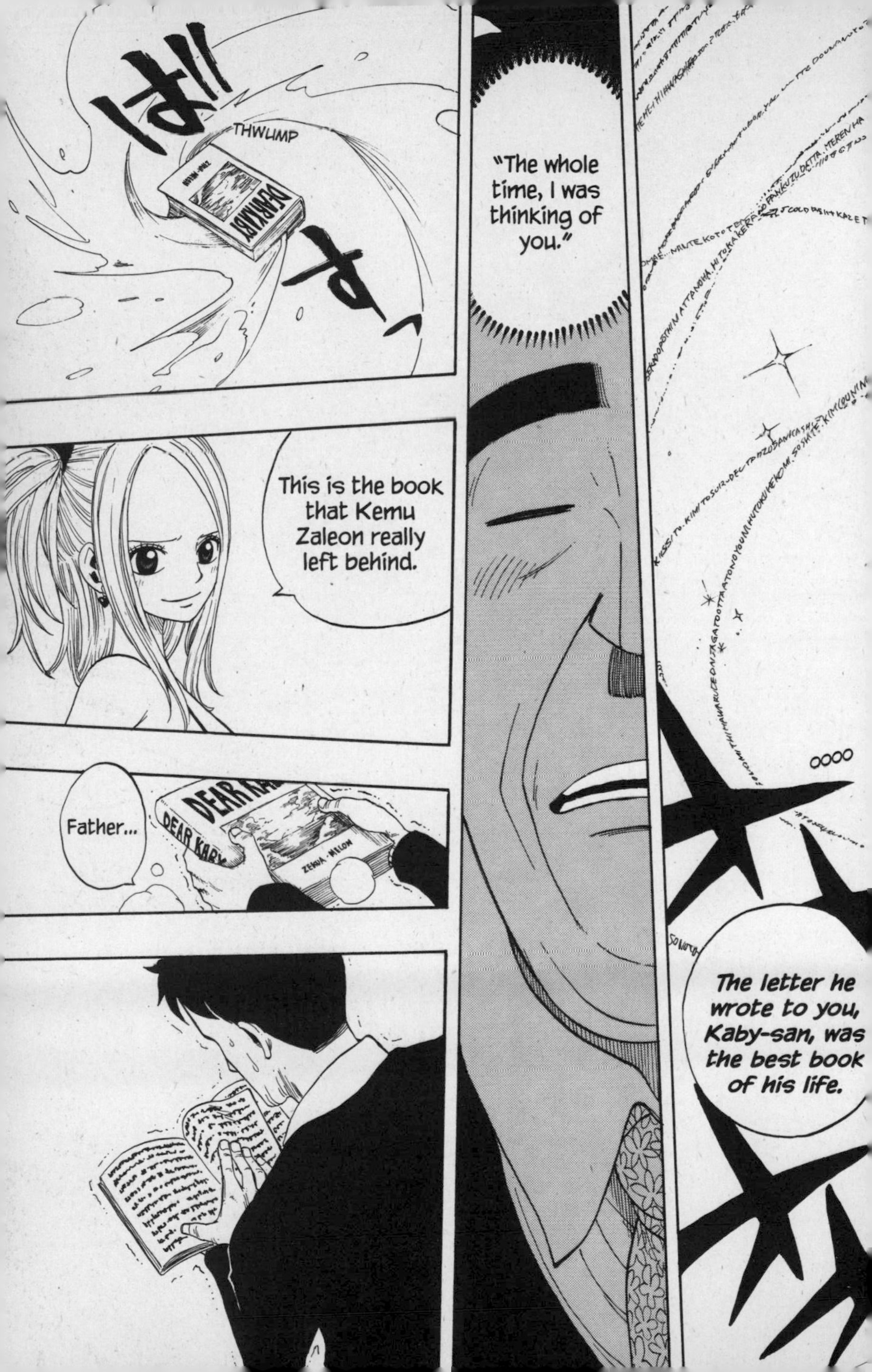
OOOO
The letter he wrote to you, Kaby-san, was the best book of his life.
"The whole time, I was thinking of you."
THWUMP
This is the book that Kemu Zaleon really left behind.
Father...
DEAR KARY
ZEKUA · MELON

But how did you know it wasn't their house?

Hm?

Well, I would have!!!

Do you really think so?

Maybe...

They didn't have to go to the trouble. We would have taken their mission.

So they borrowed the house of a friend to make it look like they had money?

But that author was really an incredible wizard.

For someone to cast a spell and have it last perfectly intact for thirty years shows some powerful skills.

I'm not an animal, so I didn't!!!!

Their smell and the smell of the house were completely different.

Anybody would notice.

It makes me want to follow in his footsteps.

I guess it's because he was a member of a magic guild in his youth, huh?

And he turned his many adventures into novels later on.

DEARKABY

DEARKABY

104

FAIRY TAIL

Chapter 10:
The Armored Wizard

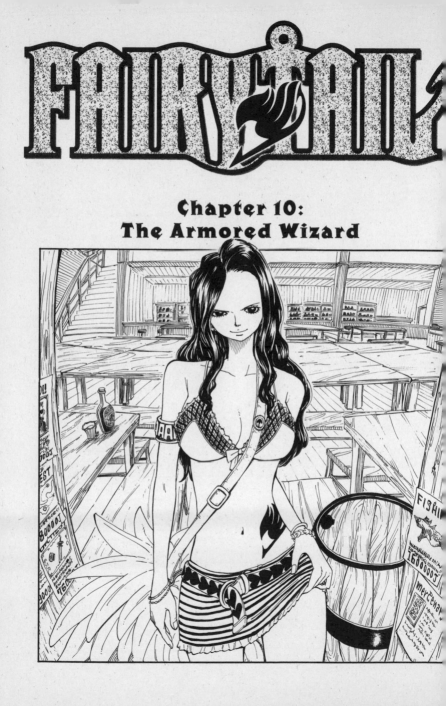

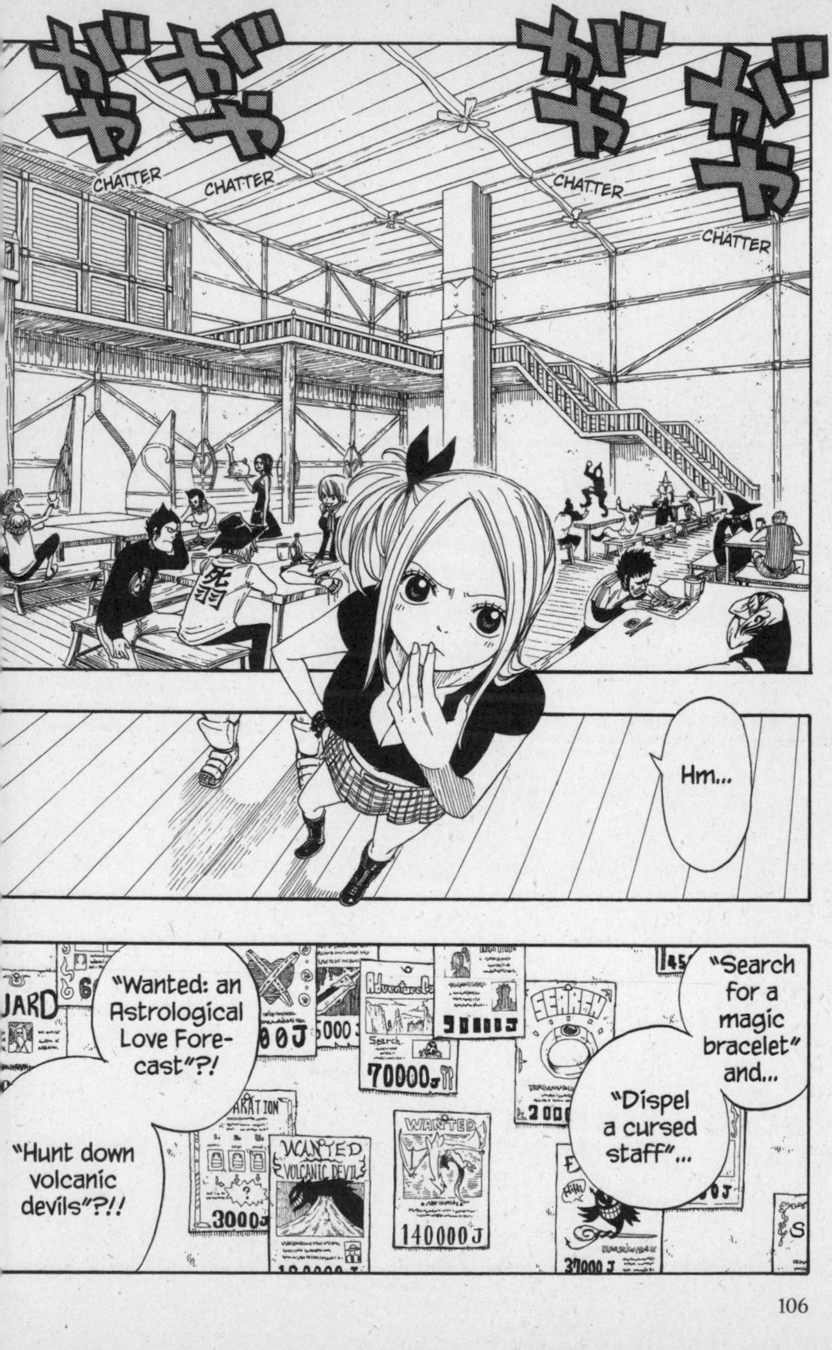
ガヤガヤ
ガヤガヤ
CHATTER
CHATTER
ガヤガヤ
ガヤガヤ
CHATTER
CHATTER
Hm...
"Search for a magic bracelet" and...
"Dispel a cursed staff"...
"Wanted: an Astrological Love Forecast"?!
"Hunt down volcanic devils"?!!
SEARCH
70000J
WANTED
140000J
37000 J
WANTED
VOLCANIC DEVIL
3000J

What? Oh, you're right.

He's attending the regularly scheduled League meeting, so he'll be gone for a while.

The Master isn't around right now.

If you see any that you like, let me know.

Wow. There really are all sorts of missions, huh?

It's different from the Council, though...

That's a little difficult to understand, isn't it?

The masters of the regional guilds gather to make their periodic reports.

League meeting?

I doubt anyone new to the guilds can easily figure out the Magic World Organizational Chart.

SQUEE
SQUEE
SQUEE

Reedus, can I borrow your light pen for a moment?

Oui.

SST

Light Pen (Magic Item)
Writes letters in the air. There are currently seventy-two colors for sale.

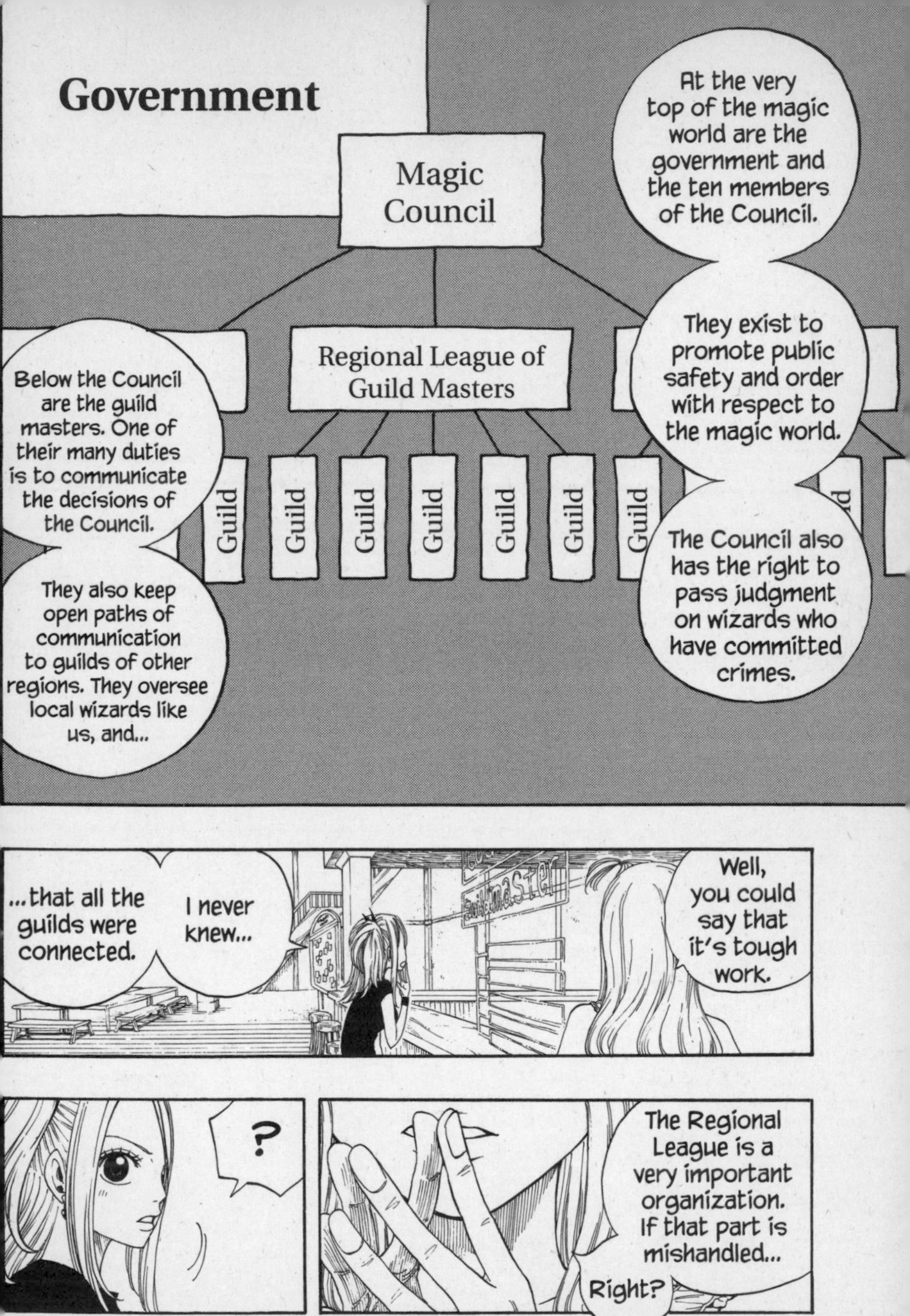

Government

Magic Council

At the very top of the magic world are the government and the ten members of the Council.

Regional League of Guild Masters

They exist to promote public safety and order with respect to the magic world.

Below the Council are the guild masters. One of their many duties is to communicate the decisions of the Council.

Guild Guild Guild Guild Guild Guild Guild

Guild

The Council also has the right to pass judgment on wizards who have committed crimes.

They also keep open paths of communication to guilds of other regions. They oversee local wizards like us, and...

...that all the guilds were connected.

I never knew...

Well, you could say that it's tough work.

?

The Regional League is a very important organization. If that part is mishandled...

Right?

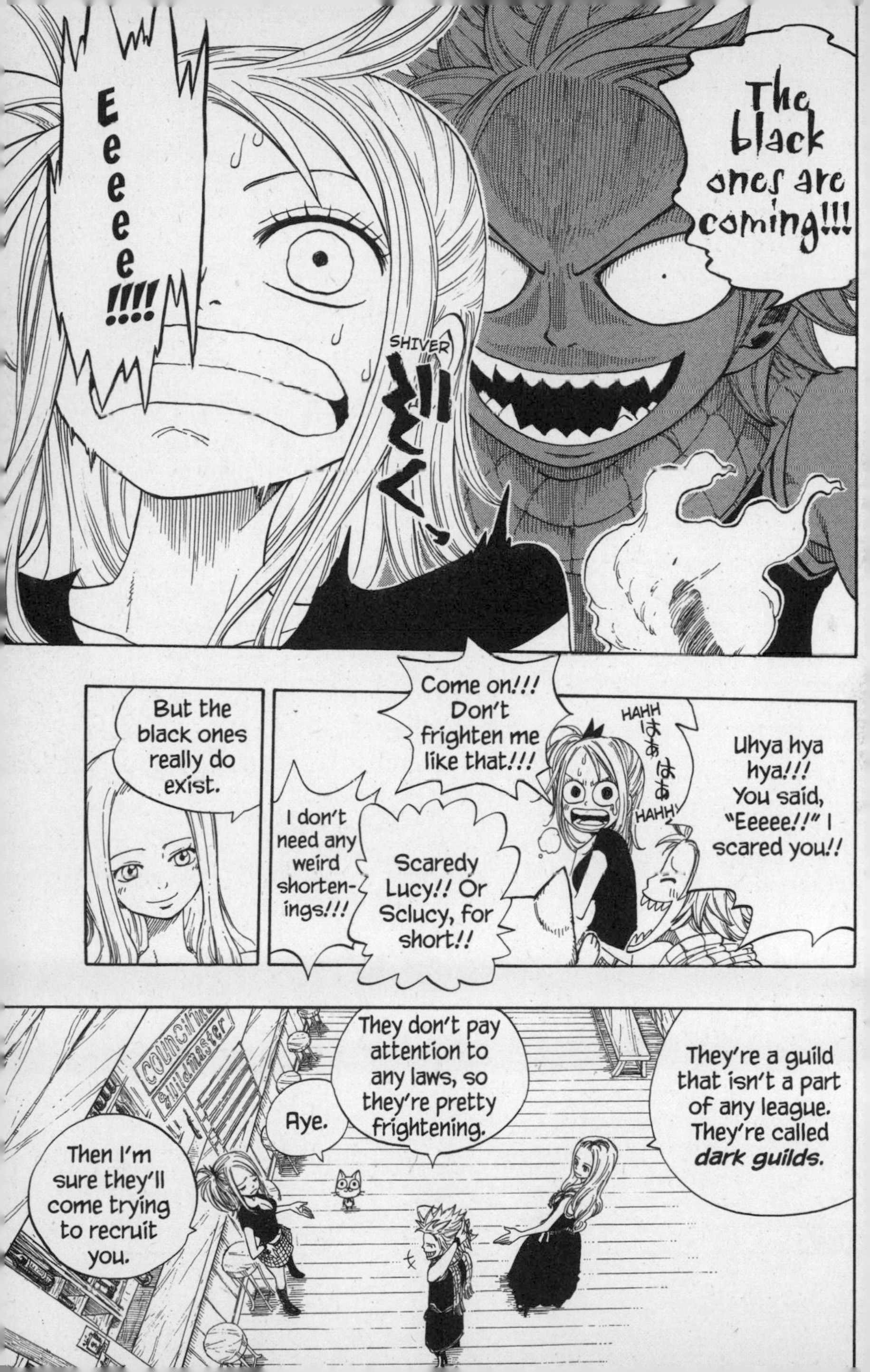

The black ones are coming!!!
Eeeee!!!!
SHIVER
Come on!!! Don't frighten me like that!!!
Uhya hya hya!!! You said, "Eeeee!!" I scared you!!
HAHH HAHH
Scaredy Lucy!! Or Sclucy, for short!!
I don't need any weird shorten-ings!!!
But the black ones really do exist.
They're a guild that isn't a part of any league. They're called *dark guilds.*
They don't pay attention to any laws, so they're pretty frightening.
Aye.
guildmaster
Then I'm sure they'll come trying to recruit you.

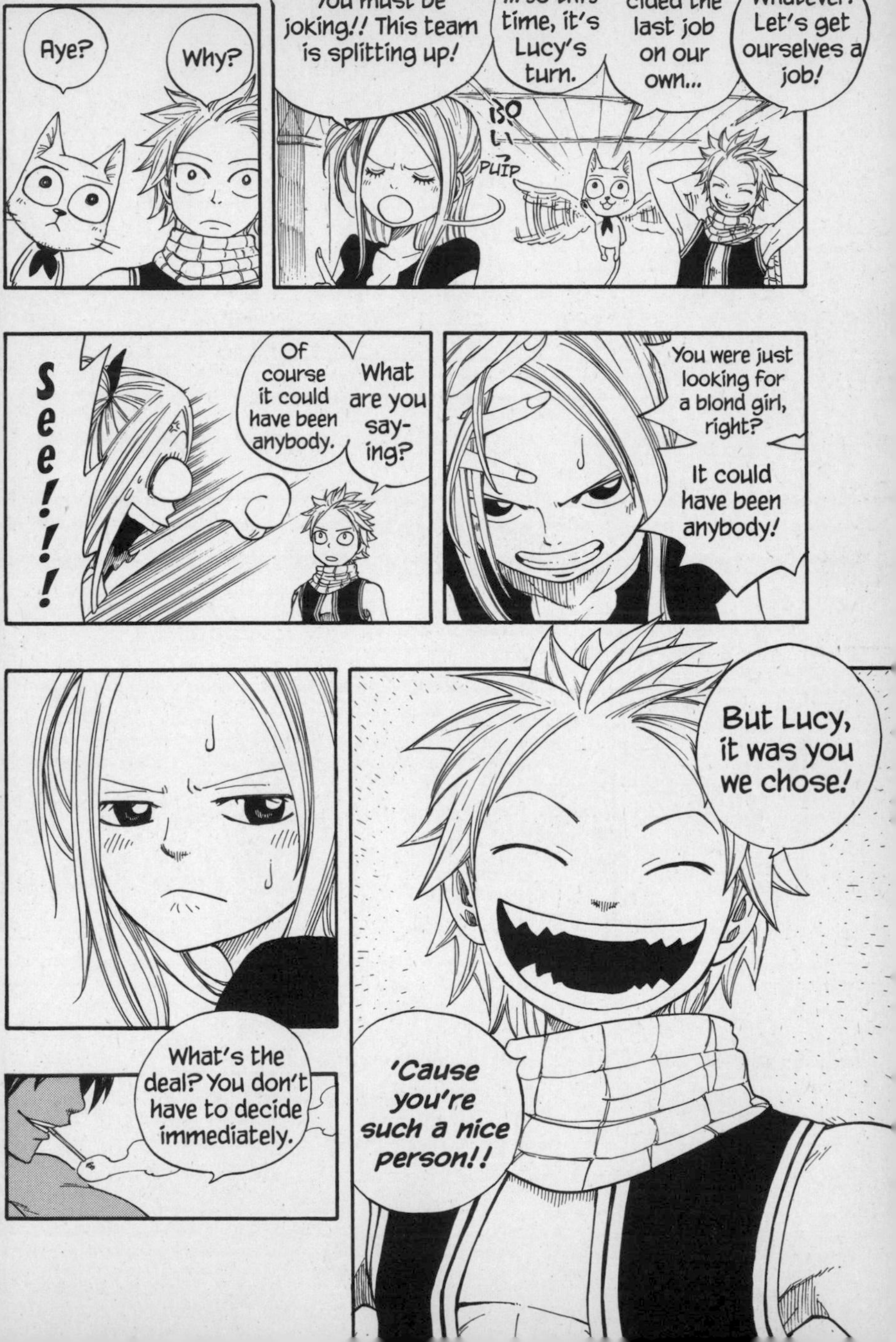
Whatever. Let's get ourselves a job!
We decided the last job on our own...
...so this time, it's Lucy's turn.
You must be joking!! This team is splitting up!
Why?
Aye?
You were just looking for a blond girl, right?
It could have been anybody!
What are you saying?
Of course it could have been anybody.
See!!!
But Lucy, it was you we chose!
'Cause you're such a nice person!!
What's the deal? You don't have to decide immediately.

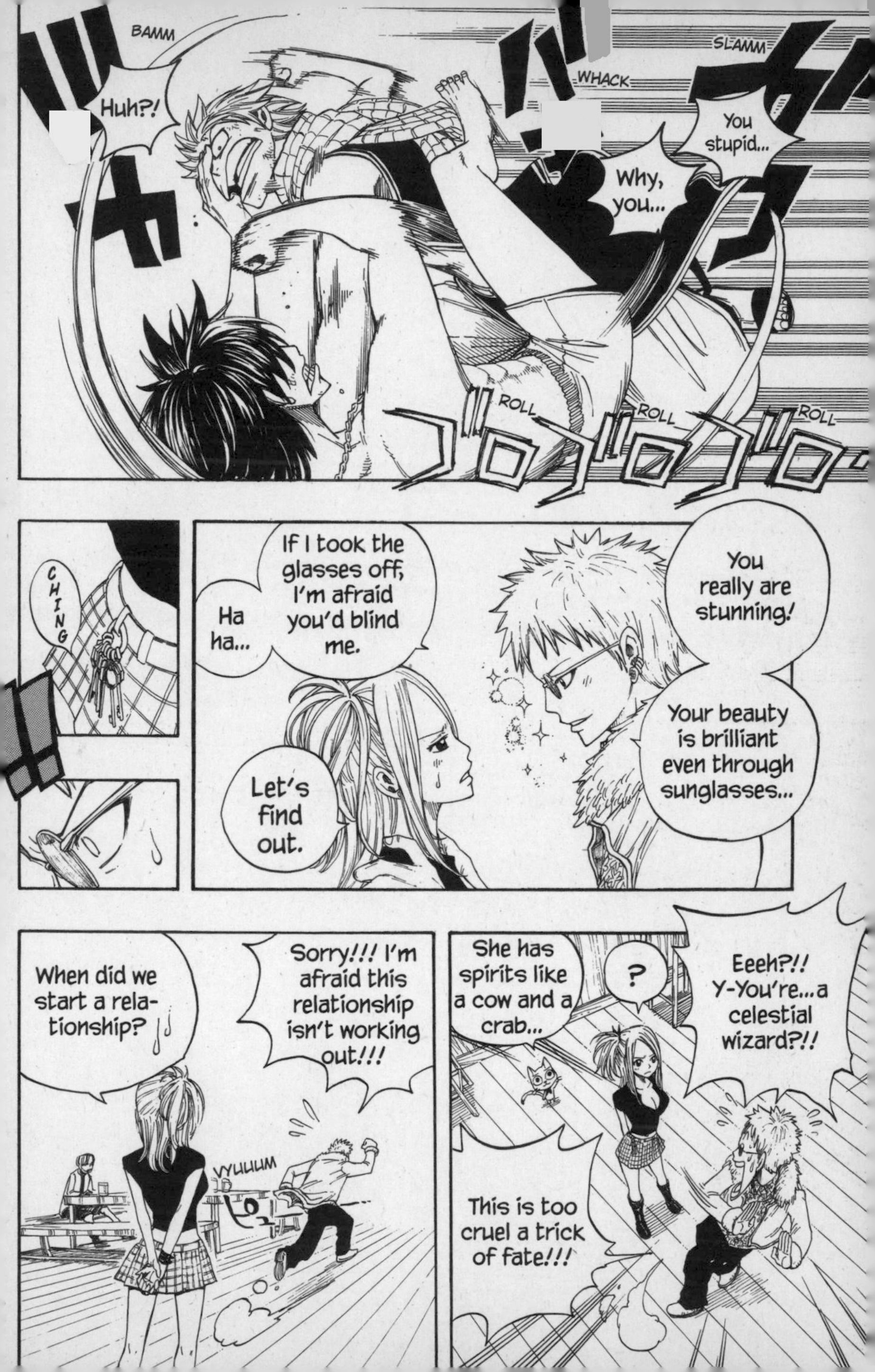
SLAMM
You stupid...
WHACK
Why, you...
BAMM
Huh?!
ROLL
ROLL
ROLL
You really are stunning!
Your beauty is brilliant even through sunglasses...
If I took the glasses off, I'm afraid you'd blind me.
Ha ha...
Let's find out.
CHING
Eeeh?!! Y-You're...a celestial wizard?!!
?
She has spirits like a cow and a crab...
This is too cruel a trick of fate!!!
Sorry!!! I'm afraid this relationship isn't working out!!!
When did we start a relationship?
VYUUUM

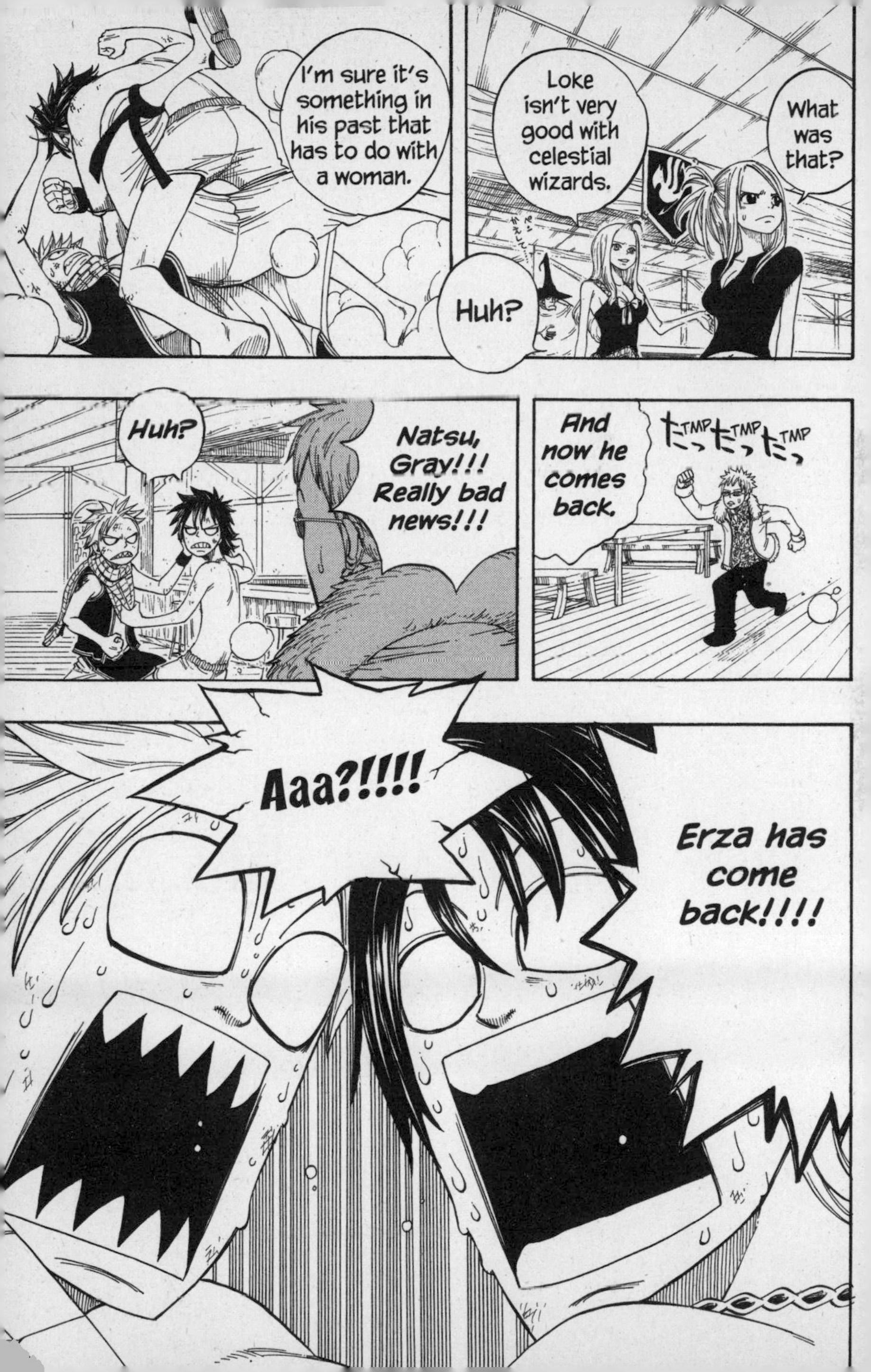
What was that?
Loke isn't very good with celestial wizards.
Huh?
I'm sure it's something in his past that has to do with a woman.
TMP TMP TMP
And now he comes back.
Natsu, Gray!!! Really bad news!!!
Huh?
Erza has come back!!!!
Aaa?!!!!

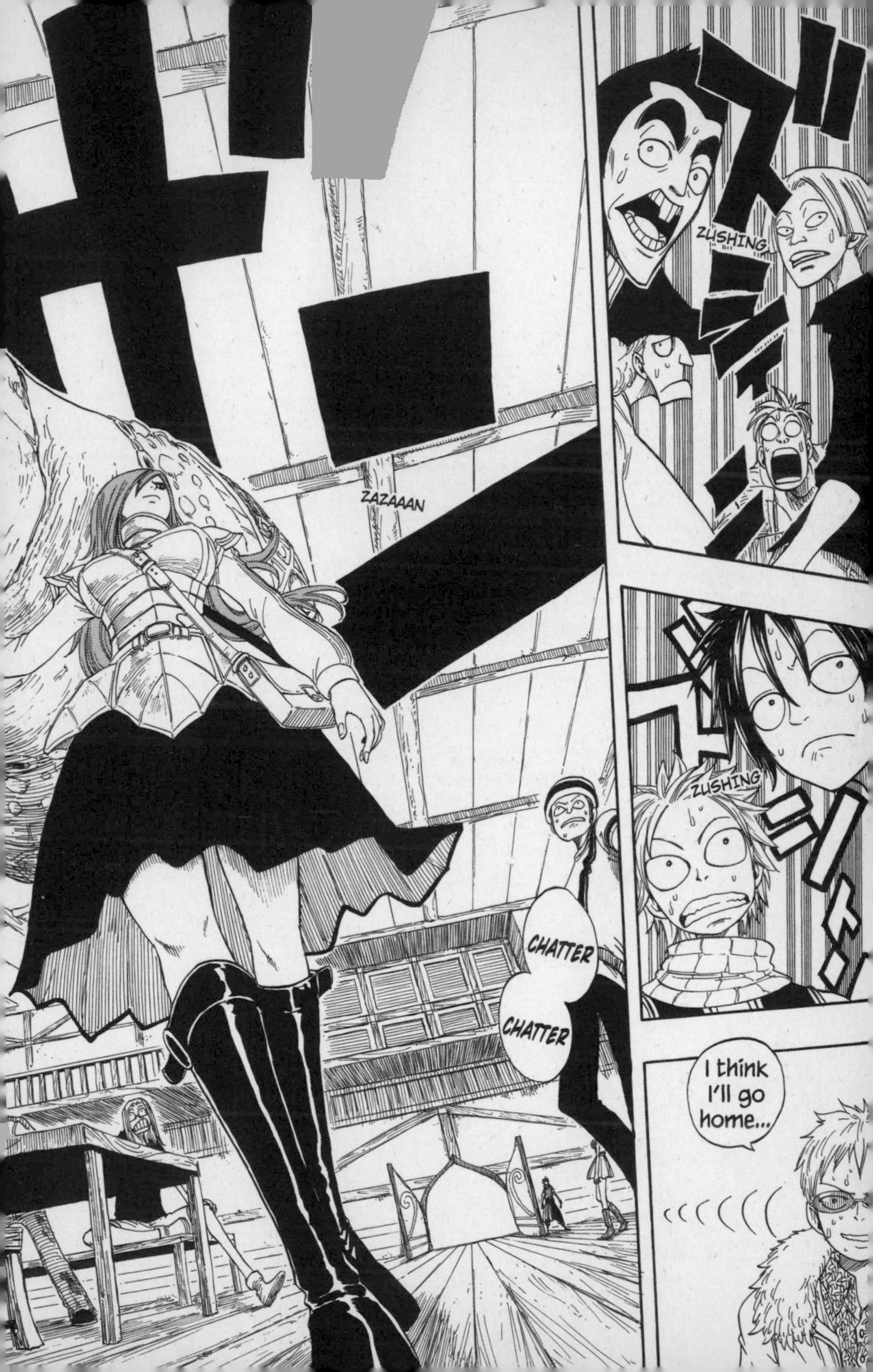
ZUSHING
ZUSHING
I think I'll go home...
ZAZAAAN
CHATTER
CHATTER

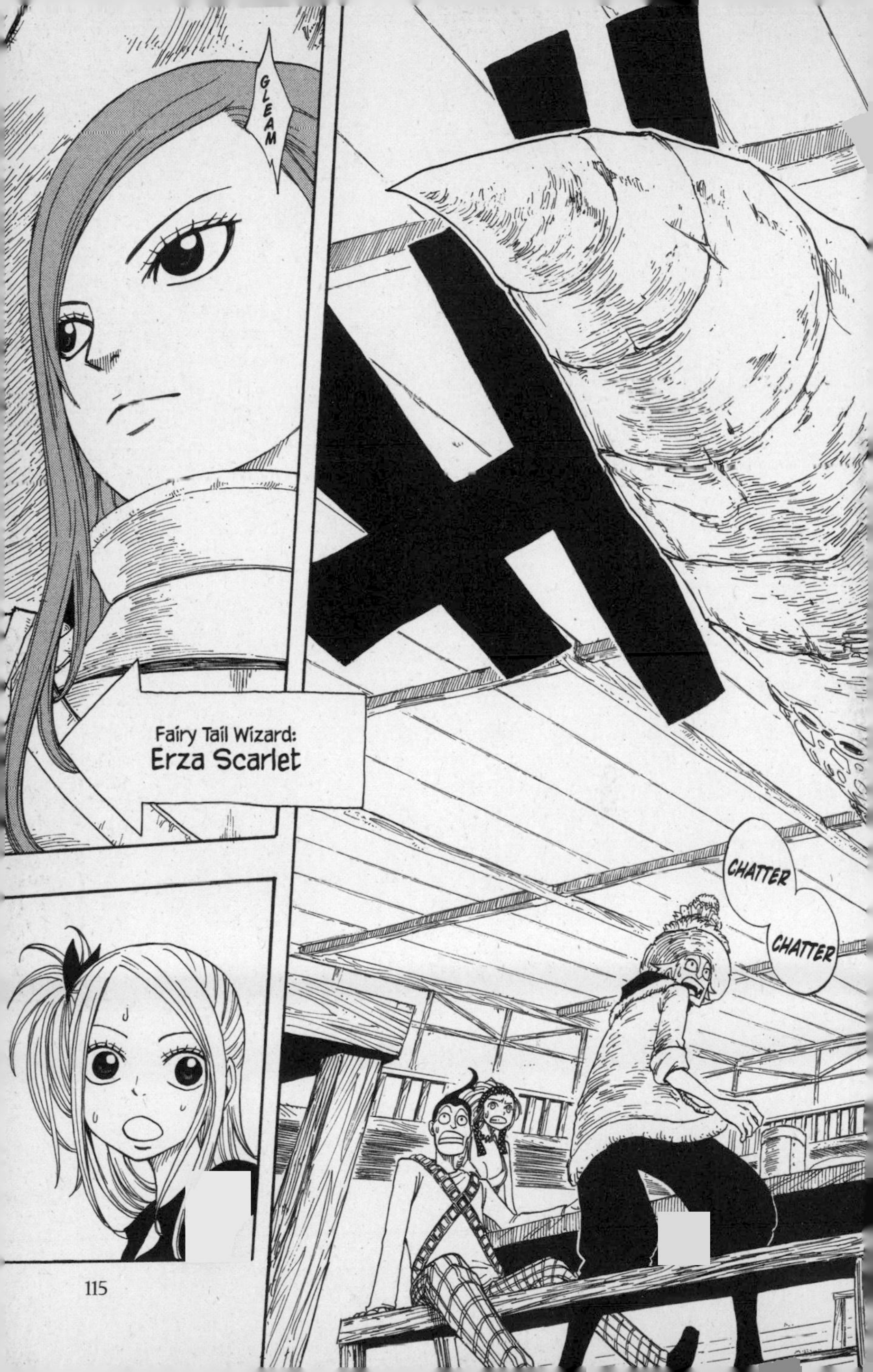
CHATTER
CHATTER
GLEAM
Fairy Tail Wizard:
Erza Scarlet

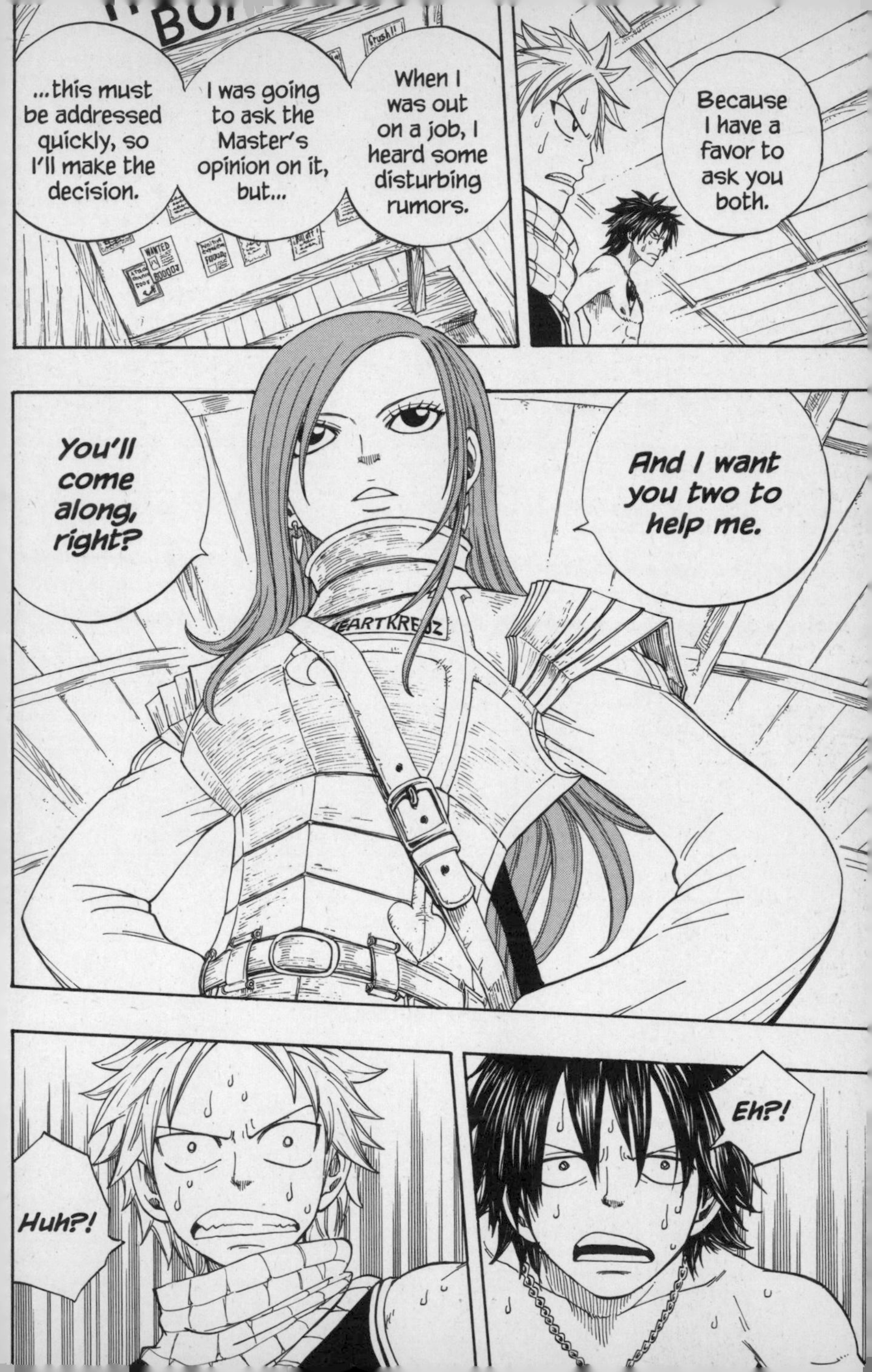
Because I have a favor to ask you both.
When I was out on a job, I heard some disturbing rumors.
I was going to ask the Master's opinion on it, but...
...this must be addressed quickly, so I'll make the decision.
And I want you two to help me.
You'll come along, right?
Eh?!
Huh?!

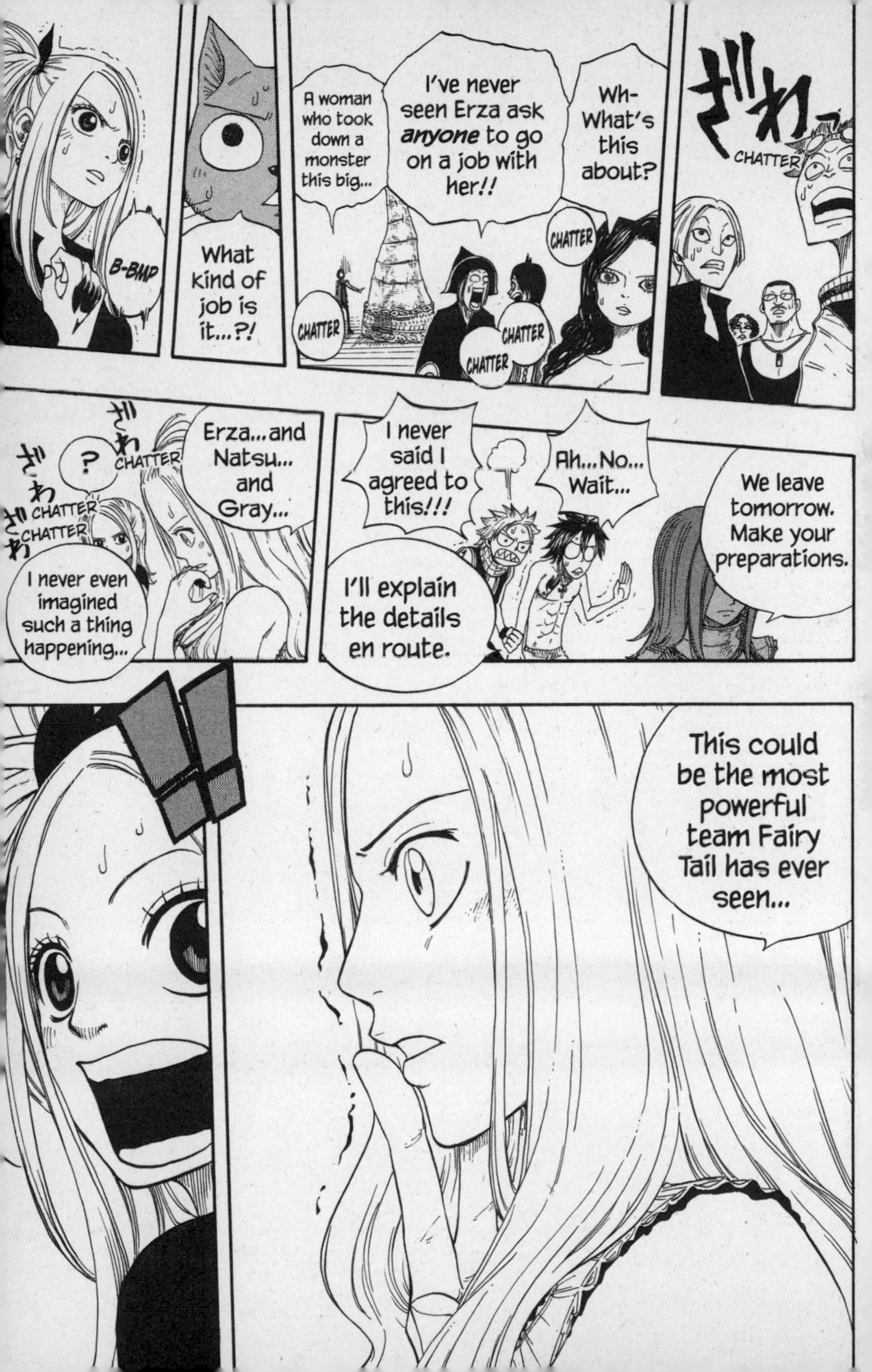
ざわ
CHATTER
Wh- What's this about?
CHATTER
I've never seen Erza ask *anyone* to go on a job with her!!
A woman who took down a monster this big...
CHATTER
CHATTER
CHATTER
What kind of job is it...?!
B-BMP
We leave tomorrow. Make your preparations.
Ah...No... Wait...
I never said I agreed to this!!!
I'll explain the details en route.
Erza...and Natsu... and Gray...
ざわ
CHATTER
?
ざわ
CHATTER
ざわ
CHATTER
I never even imagined such a thing happening...
This could be the most powerful team Fairy Tail has ever seen...

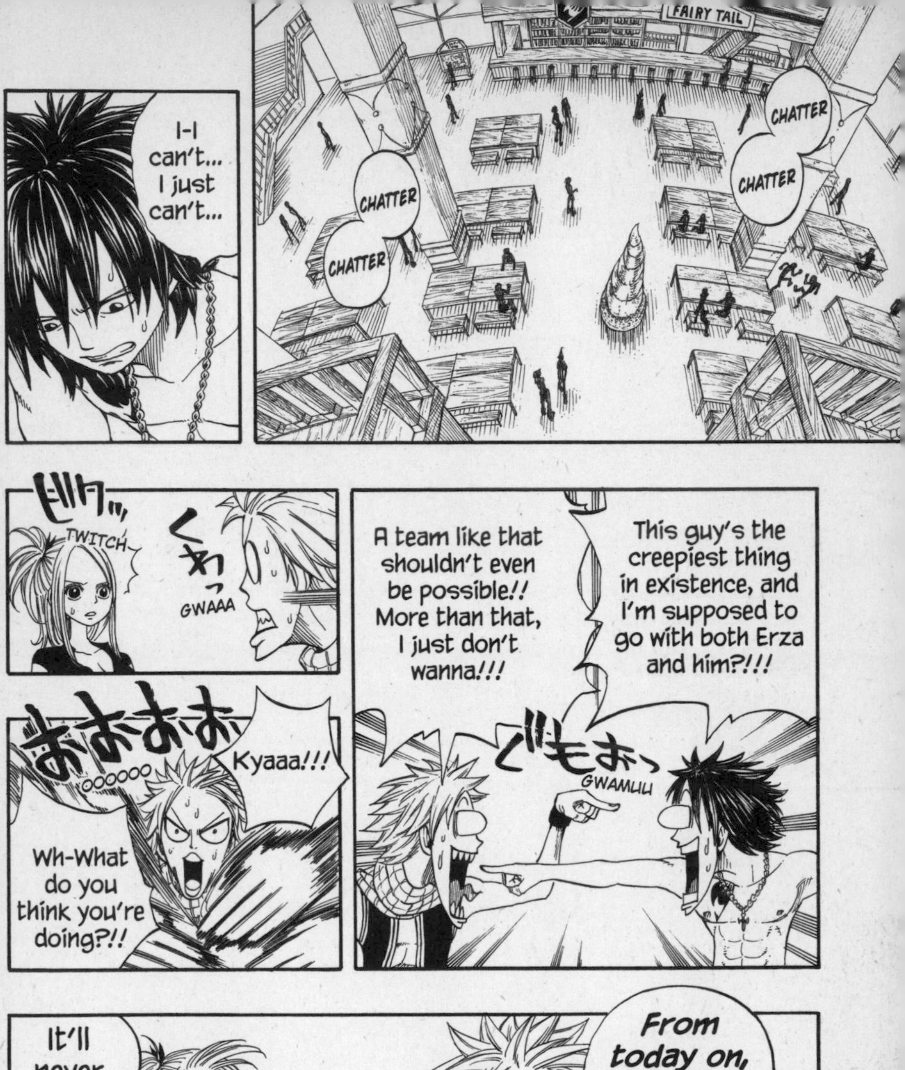
FAIRY TAIL
CHATTER
CHATTER
CHATTER
CHATTER
I-I can't... I just can't...
This guy's the creepiest thing in existence, and I'm supposed to go with both Erza and him?!!!
A team like that shouldn't even be possible!! More than that, I just don't wanna!!!
ぐもぉっ
GWAMUU
くわっ
GWAAA
ビクッ
TWITCH
Kyaaa!!!
おおおお
OOOOOO
Wh-What do you think you're doing?!!
From today on, you are Natsu!
ふぅ…
HEH!
It'll never work!
Aye.

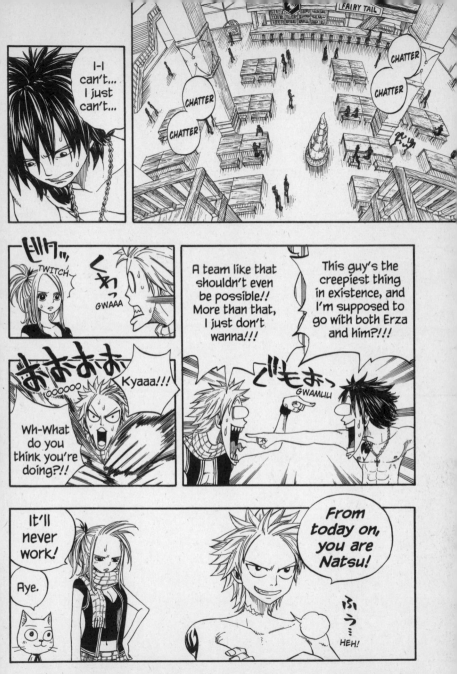

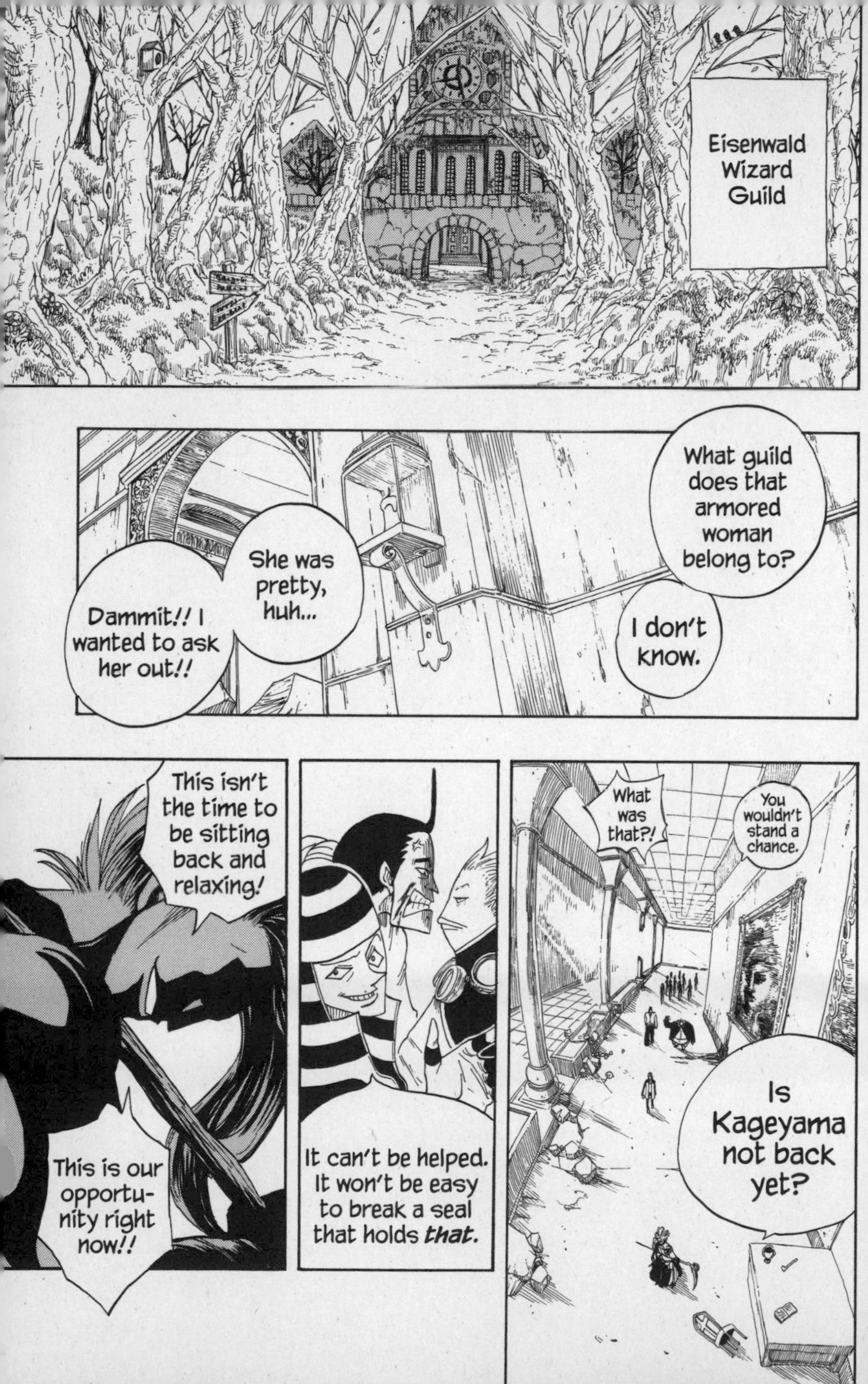
Eisenwald Wizard Guild
What guild does that armored woman belong to?
I don't know.
She was pretty, huh...
Dammit!! I wanted to ask her out!!
You wouldn't stand a chance.
What was that?!
Is Kageyama not back yet?
It can't be helped. It won't be easy to break a seal that holds *that*.
This isn't the time to be sitting back and relaxing!
This is our opportu-nity right now!!

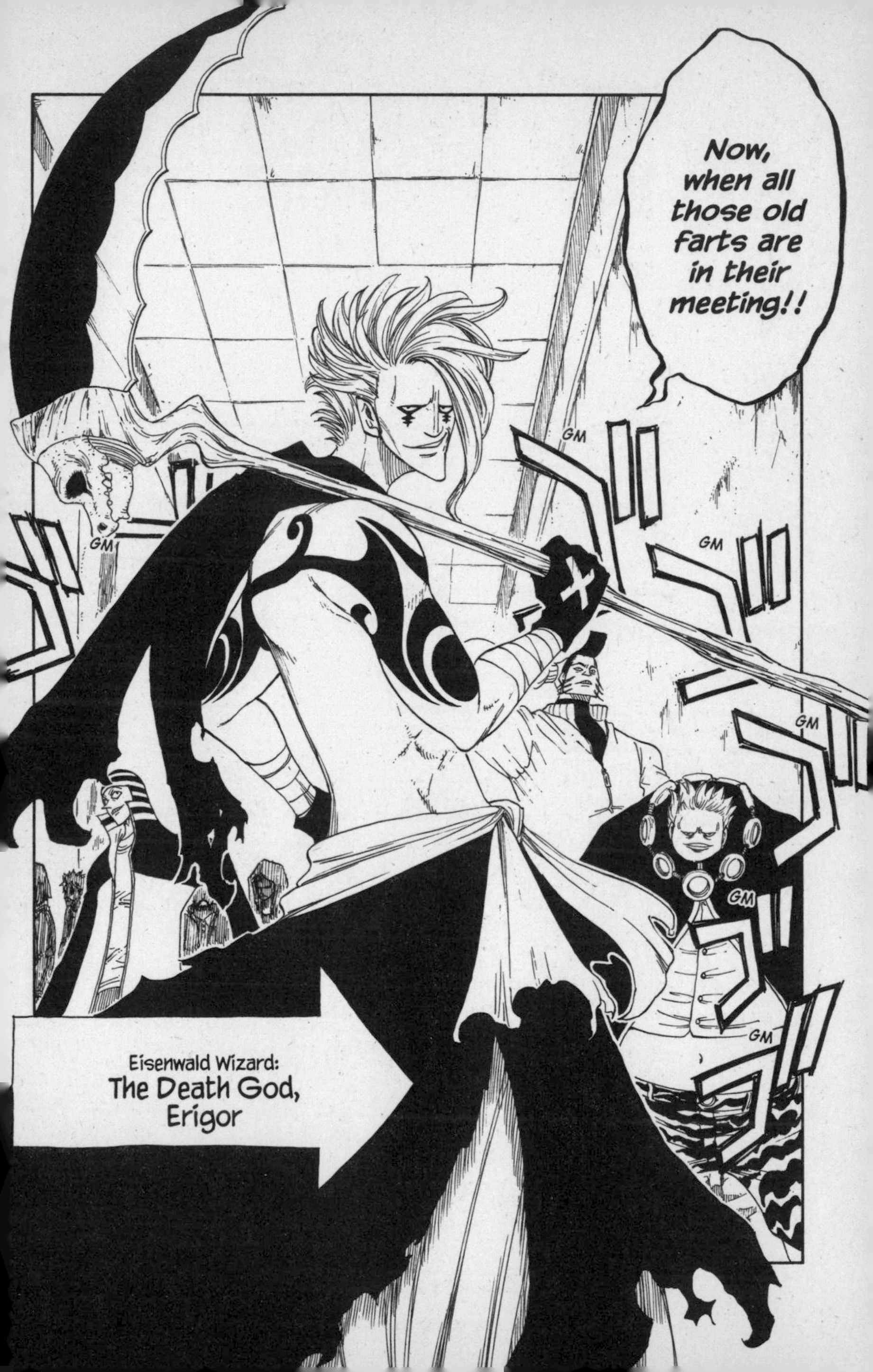
Now, when all those old farts are in their meeting!!
GM
GM
GM
GM
GM
GM
Eisenwald Wizard:
The Death God, Erigor

FAIRY TAIL

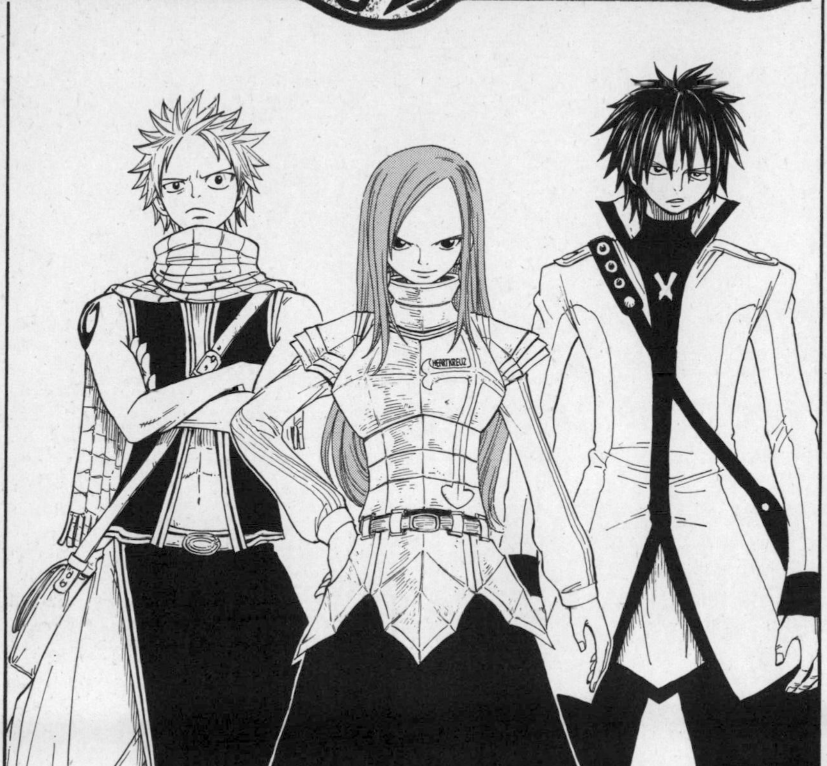

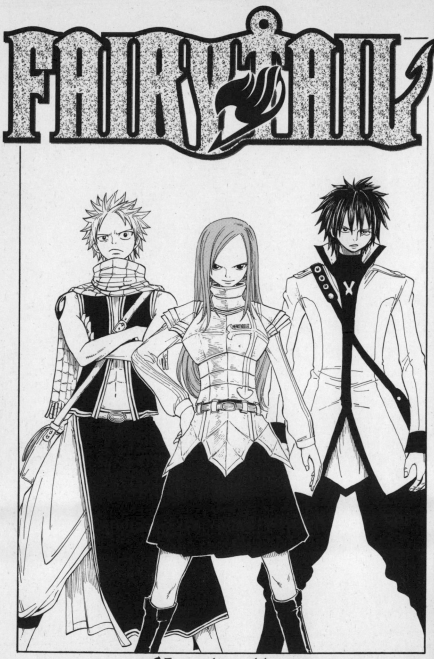

Chapter 11: Natsu on the Train

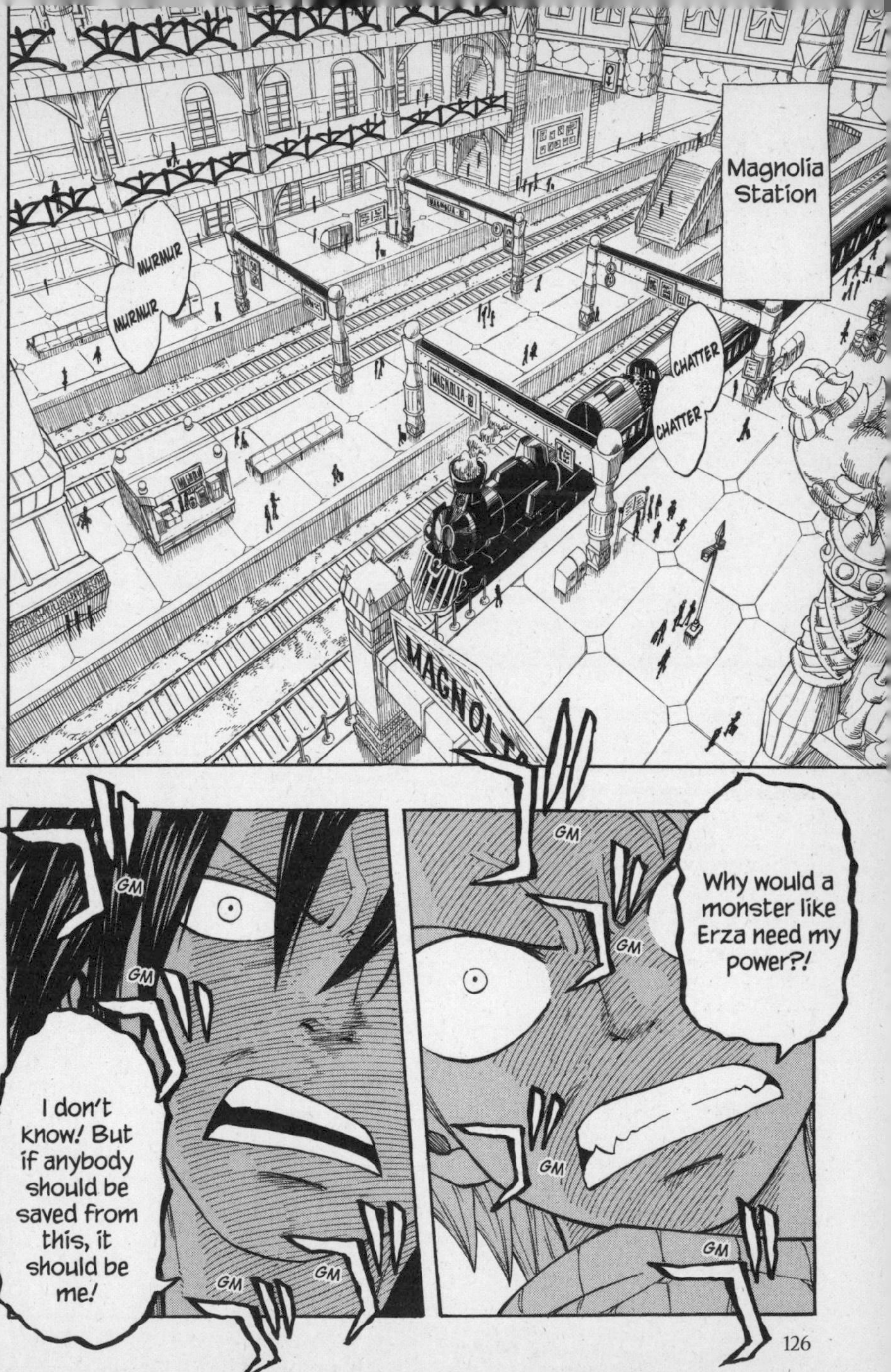
Magnolia Station
CHATTER
CHATTER
MAGNOLIA
MURMUR
MURMUR
GM
Why would a monster like Erza need my power?!
GM
GM
GM
GM
I don't know! But if anybody should be saved from this, it should be me!
GM
GM
GM

128

130

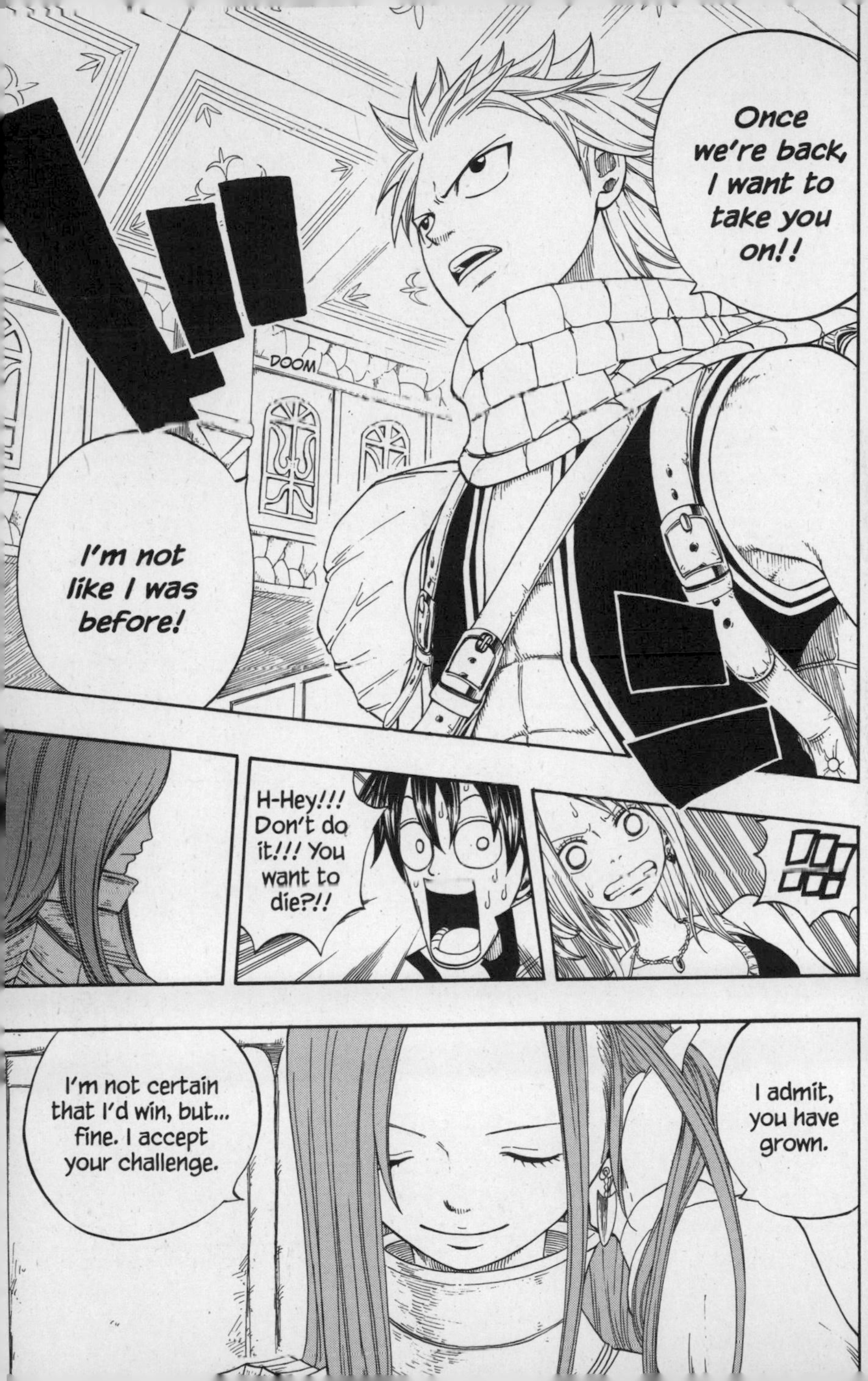
Once we're back, I want to take you on!!
DOOM
I'm not like I was before!
H-Hey!!! Don't do it!!! You want to die?!!
I admit, you have grown.
I'm not certain that I'd win, but... fine. I accept your challenge.

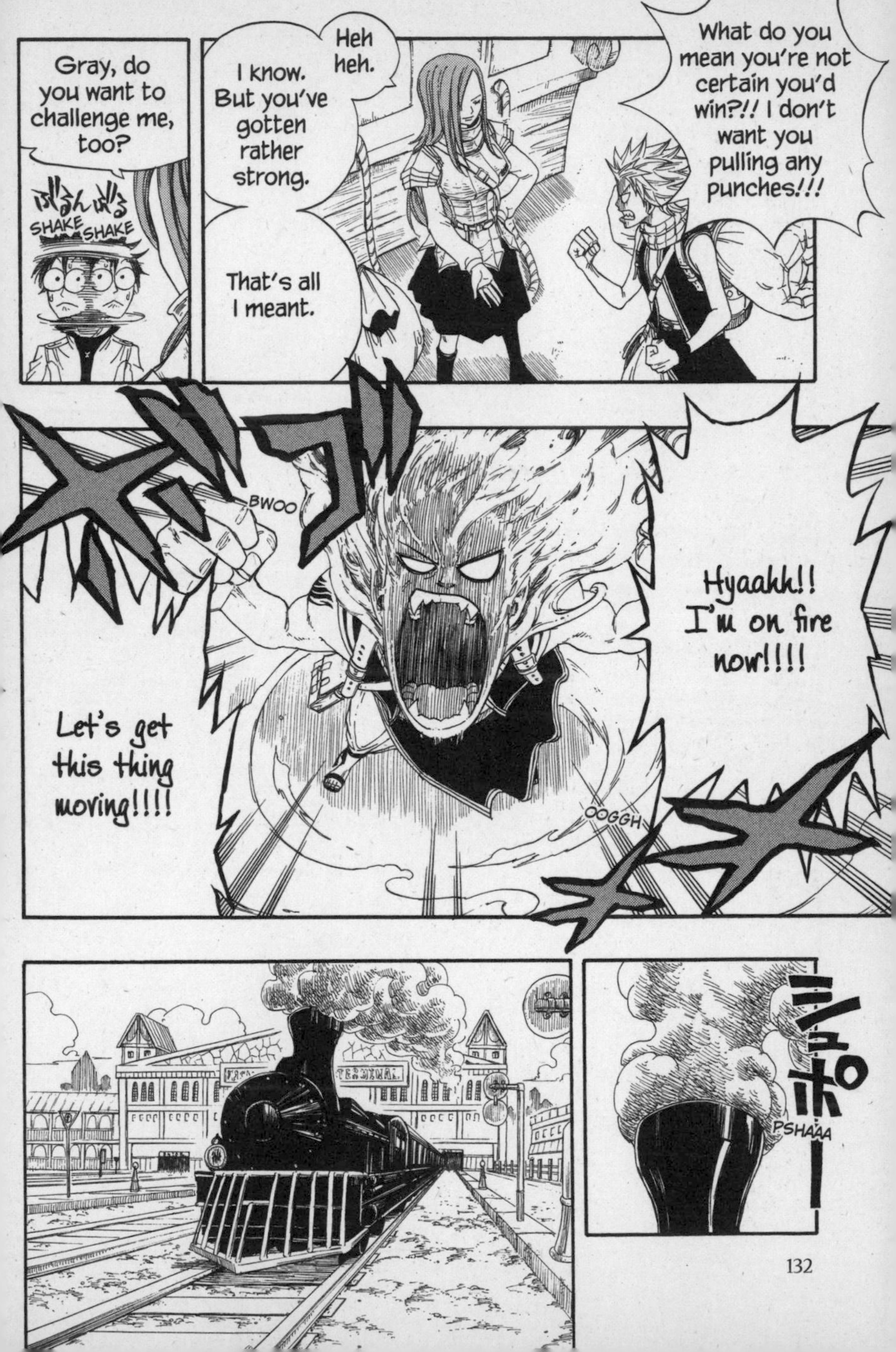
What do you mean you're not certain you'd win?!! I don't want you pulling any punches!!!
Heh heh.
I know. But you've gotten rather strong.
That's all I meant.
Gray, do you want to challenge me, too?
SHAKE SHAKE
Hyaahh!! I'm on fire now!!!!
BWOO
OOGGH
Let's get this thing moving!!!!
PSHAAA

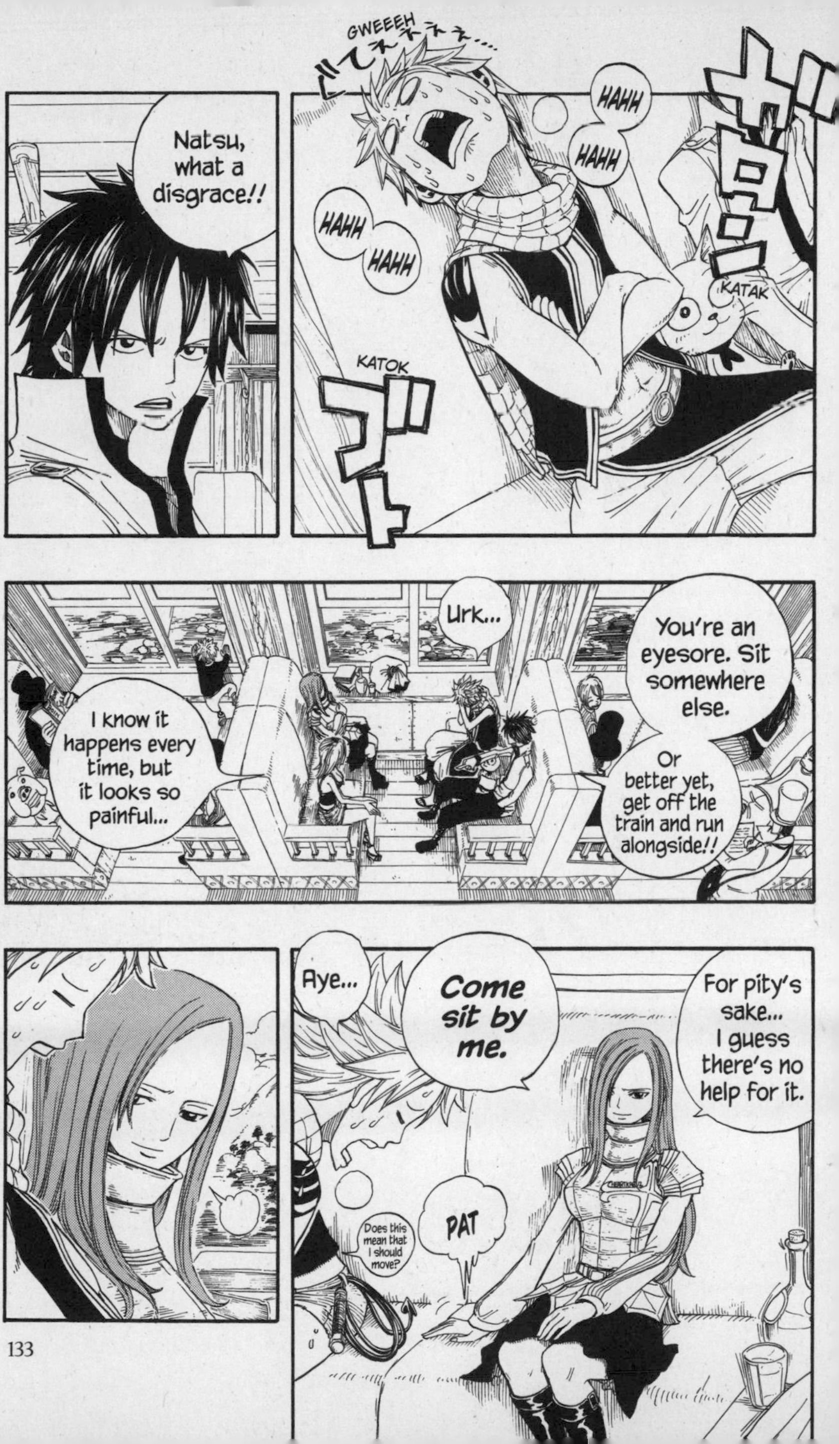
GWEEEH
HAHH
HAHH
HAHH
HAHH
KATAK
KATOK
Natsu, what a disgrace!!
You're an eyesore. Sit somewhere else.
Or better yet, get off the train and run alongside!!
Urk...
I know it happens every time, but it looks so painful...
For pity's sake... I guess there's no help for it.
Come sit by me.
Aye...
PAT
Does this mean that I should move?

That should settle you down a bit.

ZWAMM!!

WHUMP!!

And that's pretty? That?

Her opponent's blood...

...goes spurting everywhere!!

Erza's magic is very pretty.

Just call me Erza.

Erza-san, what kind of magic do you use?

KATAK

Come to think of it...

...I've never seen anyone other than Natsu do magic at Fairy Tail.

KATOK

SHUUUUU

FAPP

Hah!!!

You think so?

My magic isn't anything much. If you want pretty magic, Gray's is much prettier than mine.

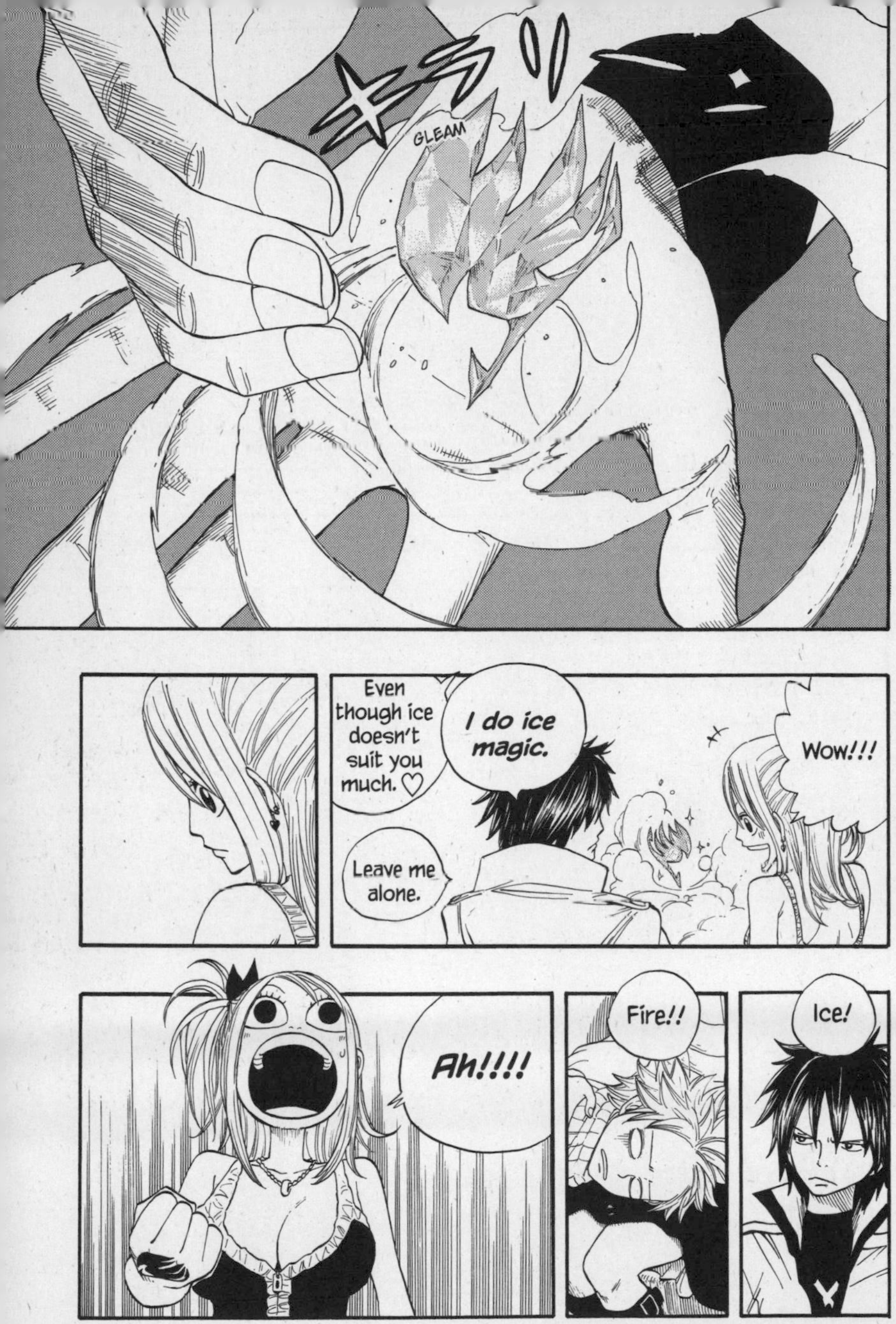
GLEAM
Wow!!!
I do ice magic.
Even though ice doesn't suit you much. ♡
Leave me alone.
Ice!
Fire!!
Ah!!!!

Who cares, anyway?!

......

Is that true?

Is that why you two don't get along?!! It's so simple, it's almost cute!

Yes... Let's discuss it.

It must be something incredible for someone like you to want help!!

But more important, isn't it about time you told us what this is about, Erza?

What are we here for?

KATAK

KATOK

KATAK

On my way back from my last job...

...I stopped by a bar where wizards gather in Onibas.

And there were a few people who drew my attention.

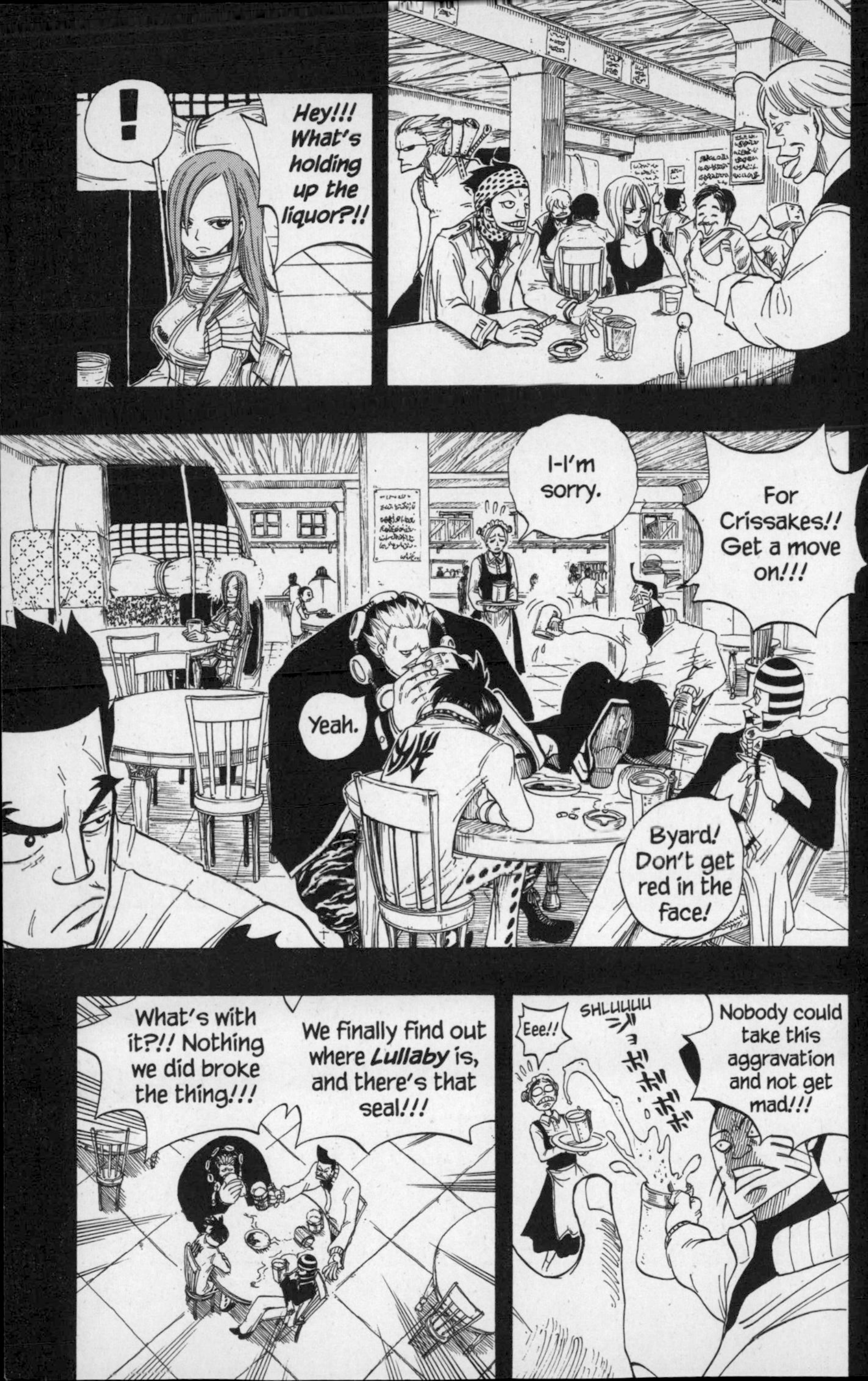
!
Hey!!! What's holding up the liquor?!!
For Crissakes!! Get a move on!!!
I-I'm sorry.
Yeah.
Byard! Don't get red in the face!
Nobody could take this aggravation and not get mad!!!
SHLUUUU
ジョボボボ
Eee!!
We finally find out where *Lullaby* is, and there's that seal!!!
What's with it?!! Nothing we did broke the thing!!!

That magic seal can't be broken simply by numbers alone.

Huh?

I'll take it from here. You all can return to the guild now.

GLUG GLUG

Dammit!!

GLUG GLUG

Yeah.

You're too loud!

Idiot!! Pipe down!!

Are you serious?! You've figured out a way to break the seal?

Wow! That's Kage-chan for you!!

...I will return in three days with *Lullaby* in hand.

And tell Erigor...

KATOK

I figured it must have some strong magic.

I don't know. But when I heard that it was sealed...

KATAK

A child's bedtime song? Might it be some kind of sleep magic?

Lullaby?

KATAK

KATOK

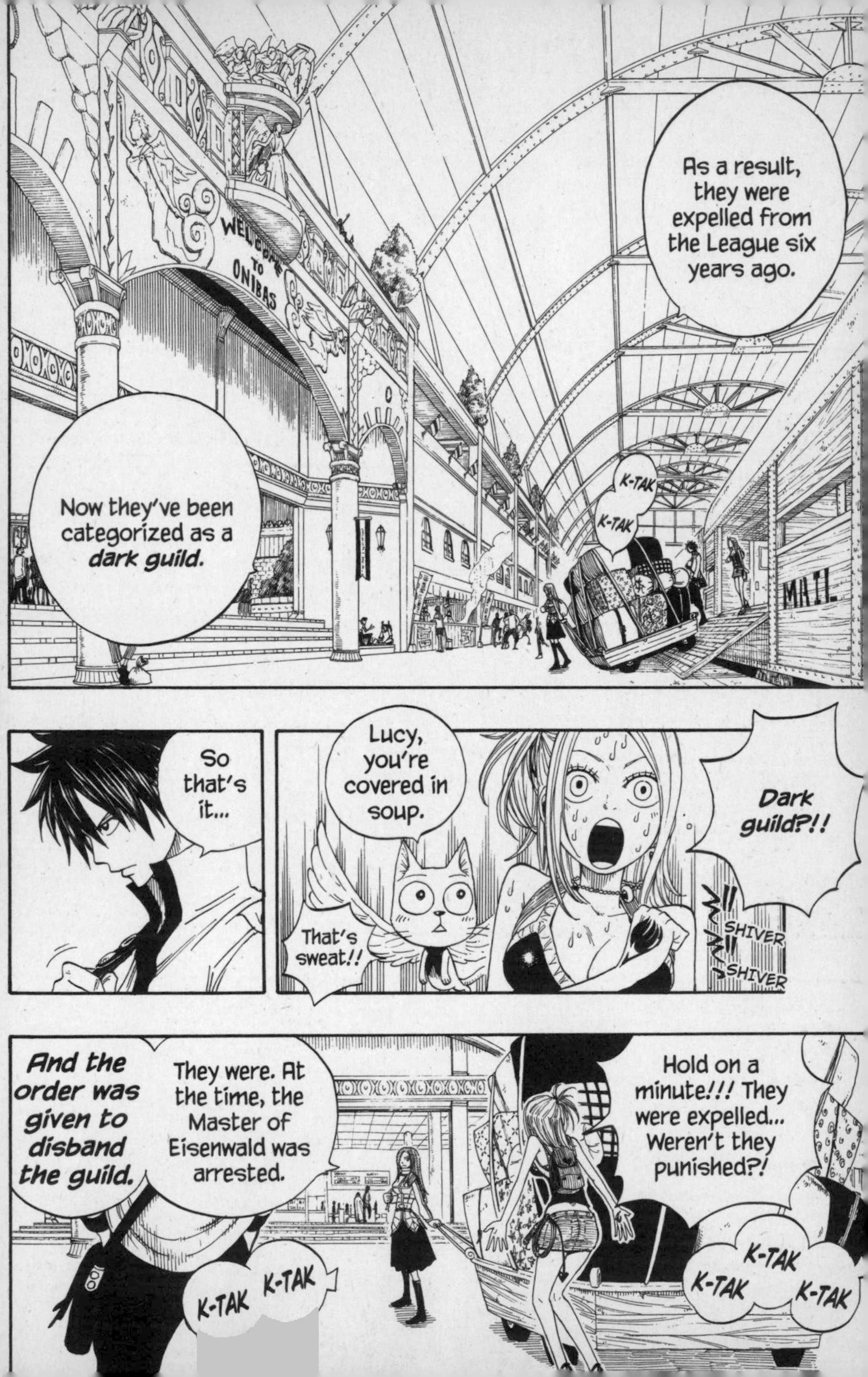
As a result, they were expelled from the League six years ago.
K-TAK
K-TAK
MAIL.
Now they've been categorized as a *dark guild.*
Dark guild?!!
SHIVER
SHIVER
Lucy, you're covered in soup.
That's sweat!!
So that's it...
Hold on a minute!!! They were expelled... Weren't they punished?!
K-TAK
K-TAK
K-TAK
They were. At the time, the Master of Eisenwald was arrested.
And the order was given to disband the guild.
K-TAK
K-TAK

GWAAAN
ぐもぉーん

Maybe I should go home...

I knew that was coming!!

......!!

But the majority of all guilds that they call dark guilds...

...have ignored the order and continued acting as guilds.

I should have bled them all dry.

Eeee!!

GM
GM
GM
GM

I wasn't paying close enough attention. The moment I heard the name Erigor...

KSHHHH

What are they planning once they get this *Lullaby* magic?

I decided that I can't just disregard it.

コケ"
STK

But if it was the entire guild...

Yeah...

If it was just the four of them in the bar, you could probably have taken them all, Erza.

141

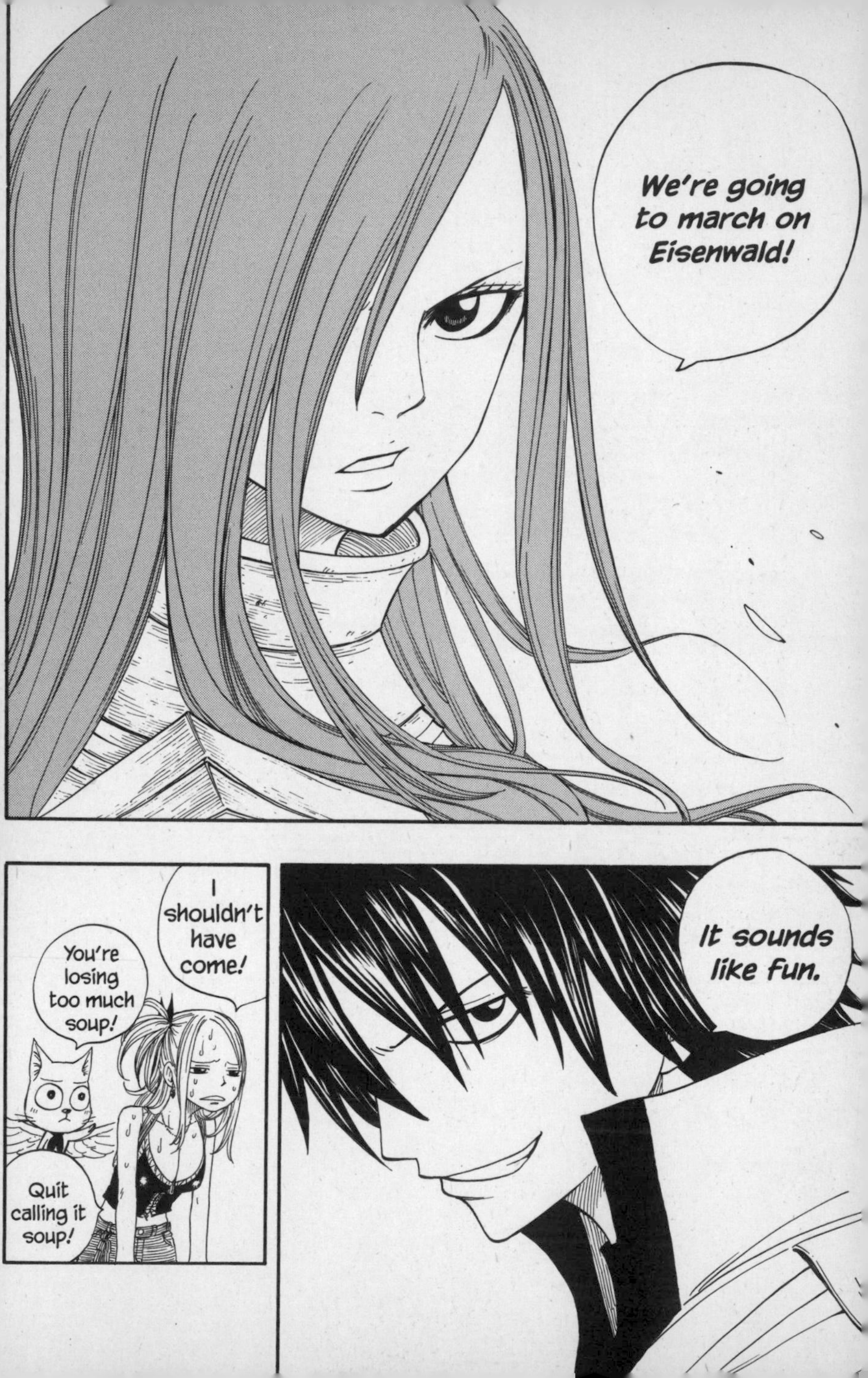
We're going to march on Eisenwald!
It sounds like fun.
I shouldn't have come!
You're losing too much soup!
Quit calling it soup!

GLANCE
GLANCE

Oh, no...

You're kidding?!!

Huh?

That's what we're in this town to investigate.

So, do you know where the Eisenwald guild is?

Natsu isn't here!!!

Young man, is this seat taken?

KATAK

HAHH
HAHH
HAHH
HAHH

KATOK

KATAK
KATOK
KATAK
KATAK

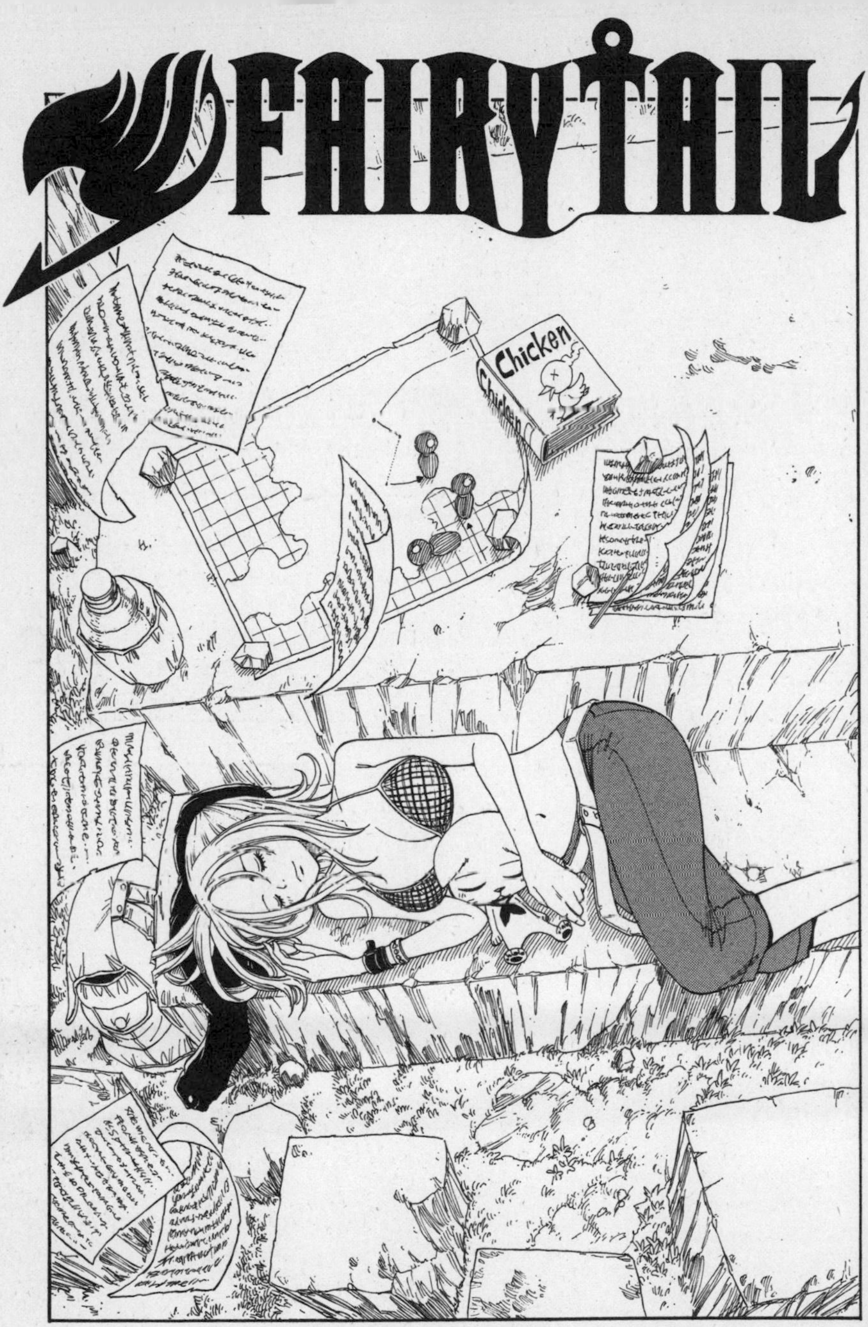
FAIRY TAIL
Chicken

Chapter 12: Spell Song

146

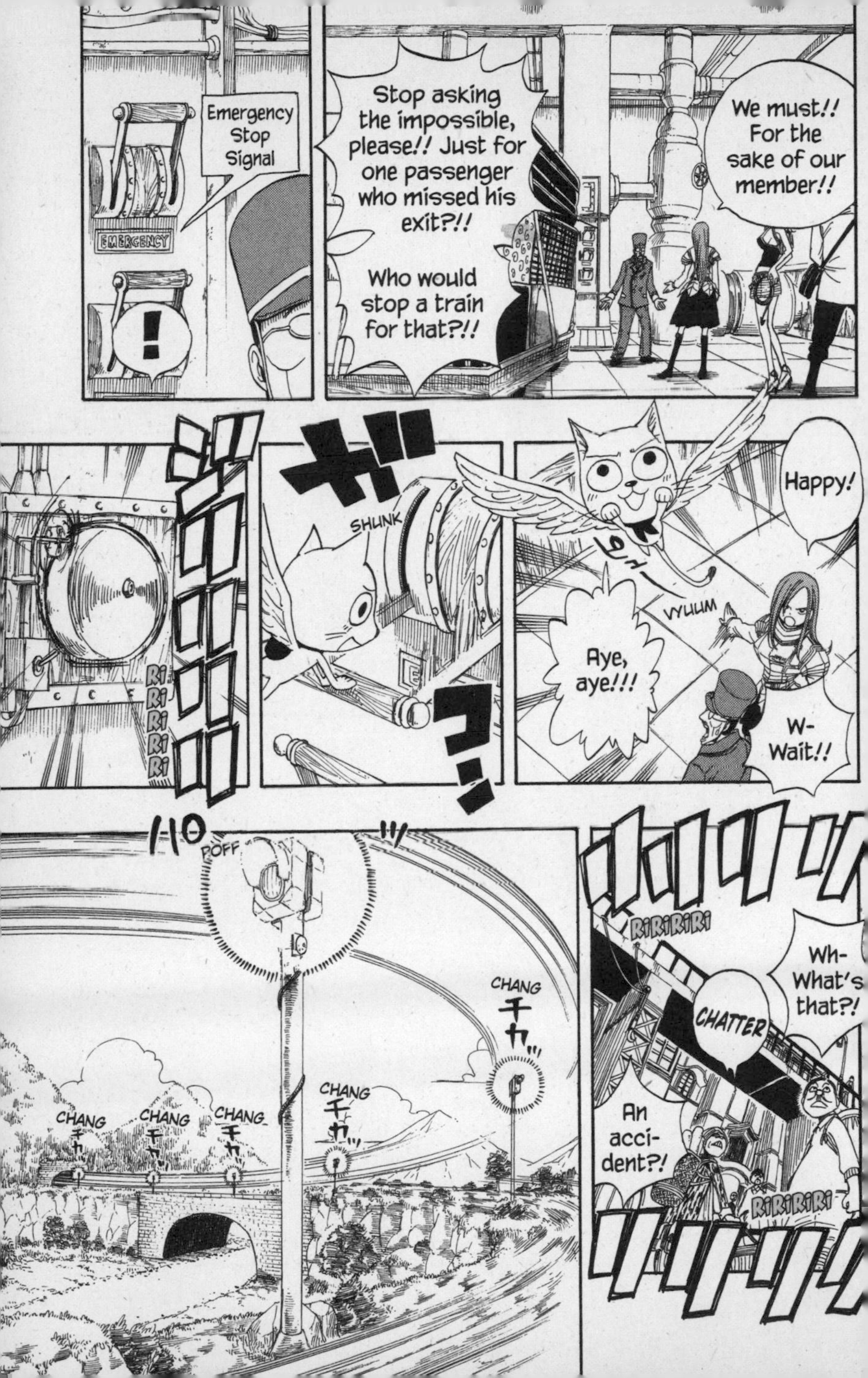
We must!! For the sake of our member!!
Stop asking the impossible, please!! Just for one passenger who missed his exit?!!
Who would stop a train for that?!!
Emergency Stop Signal
EMERGENCY
!
Happy!
Aye, aye!!!
VYUUM
W- Wait!!
SHUNK
RiRiRiRiRi
RiRiRiRi
Wh- What's that?!
CHATTER
An acci- dent?!
RiRiRiRi
CHANG
CHANG
CHANG
CHANG
CHANG
POFF

148

149

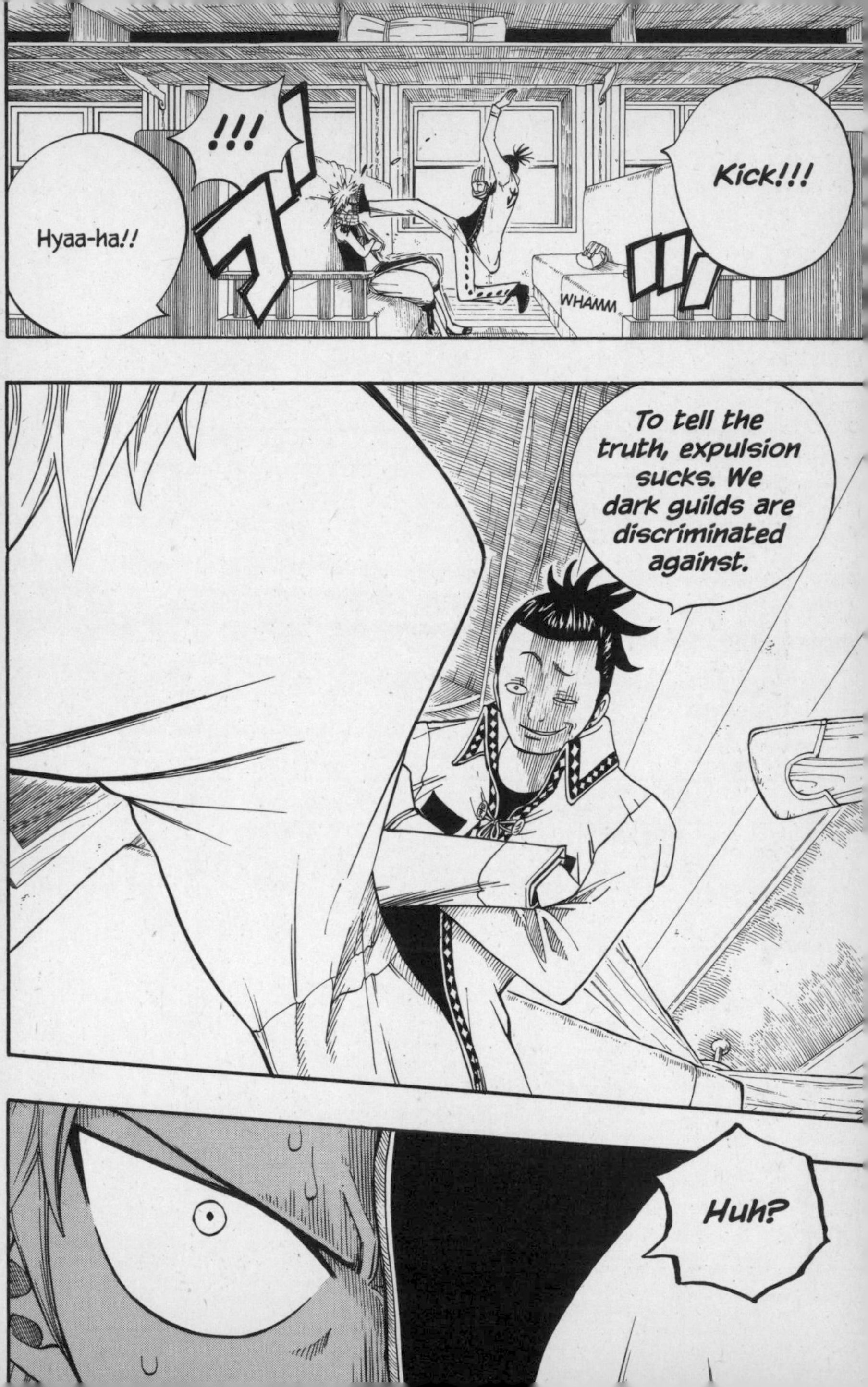
Kick!!!
!!!
Hyaa-ha!!
WHAMM
To tell the truth, expulsion sucks. We dark guilds are discriminated against.
Huh?

151

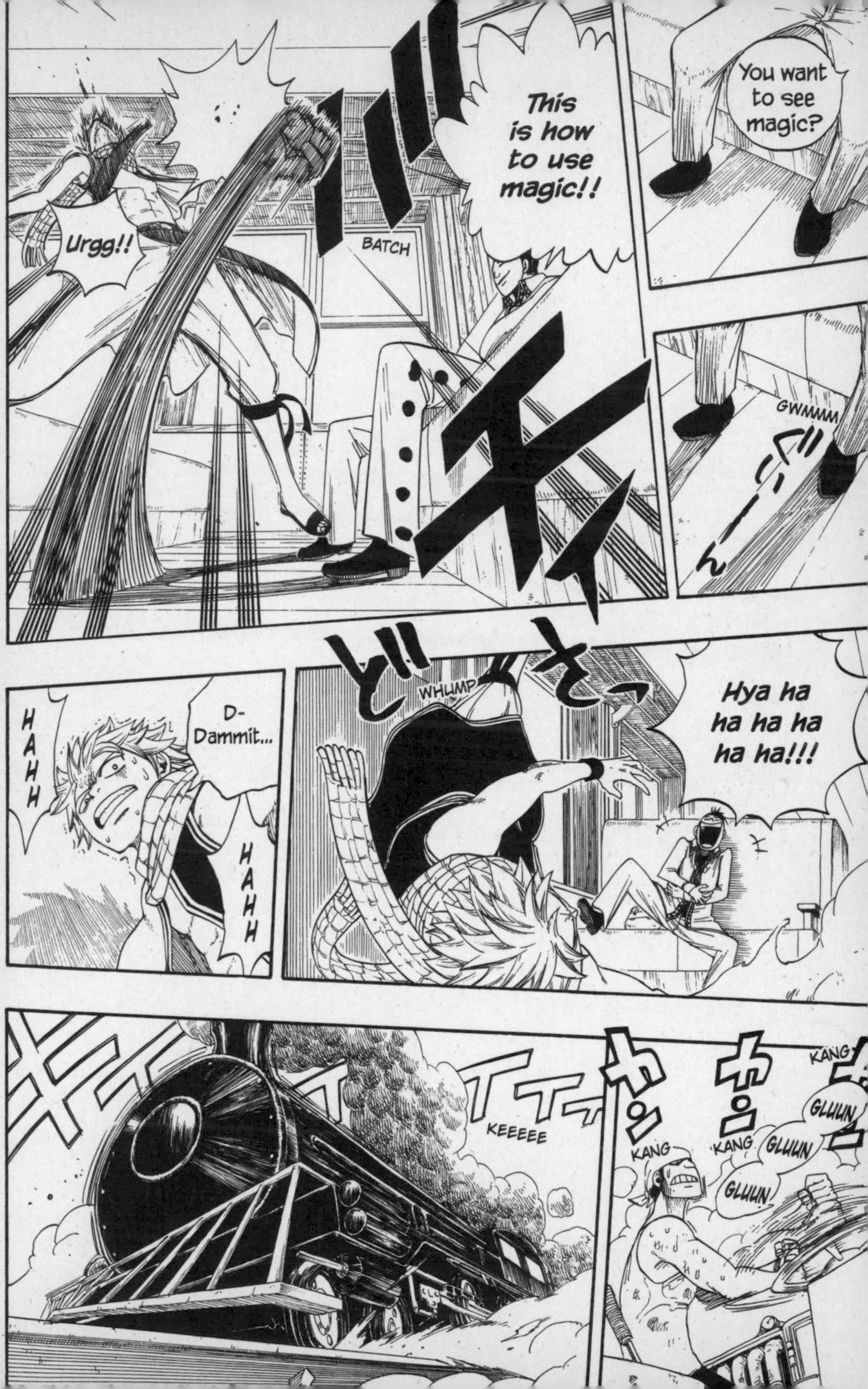

You want to see magic?
GWMMM
This is how to use magic!!
BATCH
Urgg!!
Hya ha ha ha ha ha ha!!!
WHUMP
D- Dammit...
HAHH
HAHH
KANG
GLUUN
KANG
GLUUN
KANG
GLUUN
KEEEEE

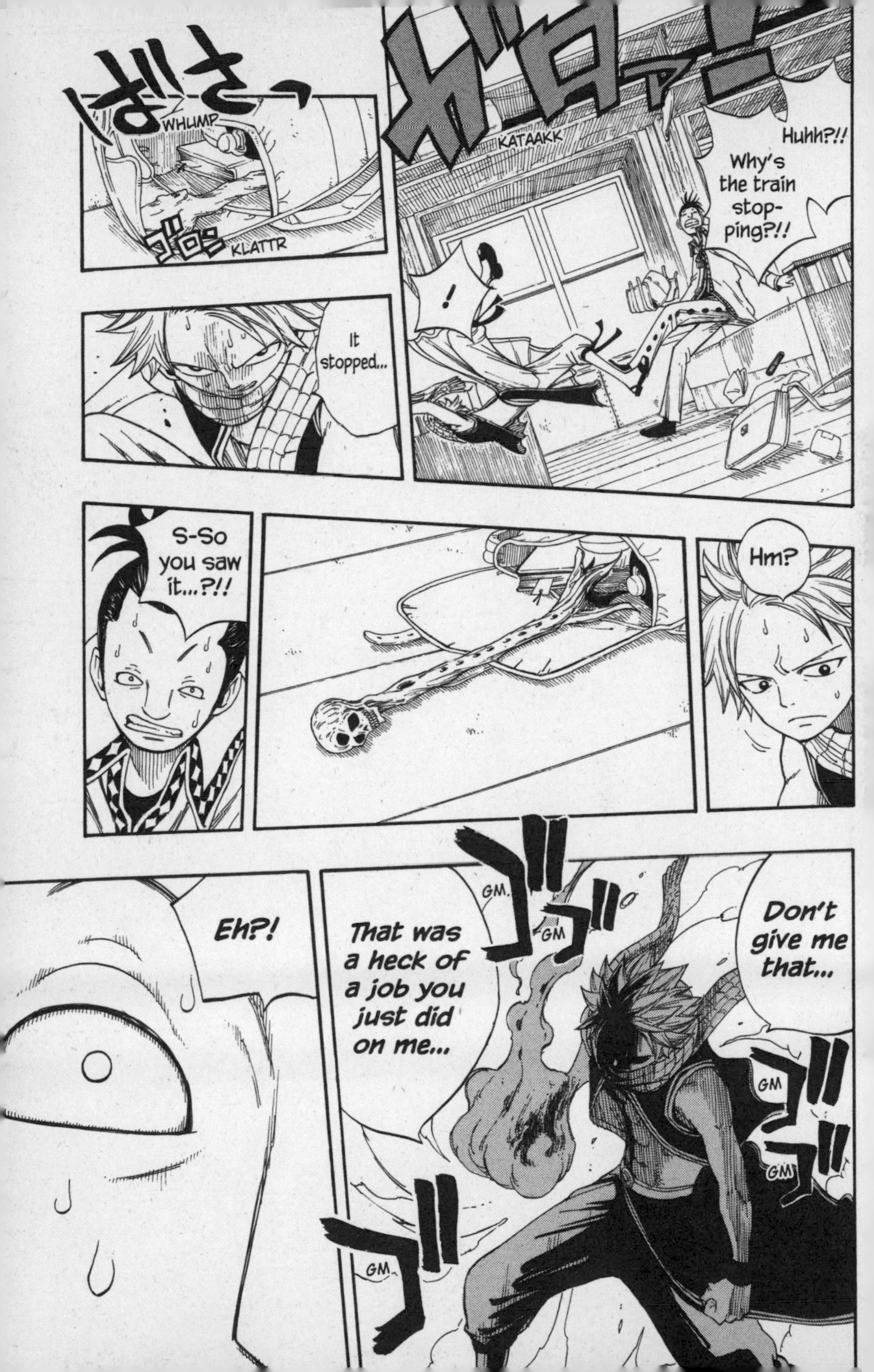
KATAAKK
Huhh?!!
Why's the train stopping?!!
!
WHUMP
KLATTR
It stopped...
Hm?
S-So you saw it...?!!
Don't give me that...
GM
GM
GM
That was a heck of a job you just did on me...
GM
GM
Eh?!

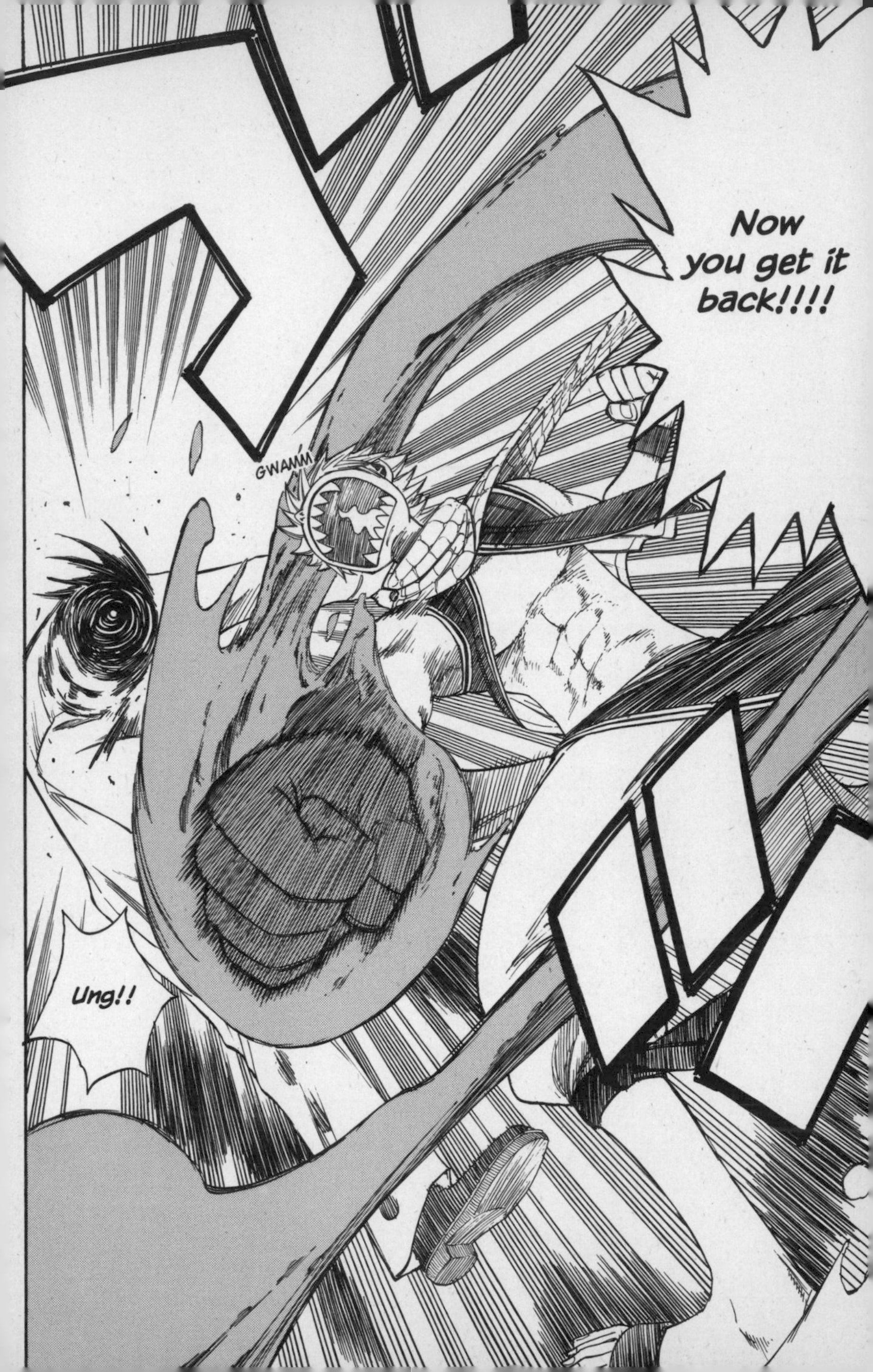
Now you get it back!!!!
GWAMM
Ung!!

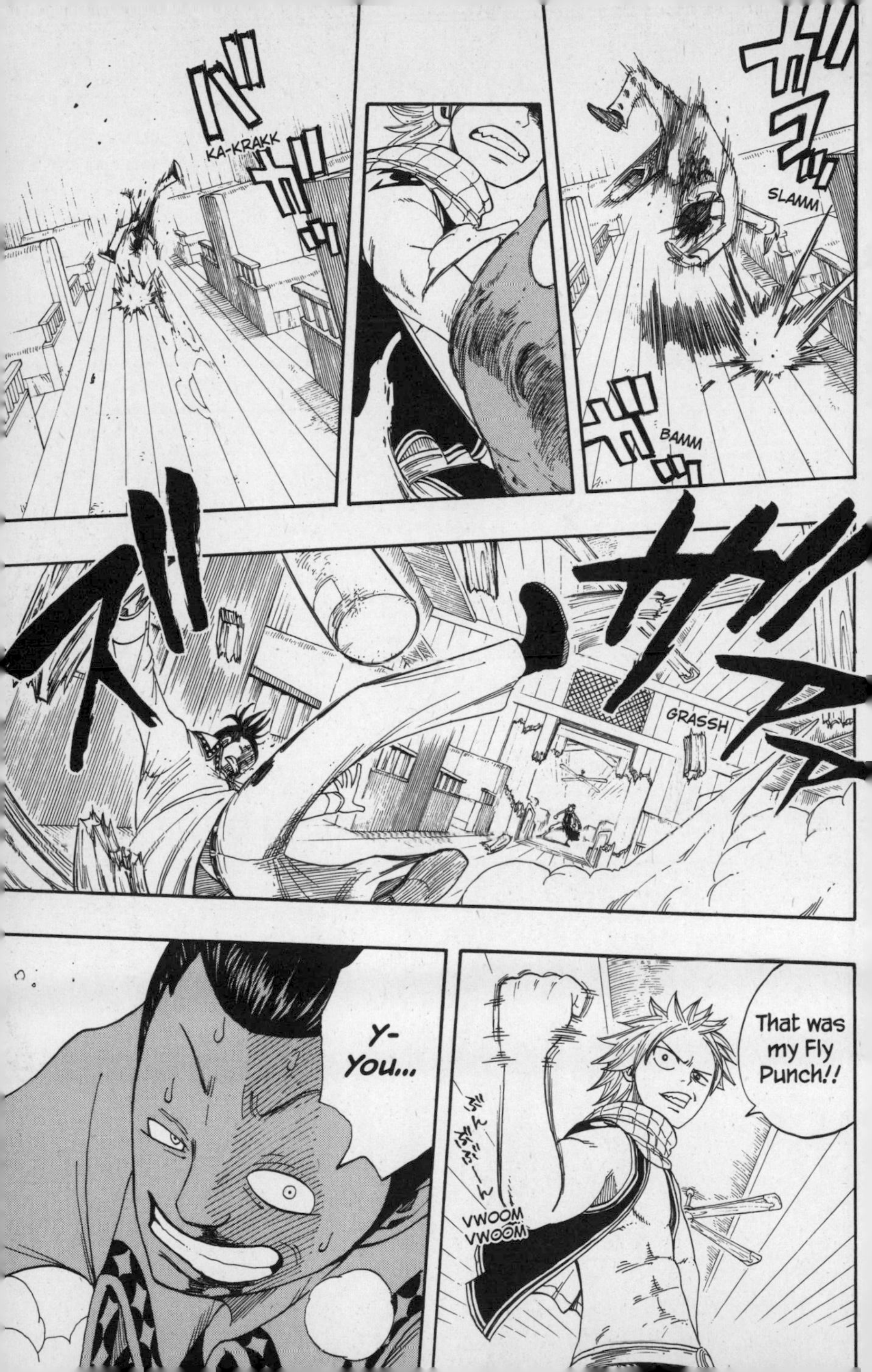
SLAMM
BAMM
KA-KRAKK
GRASSH
That was my Fly Punch!!
VWOOM VWOOM
Y- You...

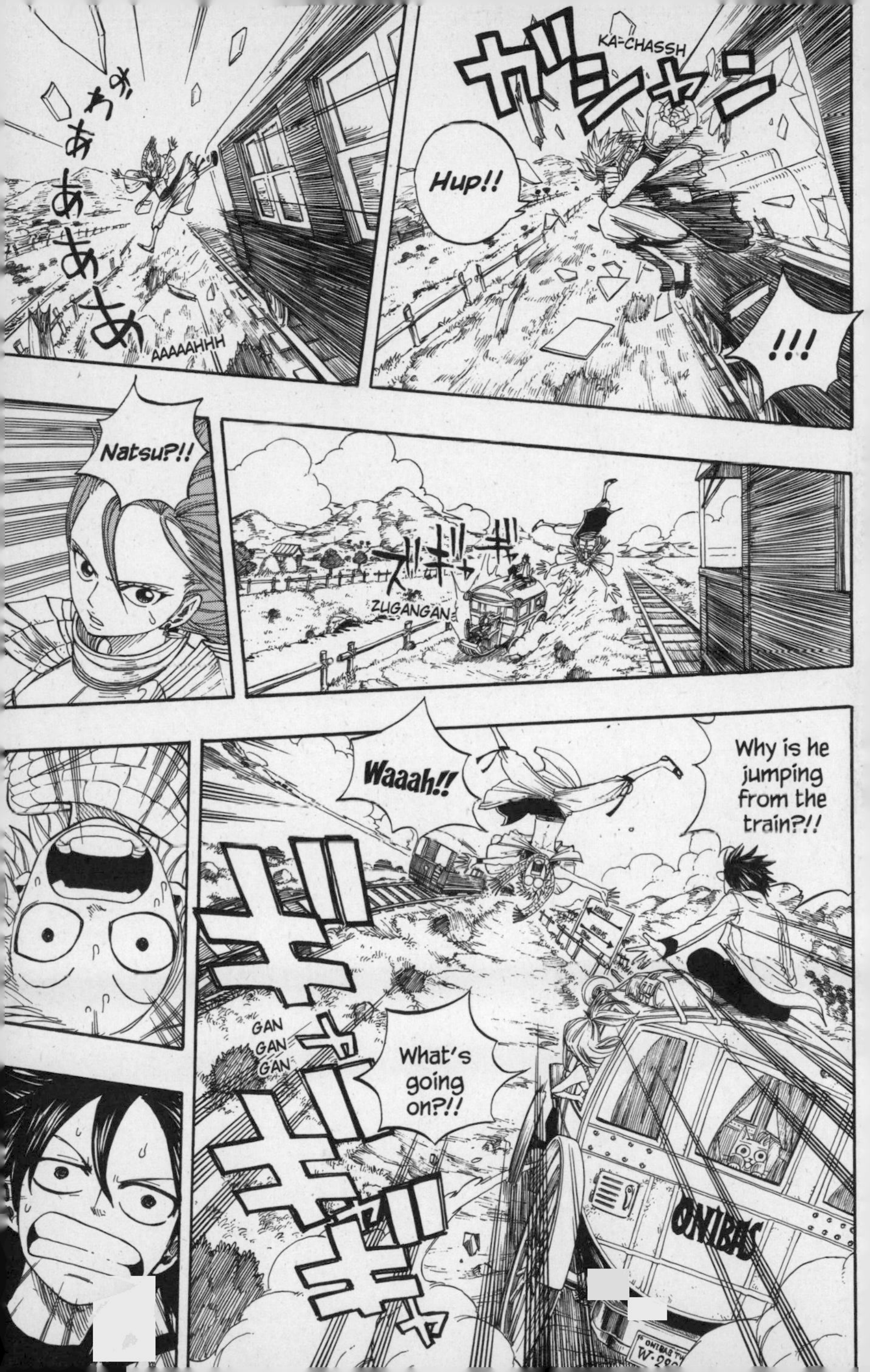
KA-CHASSH
Hup!!
!!!
AAAAAHHH
ZUGANGAN
Natsu?!!
Why is he jumping from the train?!!
Waaah!!
GAN GAN GAN
What's going on?!!
ONIBAS

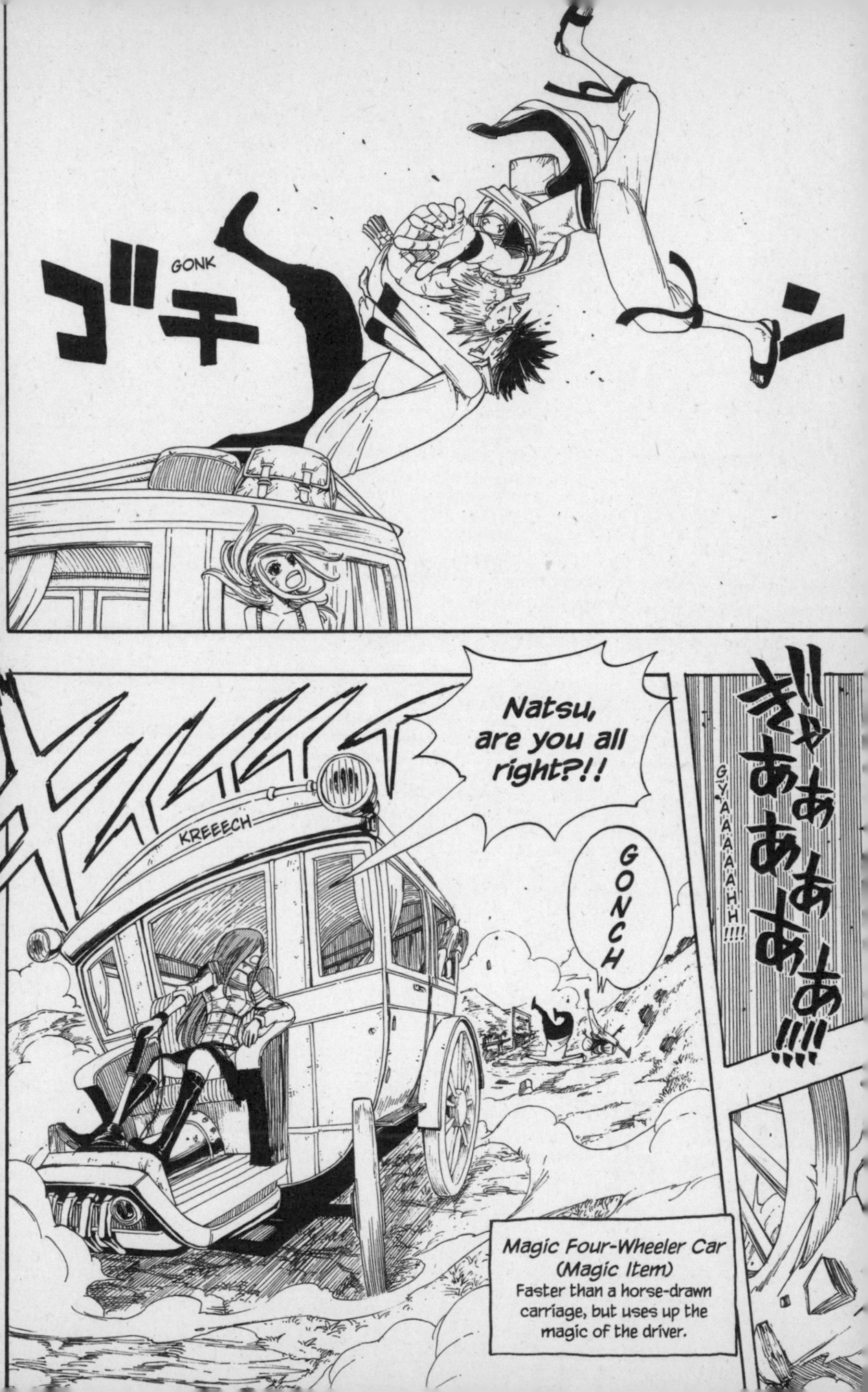
ゴチン
GONK
ぎゃあああああ!!!!
GYAAAAAAH!!!!
GONCH
Natsu, are you all right?!!
KREEECH
Magic Four-Wheeler Car
(Magic Item)
Faster than a horse-drawn carriage, but uses up the magic of the driver.

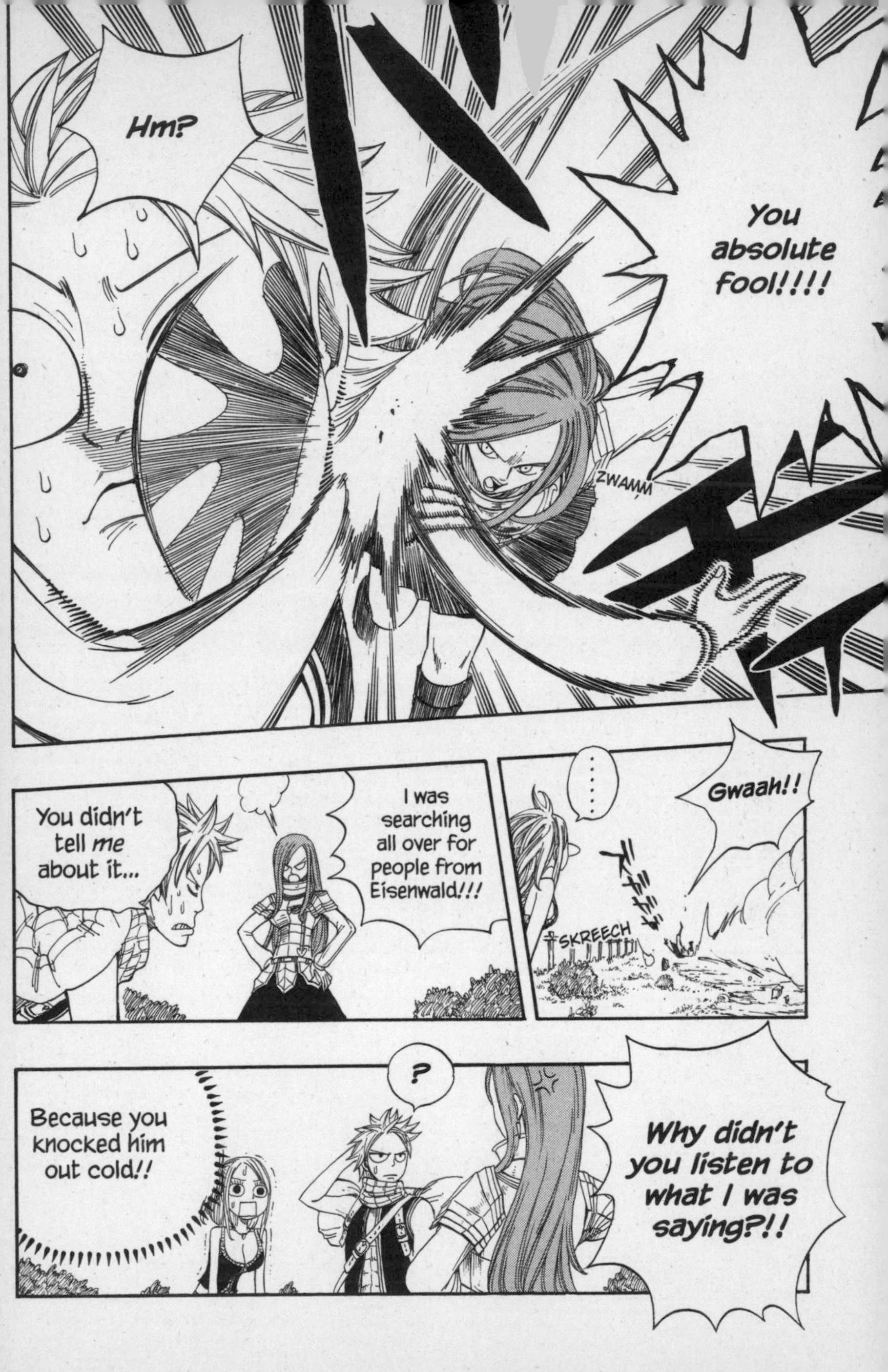

Hm?
You absolute fool!!!!
ZWAMM
Gwaah!!
......
SKREECH
I was searching all over for people from Eisenwald!!!
You didn't tell *me* about it...
Why didn't you listen to what I was saying?!!
?
Because you knocked him out cold!!

He didn't have much that was special...

Did you notice anything special about him?

ZLIP

He was on that train, huh? Well, we'll have to go after him.

What's that mean? What a creepy guy!!

He did have this skull-like flute...

The skull had three eyes in it...

That was just a made-up story.

But...

No... It couldn't be...

What's wrong, Lucy...?

A flute with a skull that had three eyes...

...Lullaby... sleep...death...

!!!

But if that flute could put out a *spell song*...

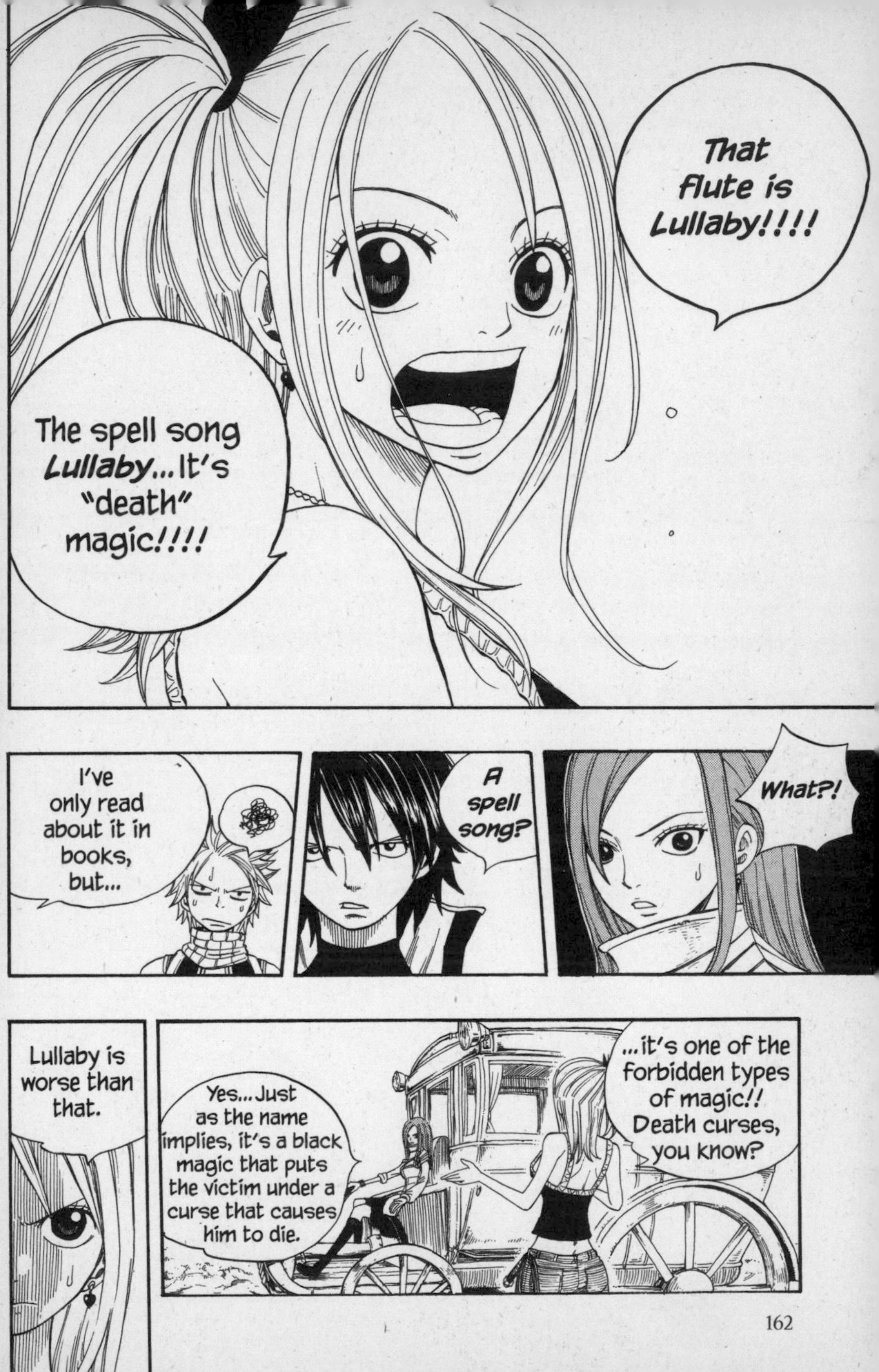
That flute is Lullaby!!!!
The spell song Lullaby... It's "death" magic!!!!
What?!
A spell song?
I've only read about it in books, but...
...it's one of the forbidden types of magic!! Death curses, you know?
Yes... Just as the name implies, it's a black magic that puts the victim under a curse that causes him to die.
Lullaby is worse than that.

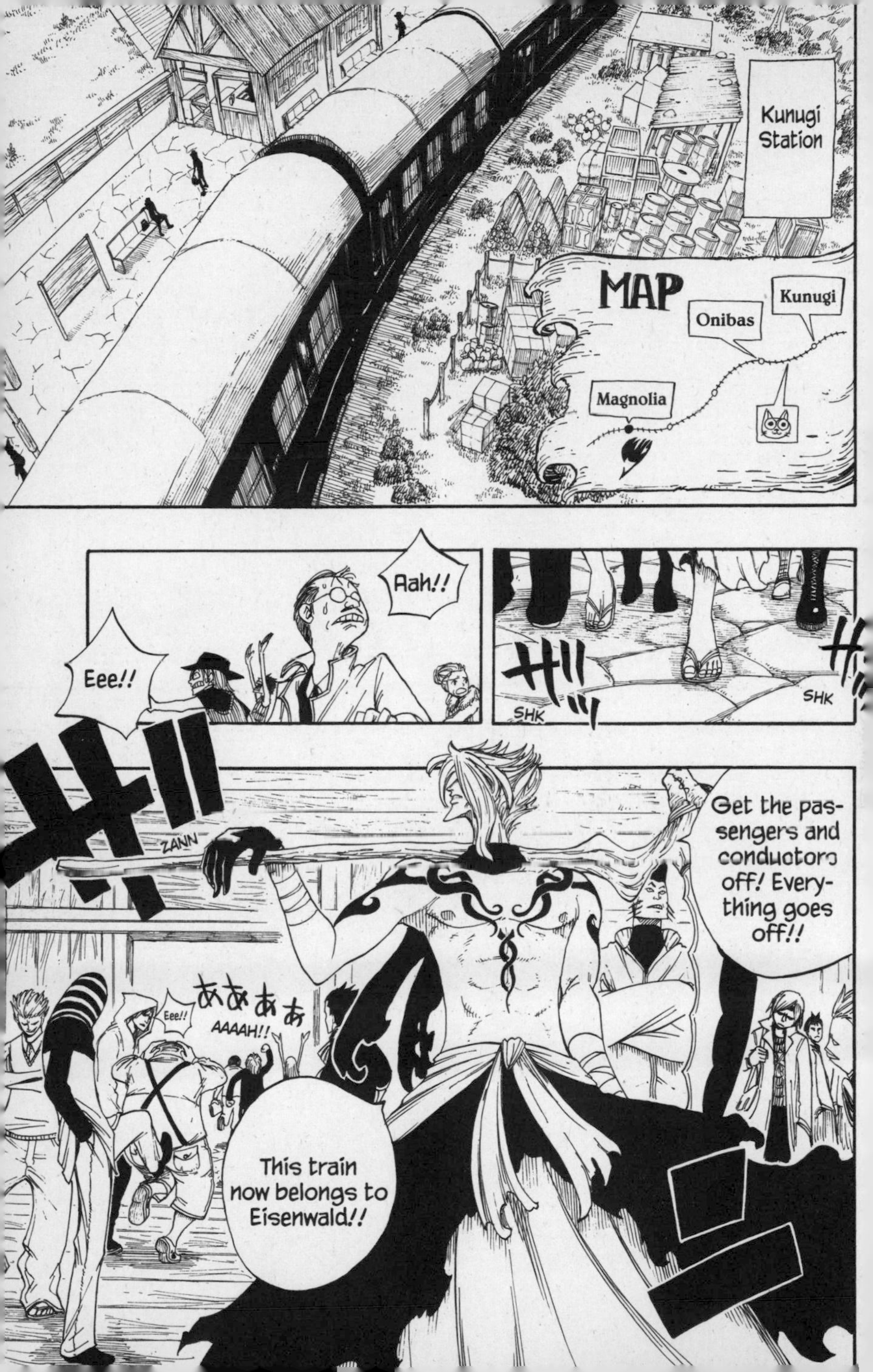
Kunugi Station
MAP
Kunugi
Onibas
Magnolia
SHK
SHK
Aah!!
Eee!!
Get the pas-sengers and conductors off! Every-thing goes off!!
ZANN
Eee!!
AAAAH!!
This train now belongs to Eisenwald!!

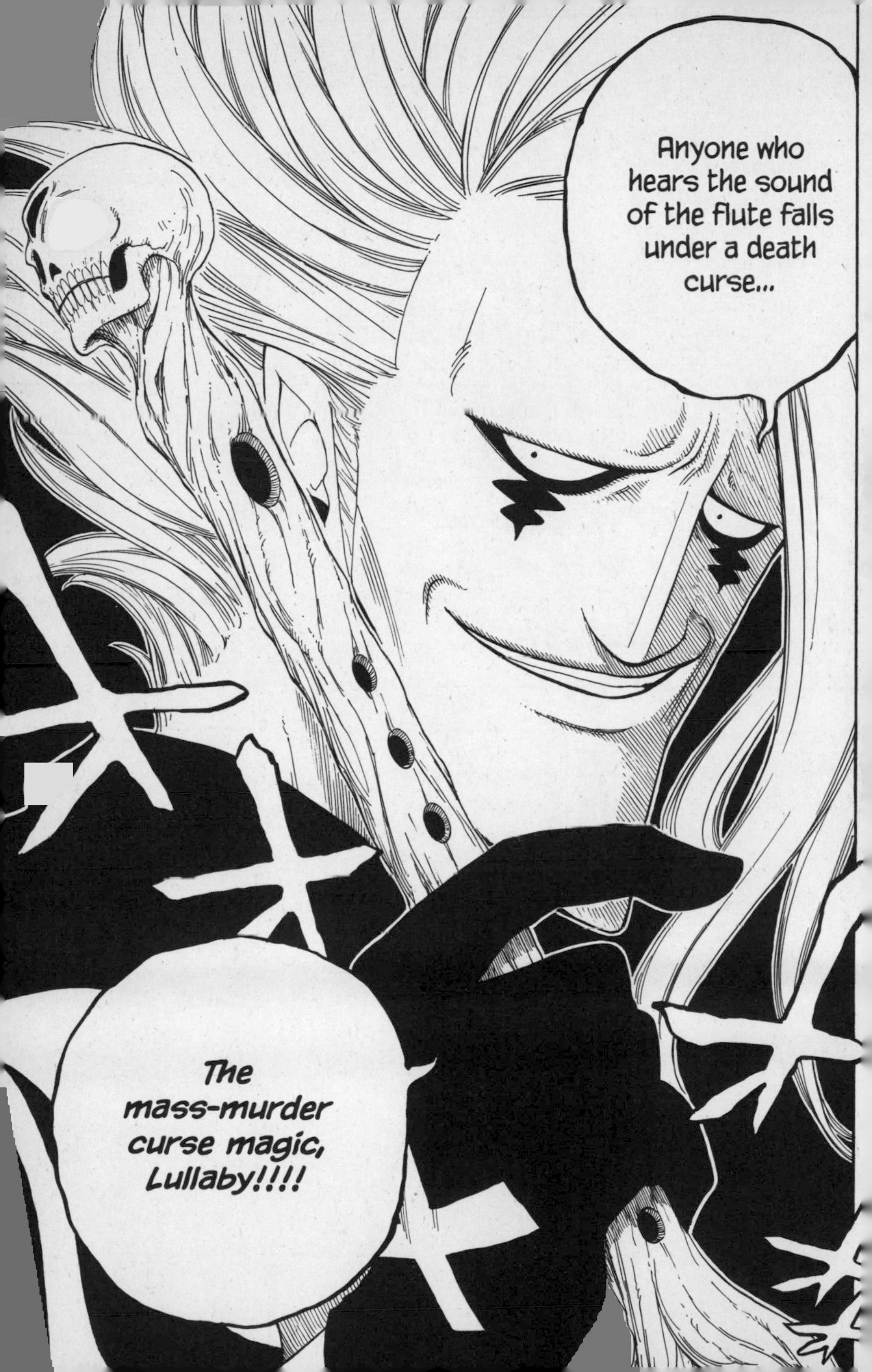
Anyone who hears the sound of the flute falls under a death curse...
The mass-murder curse magic, Lullaby!!!!

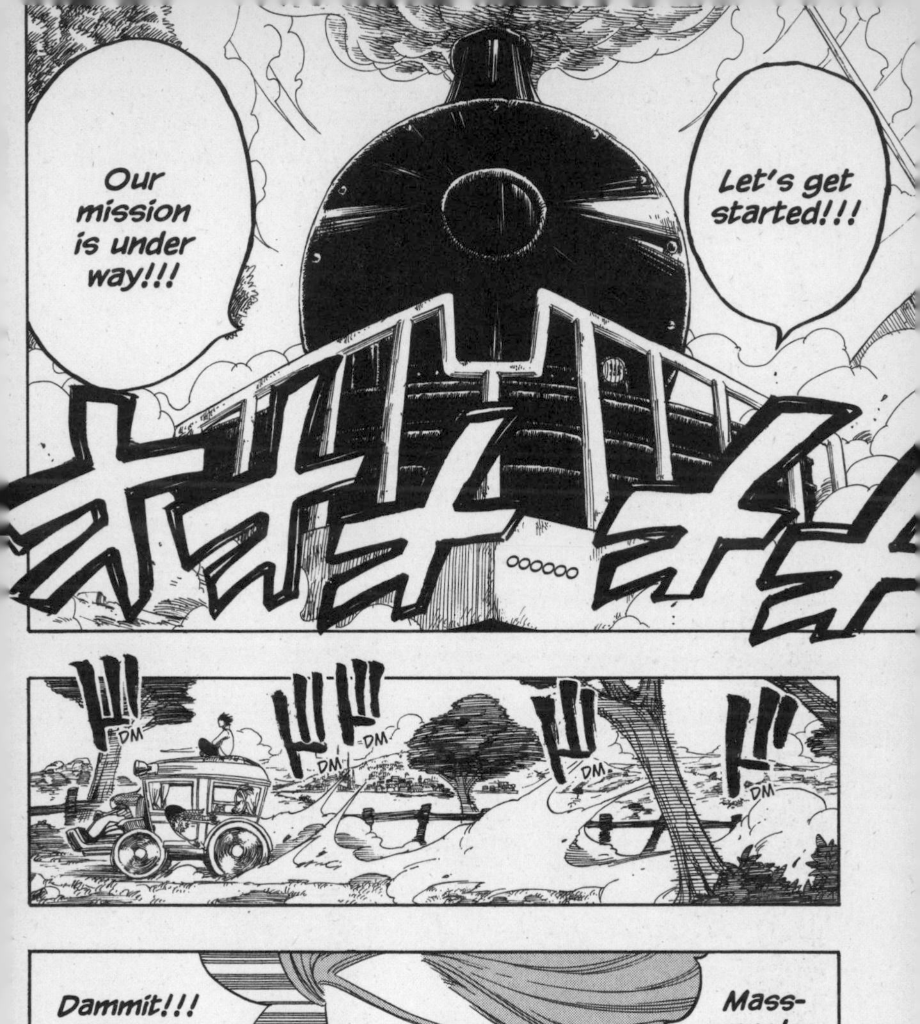
Let's get started!!!
Our mission is under way!!!
oooooo
DM DM DM DM DM
Mass-murder curse magic?!!
If that kind of thing gets into Erigor's hands...
Dammit!!! Who are they planning to use it against?!!!

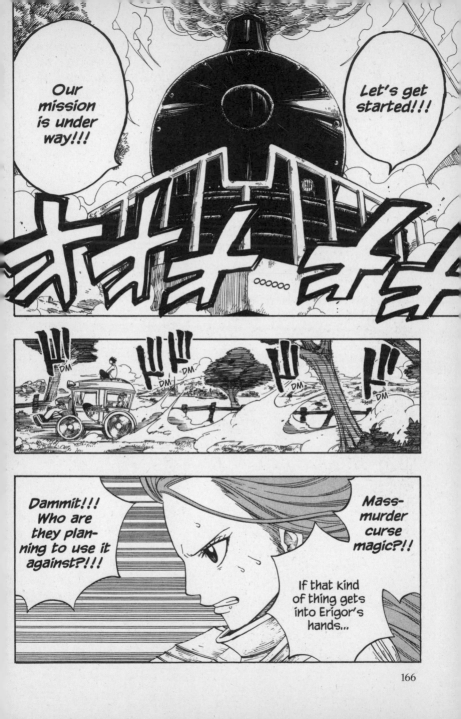

FAIRY TAIL

Chapter 13: Death Laughs Twice

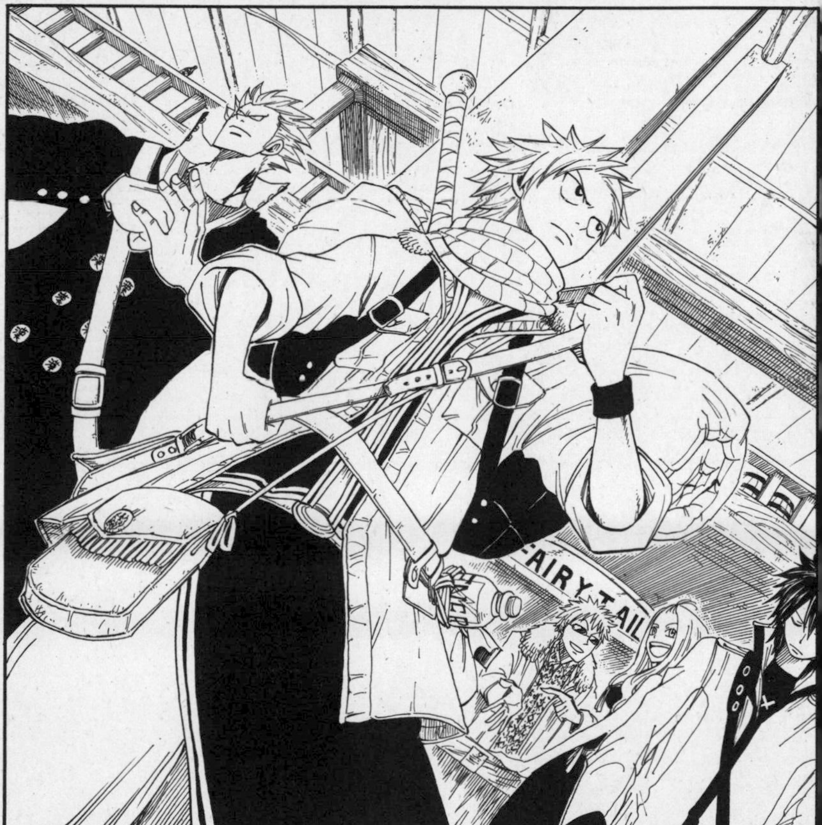
FAIRYTAIL

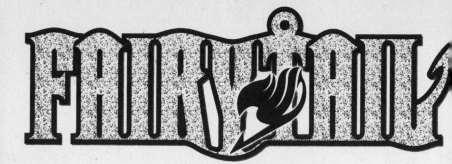

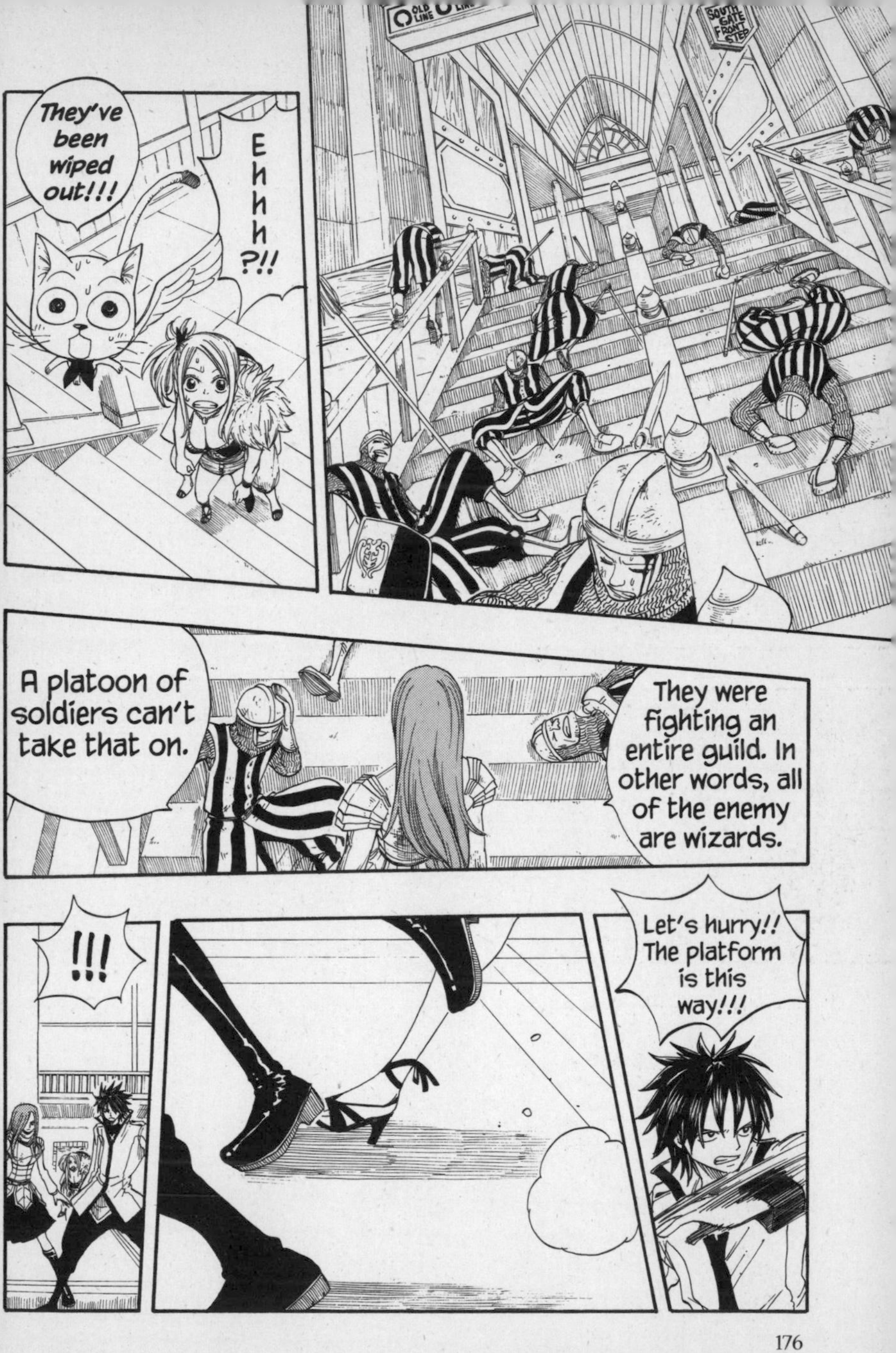
SOUTH GATE FRONT STEP
OLD LINE
Ehhh?!!
They've been wiped out!!!
They were fighting an entire guild. In other words, all of the enemy are wizards.
A platoon of soldiers can't take that on.
Let's hurry!! The platform is this way!!!
!!!

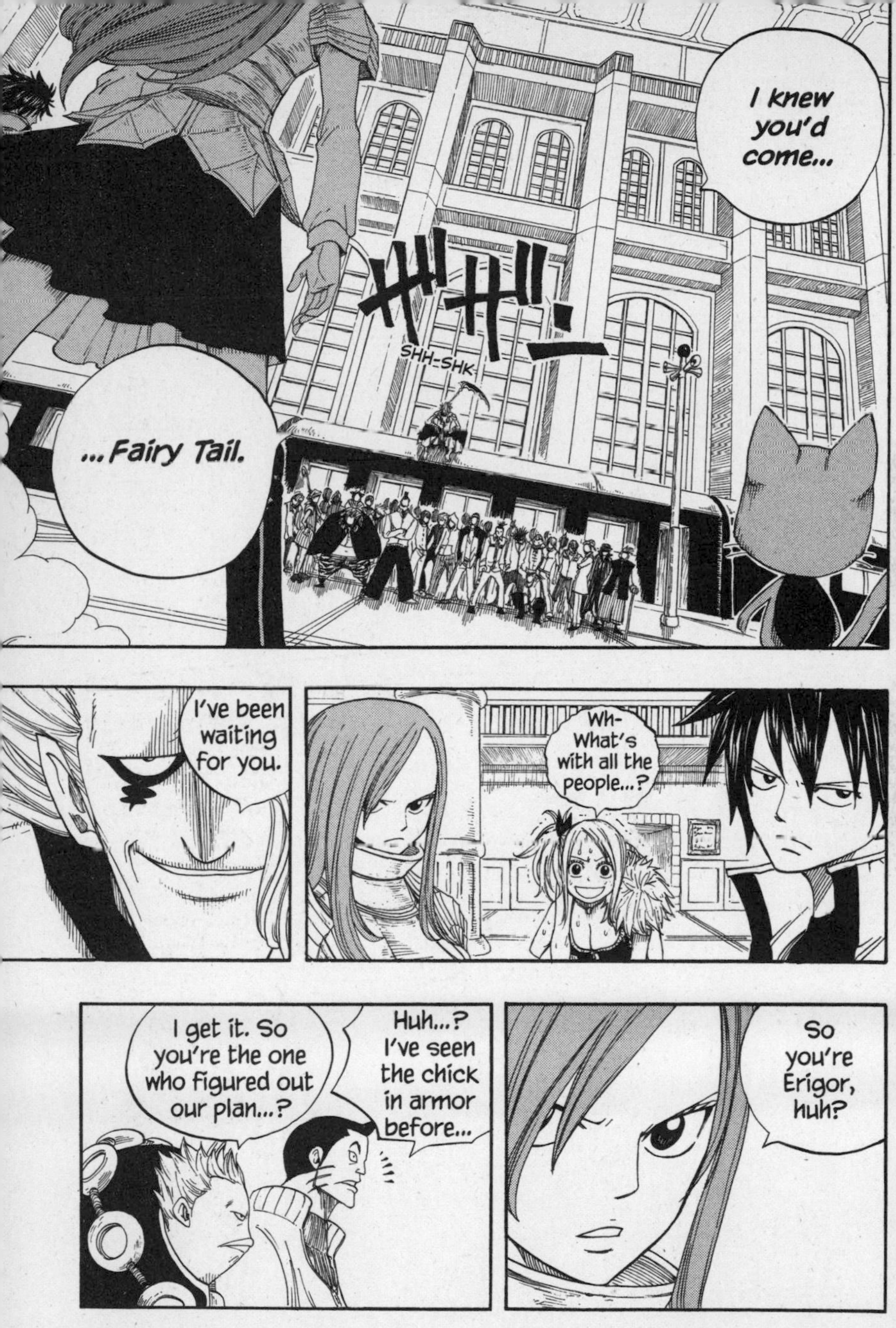
I knew you'd come...
SHH-SHK
...Fairy Tail.
Wh- What's with all the people...?
I've been waiting for you.
So you're Erigor, huh?
Huh...? I've seen the chick in armor before...
I get it. So you're the one who figured out our plan...?

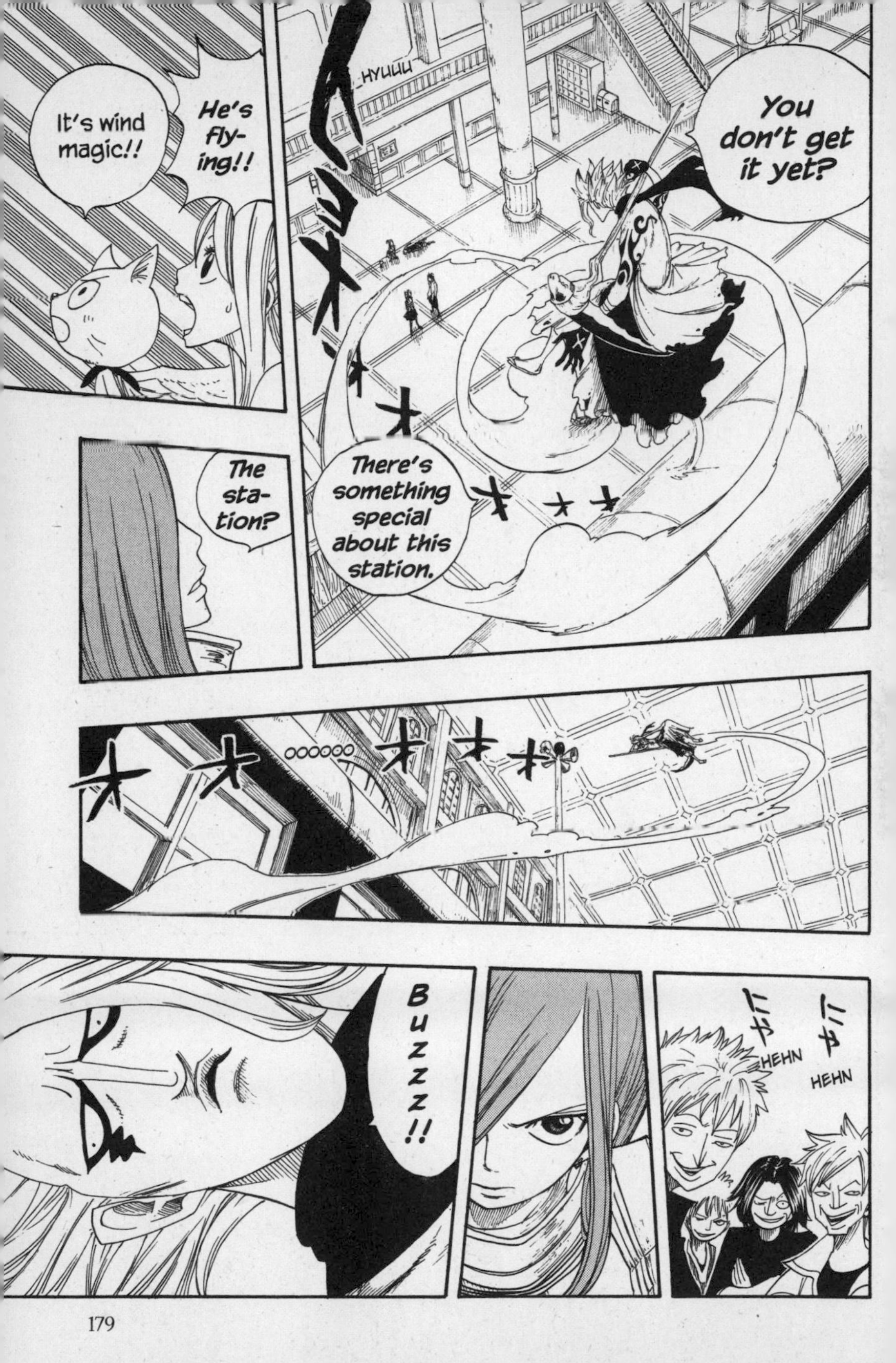
You don't get it yet?
HYUUU
There's something special about this station.
He's fly-ing!!
It's wind magic!!
The sta-tion?
OOOOOO
HEHN
HEHN
BUZZZ!!

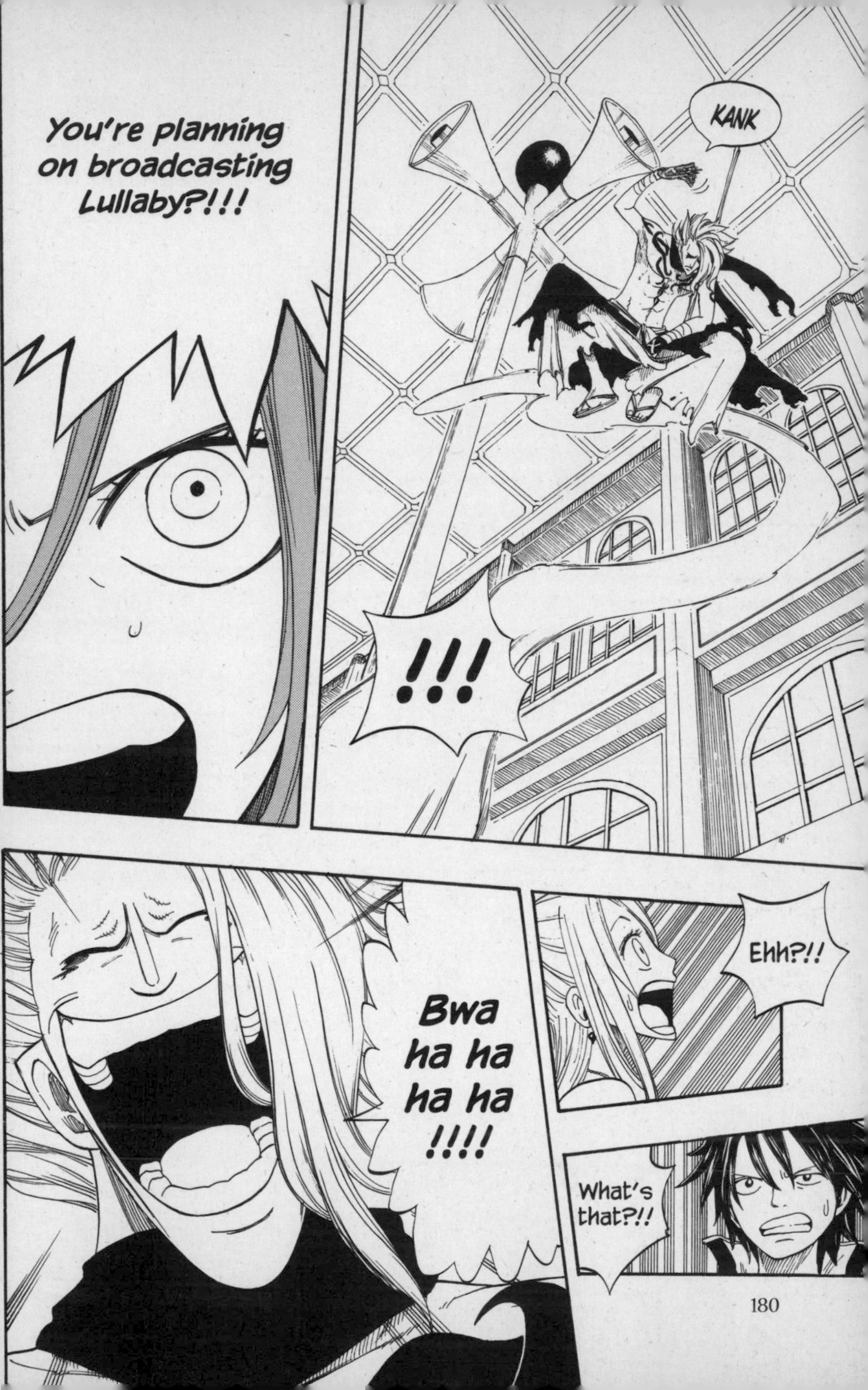

KANK
!!!
You're planning on broadcasting Lullaby?!!!
Ehh?!!
What's that?!!
Bwa ha ha ha ha !!!!

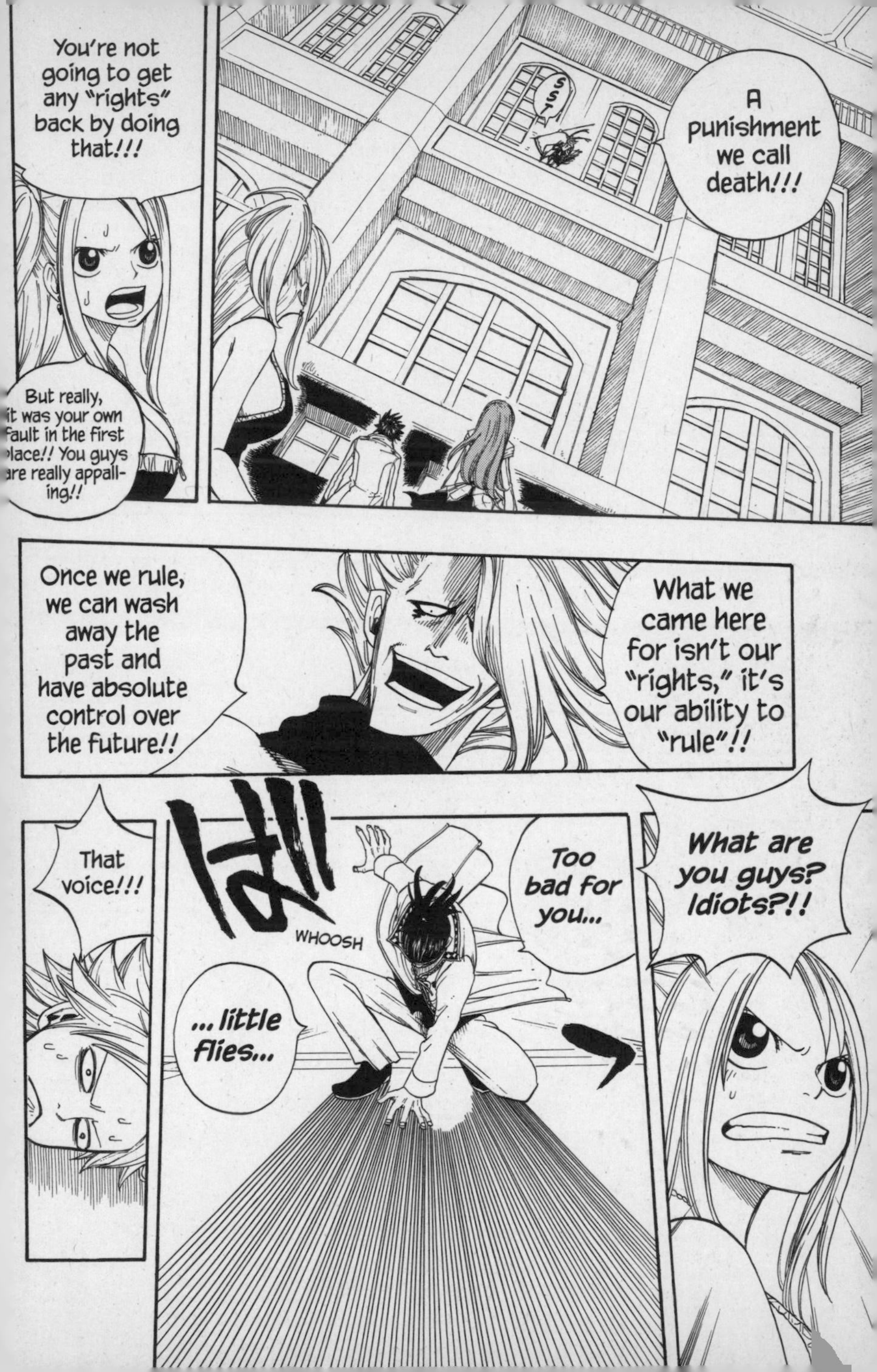
SSST
A punishment we call death!!!
You're not going to get any "rights" back by doing that!!!
But really, it was your own fault in the first place!! You guys are really appalling!!
What we came here for isn't our "rights," it's our ability to "rule"!!
Once we rule, we can wash away the past and have absolute control over the future!!
What are you guys? Idiots?!!
Too bad for you...
WHOOSH
...little flies...
That voice!!!

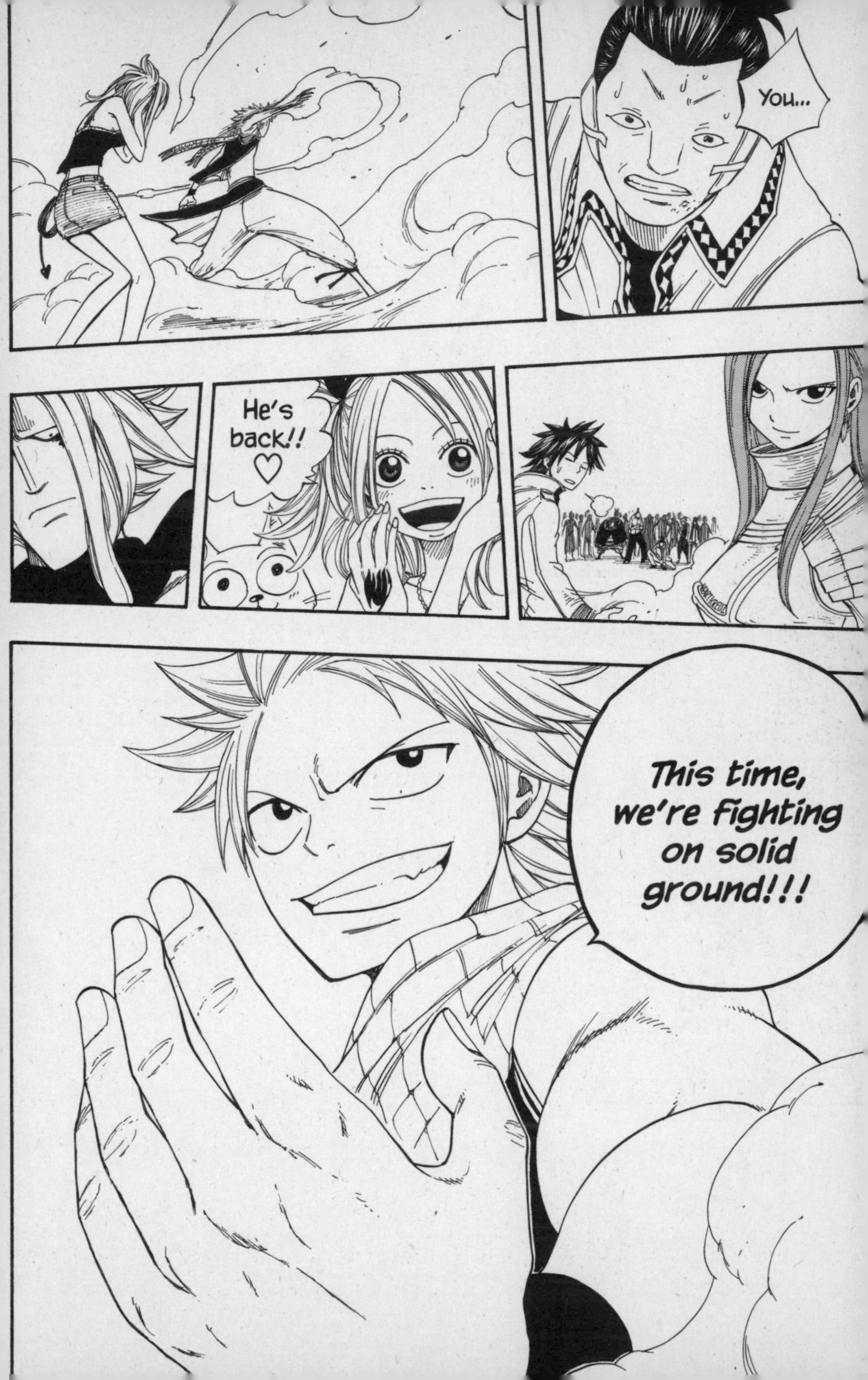
You...
He's back!! ♡
This time, we're fighting on solid ground!!!

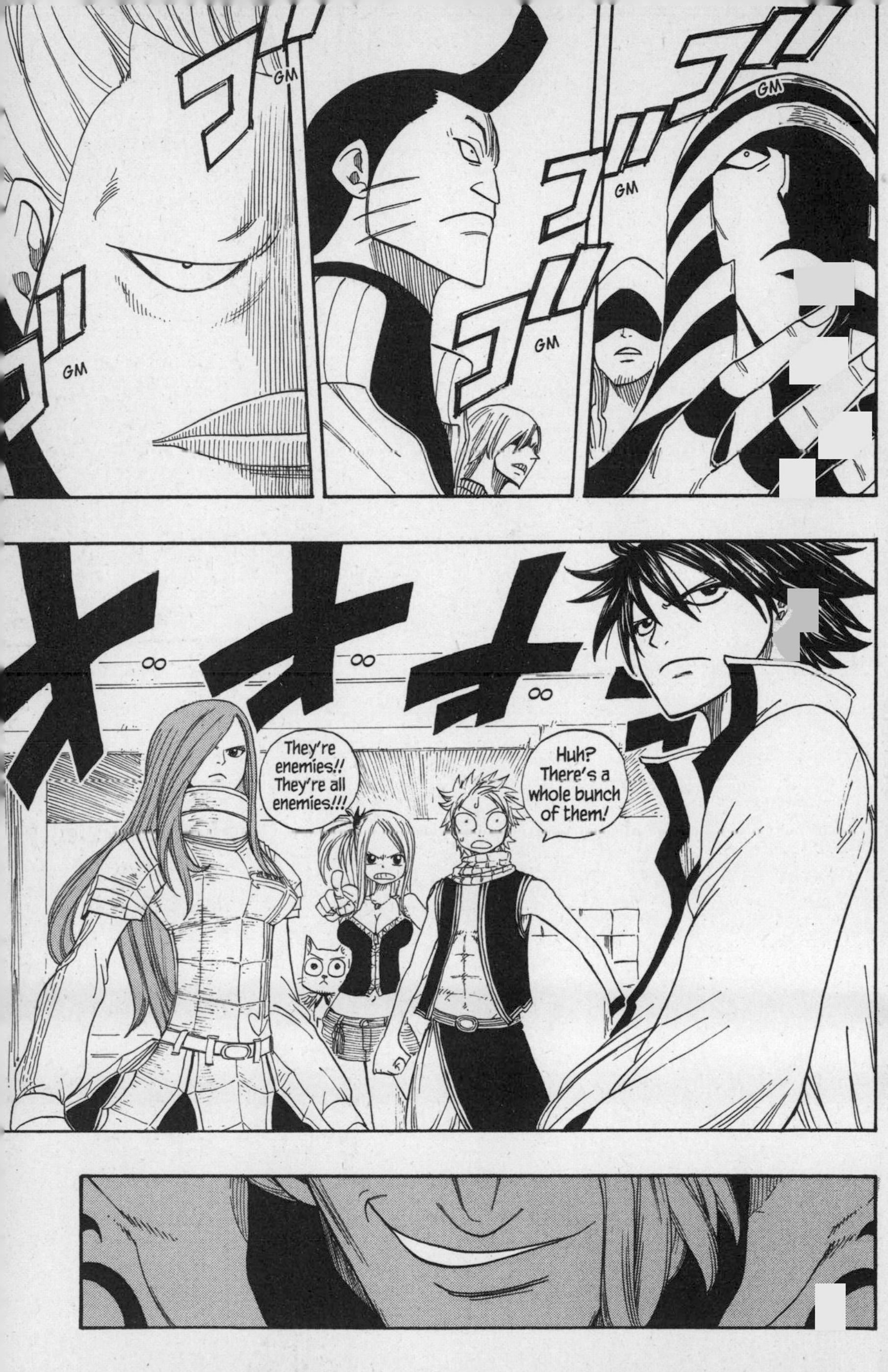
GM
GM
GM
GM
GM
Huh? There's a whole bunch of them!
They're enemies!! They're all enemies!!!

TO BE CONTINUED

The Road to the Fairy Tail Mark

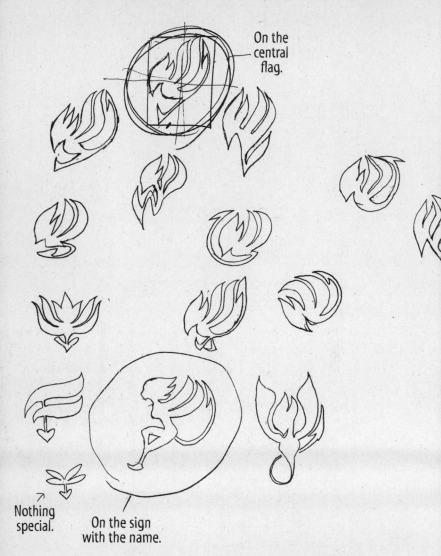

On the central flag.

On the sign with the name.

Nothing special.

The one in the circle at the very top is the final approved design. There was a lot of trial and error to get to that point, huh? I included the one on the bottom left, but it wasn't ever a serious idea.

This Is the Place Where Fairy Tail Is Made!!!

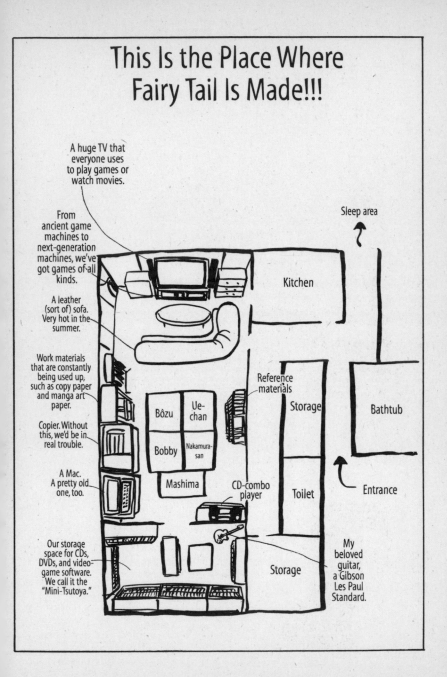

A huge TV that everyone uses to play games or watch movies.

From ancient game machines to next-generation machines, we've got games of all kinds.

A leather (sort of) sofa. Very hot in the summer.

Work materials that are constantly being used up, such as copy paper and manga art paper.

Copier. Without this, we'd be in real trouble.

A Mac. A pretty old one, too.

Our storage space for CDs, DVDs, and video-game software. We call it the "Mini-Tsutoya."

Sleep area

Kitchen

Reference materials

Storage

Bathtub

Bôzu

Ue-chan

Bobby

Nakamura-san

Mashima

CD-combo player

Toilet

Entrance

Storage

My beloved guitar, a Gibson Les Paul Standard.

This Is the Fairy Tail Staff!!!

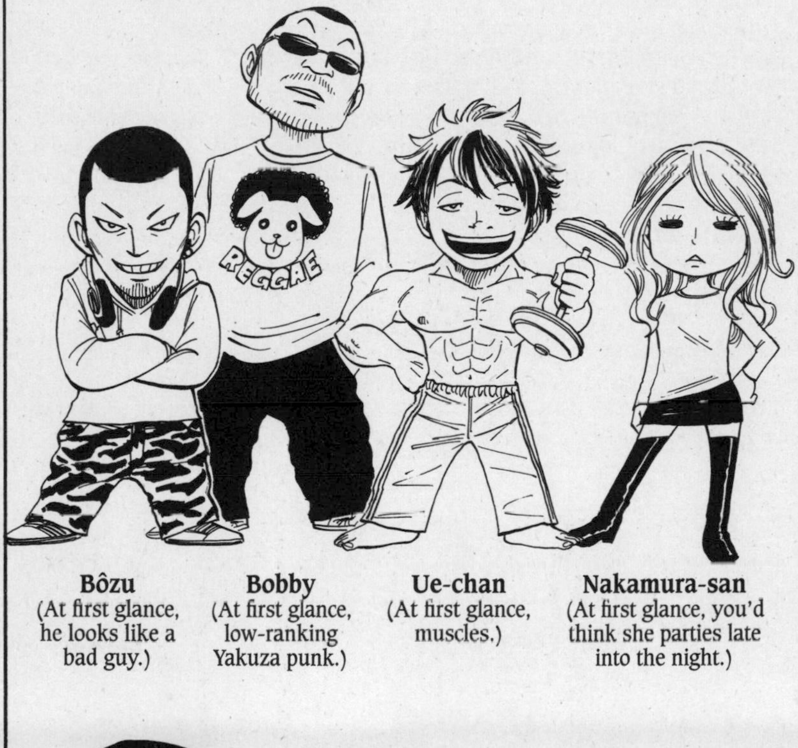
REGGAE

Bôzu
(At first glance, he looks like a bad guy.)

Bobby
(At first glance, low-ranking Yakuza punk.)

Ue-chan
(At first glance, muscles.)

Nakamura-san
(At first glance, you'd think she parties late into the night.)

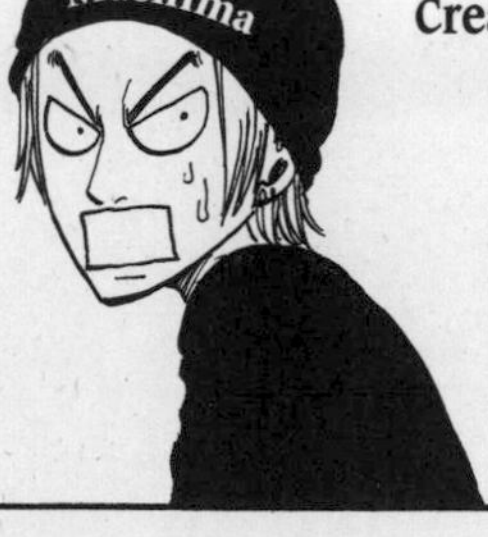
Mashima

Creator (Originally a street punk.)

When people talk about this work, they always seem to say that it's a punk fantasy, but…Maybe it's because the people making it are punks and the work itself is fantasy…? Could that be it? But really, we're all great people!

About the Naming of the Characters

The main character is named Natsu. This is the truth. The name of my last main character was Haru (Japanese for "spring"), and after Haru comes Natsu (Japanese for "summer"). Sorry. Happy was originally named Freyr. It's the name of a Norse god. That was too much for him, so I changed it to something more appropriate. Lucy is from a Beatles song. At the time I decided to name her, the song was running through my mind. I don't remember exactly what I was thinking when I named Makarov, but I recall wanting something that sounded vaguely Russian. Mirajane is the name of a character I came to know in an online game. I don't remember where I got Gray. (Ha ha!) The name of Erza came from the heroine of my ancient short story "Fairy Tale," Eru. Loke is named after the Norse god. I wanted a somewhat cute name for the Elfman character, so I came up with that name. Cana comes from the arcana of tarot cards. Hmm. Looking this over, I get the feeling that there are a lot of names I didn't think too hard about. By the way, this image of Lucy was a rejected idea from before the series was launched. I don't remember why I drew it, but it came out of a drawer of old drawings, and I thought I'd include it as a bonus.

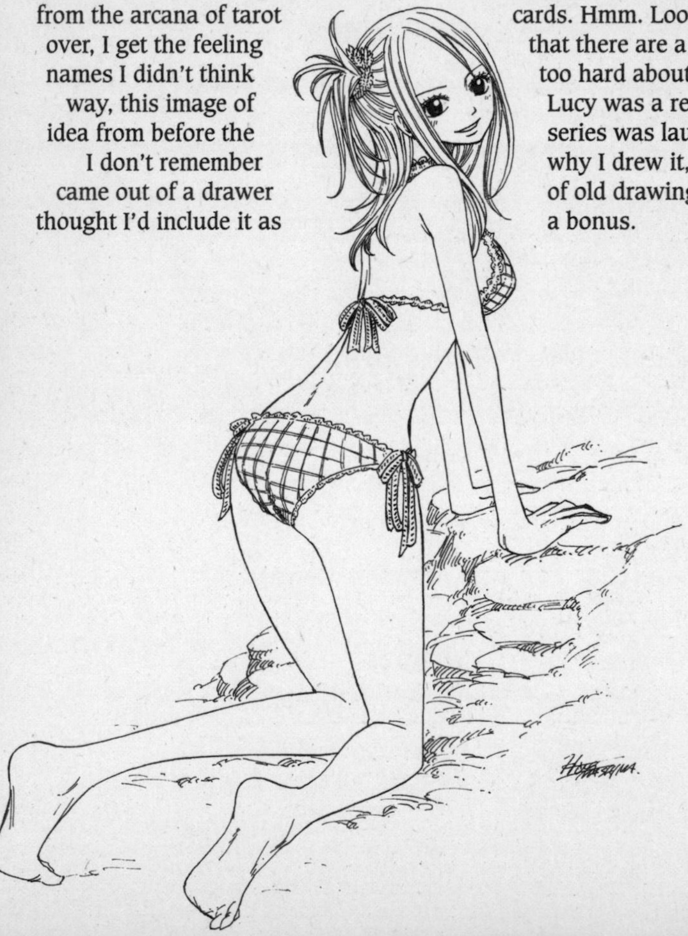

AFTERWORD

The second volume. In what seems like no time at all, we have the second volume. Boy, that was fast! What with one thing and another, I've been pretty busy lately, and the time just seems to be flying by. It only seems like a little while back that I started this series, and we're already publishing the second volume! At this pace, I'll be releasing the tenth volume in no time flat…. Naw, just kidding. I don't know if it'll even be popular enough to last that long, and I decided a while ago to stop stressing over the future. That's right, speaking of the future, I haven't given any thought to how this series is going to turn out! (Ha ha!) Other artists and editors have commented, "Your universe looks like it's going to expand to an amazing size, huh?" But to tell the truth, I haven't really thought about it. What should I do…? Series currently in planning stage. I've been simply enjoying myself for such a long time, I really should get serious!! But once I say that, I forget about the future and get absorbed in drawing pages again. Because of that, I wonder myself what's going to happen next, and without quite knowing, I just keep on going. But… that's all right for now.

And for that reason, I'm looking for letters from you fans. You can say, "I want Natsu to take on this kind of job!" Or, "I'd like to see this kind of stuff in the bonus pages of the graphic novel!" Now accepting suggestions.

DEL REY MANGA
1745 Broadway
New York, NY 10019
delreymanga@randomhouse.com

Any letters sent to this address will definitely get to me personally. Please write! And so… On to the third volume!! It will come out, right? Volume 3…

About the Creator

HIRO MASHIMA was born May 3, 1977, in the Nagano prefecture. His series *Rave Master* has made him one of the most popular manga artists in America. *Fairy Tail*, currently being serialized in *Weekly Shonen Magazine*, is his latest creation.

Translation Notes

Japanese is a tricky language for most Westerners, and translation is often more art than science. For your edification and reading pleasure, here are notes on some of the places where we could have gone in a different direction in our translation of the work, or where a Japanese cultural reference is used.

General Notes:
Wizard

In the original Japanese version of *Fairy Tail*, you'll find panels in which the English word "wizard" is part of the original illustration. So this translation has taken that as its inspiration and translated the word *madōshi* as "wizard." But *madōshi*'s meaning is similar to certain Japanese words that have been borrowed by the English language, such as *judo* (the soft way) and *kendo* (the way of the sword). *Madō* is the way of magic, and *madōshi* are those who follow the way of magic. So although the word "wizard" is used in the original dialogue, a Japanese reader would be likely to think not of traditional Western wizards such as Merlin or Gandalf, but of martial artists.

Names

Hiro Mashima has graciously agreed to provide official English spellings for just about all the characters in *Fairy Tail*. Because this version of *Fairy Tail* is the first publication of most of these spellings, there will inevitably be differences between these spellings and some of the fan interpretations that may have spread throughout the Web or in other fan circles. Rest assured that the spellings contained in this book are the spellings that Mashima-sensei wanted for *Fairy Tail*.

Greasy foods, page 7

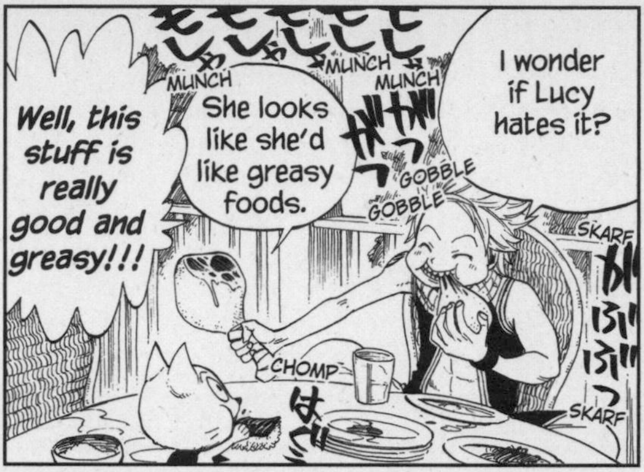
I wonder if Lucy hates it?
MUNCH
MUNCH
GOBBLE
GOBBLE
SKARF
SKARF
She looks like she'd like greasy foods.
MUNCH
Well, this stuff is really good and greasy!!!
CHOMP

The Japanese diet is famous for its low fat content, but there are many native Japanese foods that are just as artery-clogging and delicious as any famously fatty Western dish. Meats, fried foods, and other foods with high fat and oil content are called *aburakkoi*. Aside from the standard "greasy" foods like fatty pork or beef, or the cooked-in-oil foods such as tempura, the entire class of "rich" foods with a high fat or butter content are also described as *aburakkoi*. Because of its fattening reputation, women are supposed to avoid *aburakkoi* food, but the sweet taste of rich foods is hard for anybody to avoid.

Face markings, page 36

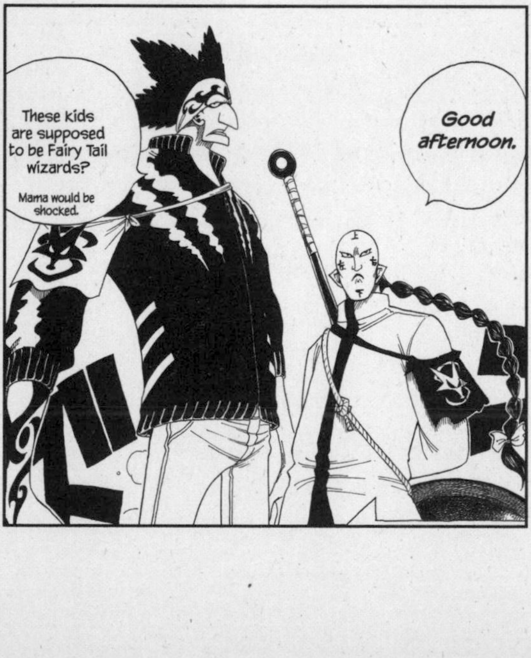
Good afternoon.
These kids are supposed to be Fairy Tail wizards?
Mama would be shocked.

The smaller of the two Vanish Brothers is dressed in the classic style of a Chinese Buddhist monk. The markings on his face, while seeming to hold deep meanings, actually only say "up" on his forehead, "down" on his chin, and "right" and "left" for his right and left cheeks, respectively.

Good afternoon, page 36

The monk-style Vanish Brother actually used the English, "Good afternoon," in his greeting to Natsu and the team. A peculiar aspect of his speech is that he often peppers it with English words (despite his distinct Chinese appearance). Since only a small minority of readers of this translation would be able to understand the Japanese equivalents of these words (let alone any other language), I decided to leave the English in English and use other ways to put across the pretentiousness of his character.

Mama, page 36

Who is the spiky-haired Vanish Brother talking about when he constantly refers to "Mama"? We don't know yet. Hopefully that question will be answered during the course of *Fairy Tail*'s development as a series.

Bodybuilding, page 48

When describing what he considered to be the main weakness of wizards, the monk-style Vanish Brother used the Japanese word *nikutai*. When taken as a whole, *nikutai* simply means "body" in the sense of a flesh-and-blood body. But the Japanese word is made up of two kanji, one that means "muscles" and another kanji which alone also means "body." Natsu, glomming on to the "muscle" meaning, thought of bodybuilders; however, just hearing the word "body" in English wouldn't give the impression of bodybuilding. So I arranged the translation so that the Vanish Brothers' dialogue causes Natsu to think of "bodybuilders" without changing the meaning of either the Vanish Brothers' lines or Natsu's.

Didn't croak, page 54

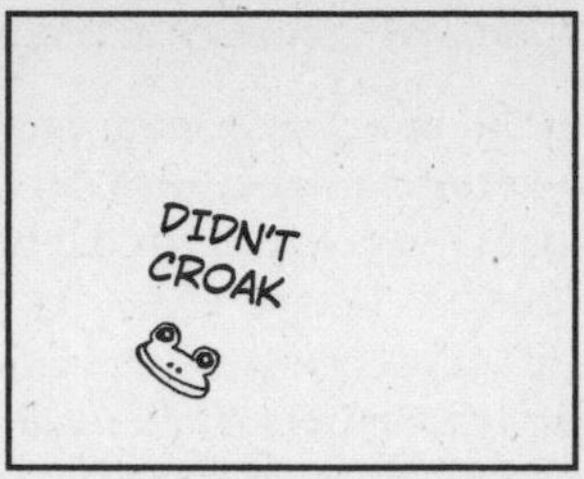
DIDN'T CROAK

The actual sound effect, *kero*, is the sound of someone bouncing back from what one would think of as a severe blow. However, it is very close in sound to *gero*, which is, to the Japanese, the sound that a frog makes. Unfortunately, "ribbit" does not have a "bouncing back" meaning in English, but since "to croak" means both "to make a sound like a frog" and "to die," that became the basis for the translation of the pun on this page.

End a sentence with "*-kani*," page 74

Many manga and anime fans are familiar with characters who end their sentences with odd syllables. The eternally popular Lum of Rumiko Takahashi's *Urusei Yatsura* manga always ended her sentences with "*-cha*." And most depictions of crabs on TV, picture books, or other media will have the crab end its sentences with "*-kani*" (a sound considered especially cute). It is so much a Japanese custom, that it's almost expected for any crab characters to end their sentences that way. So when Cancer ends his sentences with "*-ebi*" ("shrimp"), it comes as a great shock to Happy.

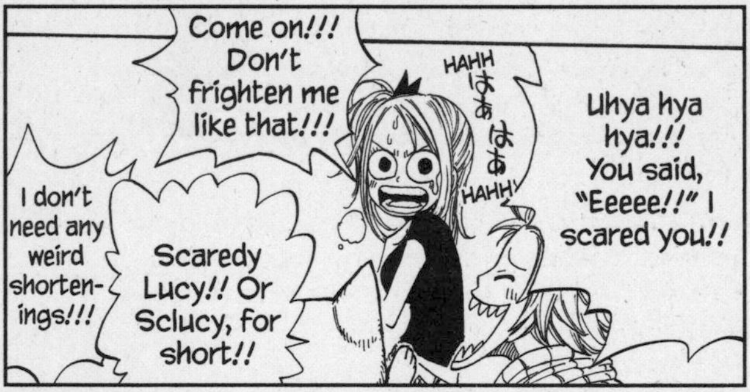
Uhya hya hya!!! You said, "Eeeee!!" I scared you!!
HAHH はあ
はあ HAHH
Come on!!! Don't frighten me like that!!!
Scaredy Lucy!! Or Sclucy, for short!!
I don't need any weird shorten-ings!!!

Sclucy, page 109

In the Japanese version, Natsu's nickname for Lucy was a combination of the Japanese word for "scaredy cat" (*bibiri*), and the Japanese pronunciation of Lucy's name (*Rushii*), shortening it to *Birii*. The Japanese nickname wouldn't work very well with English-language readers, so it was changed to Sclucy, which would be a little more familiar.

Just call me Erza, page 134

In this panel we have some of the workings of Japanese honorifics (see the list at the front of the book) in action. Erza is forgoing some of the niceties of the Japanese language, and telling Lucy that she doesn't need to add the -*san* honorific to Erza's name. There is a very similar English language situation. If you were to meet someone named Jonathan Smith, and you called him Mr. Smith, he might ask

you to instead call him Jon. The feeling implied in "Call me Jon," in this situation is almost exactly the same as Erza's "Just call me Erza," in the manga.

Buzzz, page 179

As in America, TV game shows are very popular in Japan. And the ever-popular buzzer, to tell when time is up or when an answer is wrong, is also found on both sides of the Pacific. The buzz on this page is Erigor's way of saying that time is up for the members of Fairy Tail to make their guesses.

Tsutoya, page 188

Tsutoya is a popular rental chain for CDs, DVDs, game software, and other rentable entertainment. It tends to be well stocked and is found in most parts of Japan.

Preview of Volume 3

We're pleased to present you with a preview from volume 3. Please check our website (www.delreymanga.com) to see when this volume will be available in English. For now you'll have to make do with Japanese!

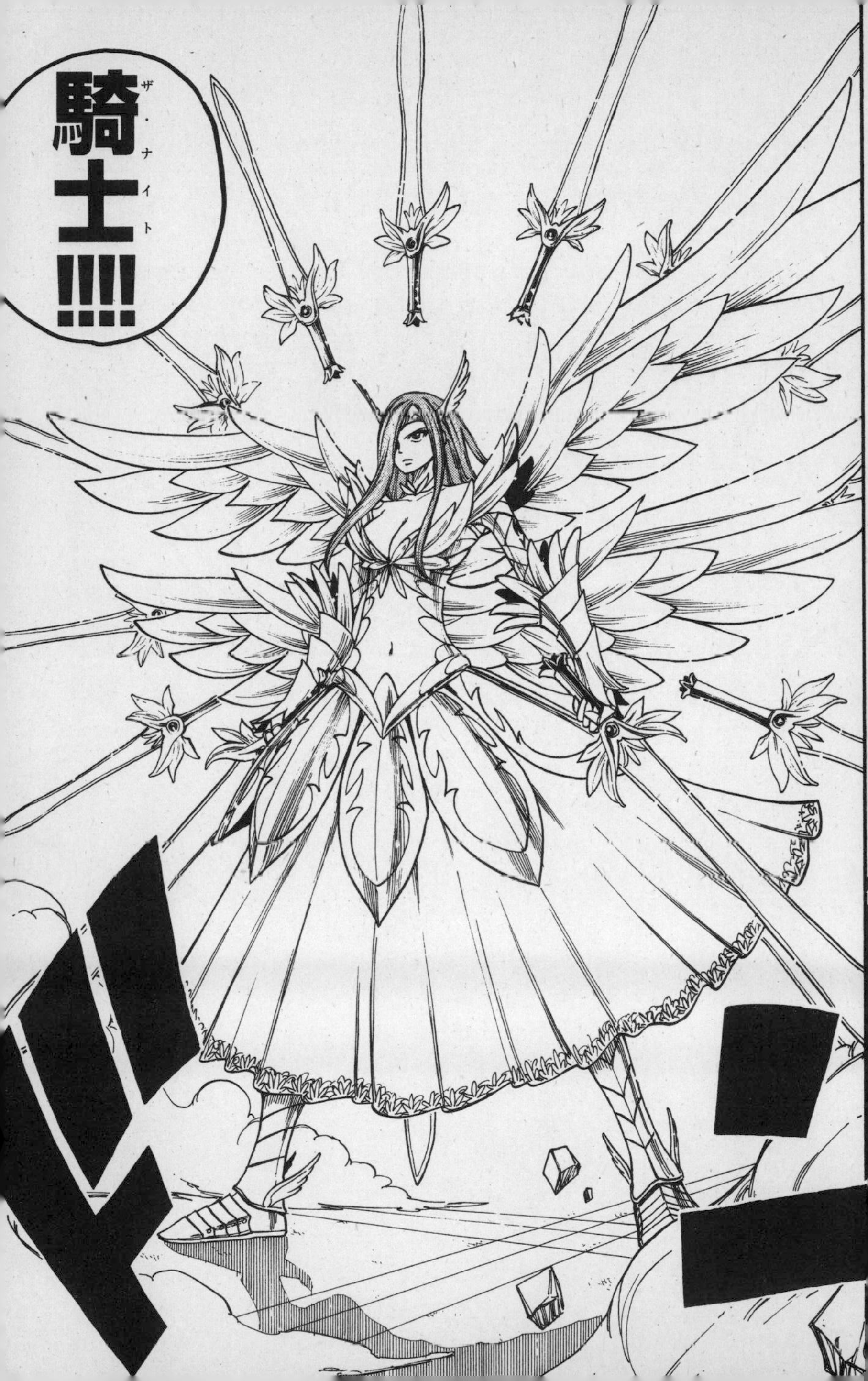
騎士（ザ・ナイト）!!!!

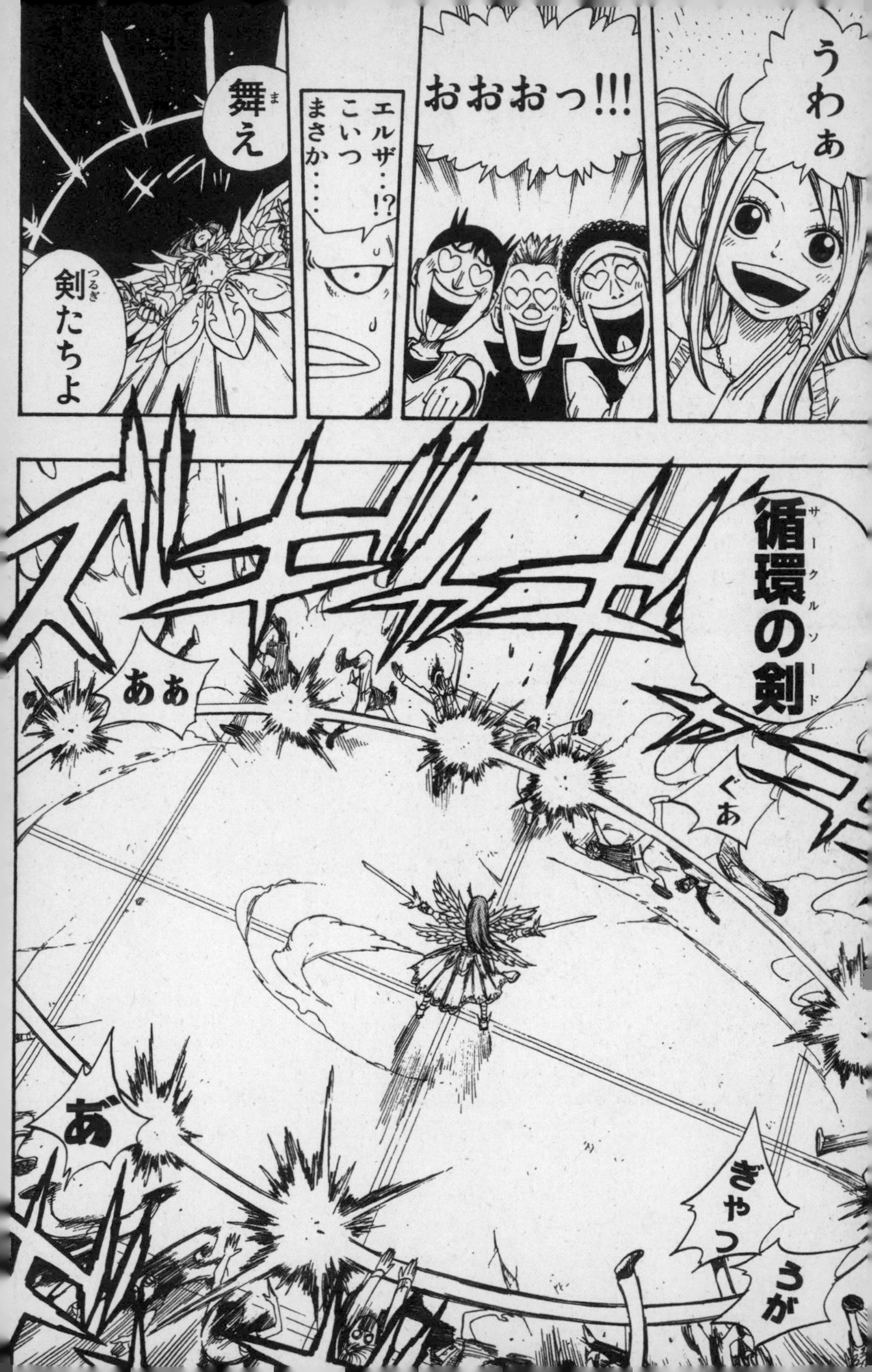
うわぁ
おおおっ!!!
エルザ…!?
こいつまさか……
舞え
剣たちよ
循環の剣
ぐあ
ぎゃっ
うが
あぁ
あ

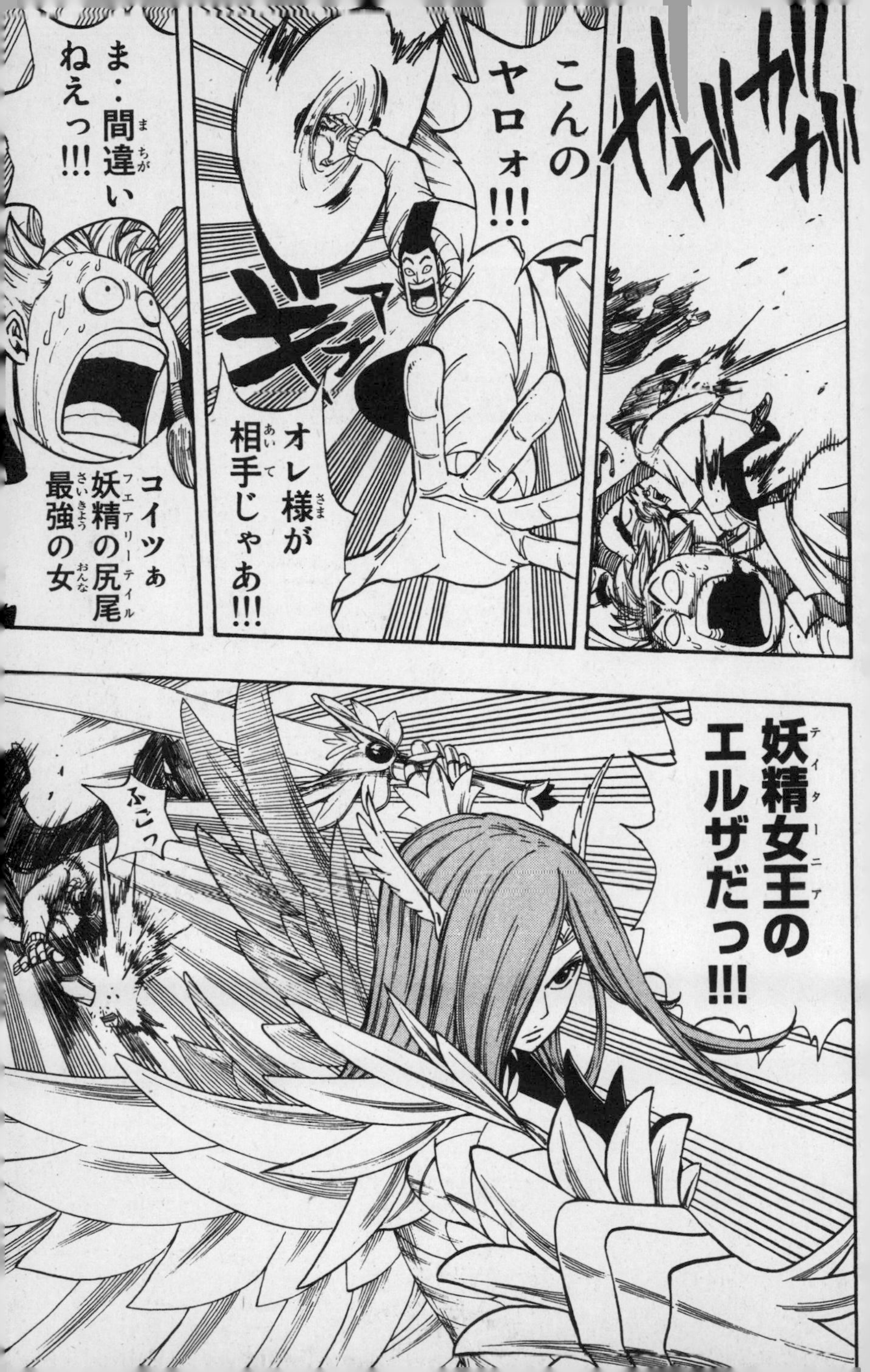
こんのヤロォ!!!
ギャア
オレ様が相手じゃあ!!!
ま・・間違いねえっ!!!
コイツぁ妖精の尻尾最強の女
妖精女王のエルザだっ!!!
ふごっ

TOMARE!

止まれ

[STOP!]

You're going the wrong way!

Manga is a completely different
type of reading experience.

To start at the *beginning*,
go to the *end*!

That's right! Authentic manga is read the traditional Japanese way—
from right to left, exactly the opposite of how American books are
read. It's easy to follow: Just go to the other end of the book and read
each page—and each panel—from right side to left side, starting at
the top right. Now you're experiencing manga as it was meant to be!